ALL IN THE DARK.

A Novel.

BY J. SHERIDAN LE FANU,

AUTHOR OF

"GUY DEVERELL," "UNCLE SILAS," ETC., ETC.

NEW YORK:

HARPER & BROTHERS, PUBLISHERS,

FRANKLIN SQUARE.

1866.

Stereotyped by W. B. Cordier & Co.

TO MY DEAR BROTHER,

WILLIAM RICHARD LE FANU,

This Tale is Inscribed

WITH GREAT AFFECTION AND ADMIRATION.

ALL IN THE DARK.

CHAPTER I.

GILROYD HALL AND ITS MISTRESS

NEAR the ancient and pretty village of Saxton, with its gabled side to the road, stands an old red-brick house of moderate dimensions, called Gilroyd Hall, with some tall elms of very old date about it; and an ancient brick-walled garden, overtopping the road with standard fruit trees, that have quite outgrown the common stature of such timber, and have acquired a sylvan and venerable appearance.

Here dwelt my aunt, an old maid, Miss Dinah Perfect by name; and here my cousin William Maubray, the nephew whom she had in effect adopted, used to spend his holidays.

I shall have a good deal to say of her by-and-by, though my story chiefly concerns William Maubray, who was an orphan, and very nearly absolutely dependent upon the kindness of his aunt. Her love was true, but crossed and ruffled now and then by temper and caprice. Not an ill temper was hers, but whimsical and despotic, and excited oftenest upon the absurdities which she liked letting into her active and perverse little head, which must have been the proper nidus of all odd fancies, they so prospered and multiplied there.

On the whole, Gilroyd Hall and the village of Saxton were rather slow quarters for the holidays. Besides his aunt, William had but one companion under that steep and hospitable roof. This was little Violet Darkwell, a child of about eleven years, when he had attained to the matured importance of seventeen, and was in the first eleven at Rugby, had his cap, and was, in fact, a person with a career to look back upon, and who had long left childish things behind him.

This little girl was—in some round-about way, which, as a lazy man, I had rather take for granted than investigate—a kinswoman; and Miss Dinah Perfect had made her in some sort her property, and had her at least eight months out of the twelve down at Gilroyd Hall. Little Violet was lonely at home—an only daughter, with a father working sternly at the bar, not every day seen by her, and who seemed like a visitor in his own house—hurried, reserved unobtrusive, and a little awful.

To the slim, prettily-formed little girl, with the large dark eyes, brown hair, and delicate bright tints, the country was delightful—the air, the flowers, the liberty; and old Aunt Dinah, though with a will and a temper, still so much kindlier and pleasanter than Miss Placey, her governess, in town; and good old Winnie Dobbs was so cosy and good-natured.

To this little maid, in her pleasant solitude, the arrival of William Maubray for the holidays, was an event full of interest and even of excitement. Shy as he was, and much in awe of all young lady-kind, she was far too young to be in his way. Her sparkling fuss and silvery prattle were even pleasant to him. There was life and something of comicality in her interruptions and unreasonableness. She made him visit her kittens and kiss them all round, and learn and recite their names; whistle after tea for her bulfinch, dig in her garden, mend and even nurse her doll, and perform many such tasks, quite beneath his dignity as a "swell" at Rugby, which, however, the gentle fellow did very merrily and industriously for the imperious little woman, with scant thanks, but some liking for his guerdon.

So, in his fancy, she grew to be mixed up with the pleasant influences of Gilroyd Hall, with the flowers and the birds, with the freaks of the little dog Pixie, with the stories he read there, and with his kindly welcomes and good-byes.

Sitting, after breakfast, deep in his novel in the "study," with his white flannel cricket trousers on, for he was to play against Winderbroke for the town of Saxton that day, he received a smart tweak by the hair, at the back of his head, and, looking round, saw little Vi, perched on the rung of his old fashioned chair, and dimly recollected having received several gentler tweaks in succession, without evincing the due attention.

"Pert little Vi! what's all this?" said the stalworth Rugby boy, turning round with a little shake of his head, and his sweet smile, and leaning on his elbow. The sunny landscape from the window, which was clustered round with roses, and a slanting sunbeam that just touched her hair, helped to make the picture very pretty.

"Great, big, old bear! you never listen to one word I say."

"Don't you call names, Miss," said Aunt Dinah, who had just glided into the room.

"What was little silver-hair saying? What does she want?" he replied, laughing at the child's indignation, and pursuing the nomenclature of Southey's pleasant little nursery tale. "Golden hair, I must call you, though," he said, looking on her sun-lit head; "and not quite golden either; it is brown, and very pretty brown, too. Who called you Violet?" He was holding the tip of her pretty chin between his fingers, and looking in her large deep eyes. "Who called you Violet?"

"How should I know, Willie?" she replied, disengaging her chin with a little toss.

"Why, your poor mamma called you Violet. I told you so fifty times," said Aunt Dinah sharply.

"You said it was my godfathers and godmothers in my baptism, grannie!" said Miss Vi, not really meaning to be pert.

"Don't answer me, Miss—that's of course, your catchism—we're speaking of your poor mamma. 'Twas her mamma who called her Violet. What about it?"

"Nothing," answered William, gently looking up at his aunt, "only it is such a pretty name;" and glancing again at the child, "it does so well with her eyes. She *is* a jolly little creature."

"She has some good features, I suppose, like every other child, and you should not try to turn her head. Nothing extraordinary. There's vanity enough in the world, and I insist, William, you don't try to spoil her."

"And what do you want of me, little woman?" asked William.

"You come out and sow my lupins for me."

"Why, foolish little woman, it isn't the season; they would not grow."

"Yes, they would though—you say that just because you don't like! you story!"

"*Violet!*" exclaimed Aunt Dinah, tapping the table with the seal end of her silver pencil-case.

"Well, but he is, grannie, very disobliging. You do nothing now but read your tiresome old books, and never do anything I bid you."

"Really! Well that's very bad; I really must do better," said William, getting up with a smile; "I *will* sow the lupins."

"What *folly!*" murmured Aunt Dinah, grimly.

"We'll get the hoe and trowel. But—but what's to be done? I forgot I'm to play for the town to-day; and I don't think I have time—no, certainly—no time to-day; for the lupins;" and William shook his head, smiling disconsolately.

"Then I'll *never* ask you to do anything for me again as long as I live—never—never—*never!*" she vowed with a tiny stamp.

"Yes you shall—you shall, indeed, and I'll do ever so much; and may she come and look at the cricket?"

So, leave granted, she did, under old Winnie's care; and when she returned, and for days after, she boasted of Willie's long score and how he caught the ball.

When he returned at the end of next "half" he found old Miss Dinah Perfect with her spectacles on, in her comfortable old drawing-room, in the cheer of a Christmas fire, with her head full of the fancies and terrors of a certain American tome, now laid with its face downwards upon the table—as she jumped up full of glee and affection, to greet him at the threshold.

It was about this period, as we all remember, that hats began to turn and heads with them, and tables approved themselves the most intelligent of quadrupeds; chests of drawers and other grave pieces of furniture babbled of family secrets, and houses resounded with those creaks and cracks with which Bacon, Shakespeare, and Lord Byron communicated their several inspirations in detestable grammar, to all who please to consult them.

Aunt Dinah was charmed. Her rapid genius loved a short-cut, and here was, by something better than a post-office, a direct gossiping intimacy opened between her and the people on t'other side of the Styx.

She ran into this as into her other whimsies, might and main, with all her heart and soul. She spent money very wildly for her, upon the gospels of the new religion, with which the transatlantic press was teeming; and in her little green-papered dressing-room was accumulating a library upon her favourite craze, which might have grown to the dimensions of Don Quixote's.

She had been practising for a year, however, and all the minor tables in her house had repeatedly prophesied before she disclosed her conversion to her nephew, or to anyone else except old Winnie.

It was no particular business of his if his aunt chose to converse with ghosts and angels by the mediation of her furniture. So, except that he now and then assisted at a *séance*, the phenomena of which were not very clear to him, though perfectly so to his aunt, and acquiesced in dimly and submissively by good old Winnie, things went on in their old course; and so, for some three or four years more, during which William Maubray read a great deal of all sorts of lore, and acquired an erudite smattering of old English authors, dramatists, divines, poets, and essayists, and time was tracing fine wrinkles about Aunt Dinah's kind eyes and candid forehead, and adding graceful inches to the lithe figure of Violet Darkwell; and the great law of decay and renewal was asserting itself everywhere, and snows shrouding the dead world in winter, and summer fragrance, and glow of many hues in the gardens and fields succeeding, and births and deaths in all the newspapers every morning.

———o———

CHAPTER II

A LETTER.

The following letter, posted at Saxton, reached a rather solitary student in ——— College, Cambridge.

"Dear William,—You will be sorry—I know you will—to hear that poor old auntie is not long for this world; I don't know exactly what is wrong, but something I am certain very bad. As for Doctor Drake, I have no faith in him, or, indeed, in medicine, and don't mean to trouble him except as a friend. I am quite happy in the expectation of the coming change, and have had within the last week, with the assistance of good old Winnie Dobbs some very delightful *communications*, you know, I dare say, what I mean. Bring with you, for you *must come immediately*, if you care to see poor Aunt Dinah before she departs---a basket-bottle of eau de Cologne, like the former, you know the kind I mean, and buy it at the same place. You need not get the cameo ring for Doctor Drake, I shan't make him a present---in fact, we are not now on terms. I had heard from many people of his incivility and want of temper; God forgive him his *ingratitude*, however, as I do. The basket-bottle holds about a pint, *remember*. I want to tell you exactly what I can do for you by my will; I always told you, dear William, it was very *small;* still, as the people used to say, 'every little makes a muckle,' and though little, it will be a *help*. I cannot rest till you come; I know, and am sure you love poor old auntie, and would like to close her eyes when the hour comes; therefore, dear Willie, come without delay. Also bring with you half a pound of the snuff, the same mixture as before; they make it up at Figgs's —*get it there*—not in paper, observe; in a canister, and *rolled in lead*, as will be poor auntie before long! Old Dobbs will have your room and bed comfortable, as usual; come by the cross coach, at eight o'clock. Tea, and anything else you like, will *await* you.

"Ever your fond old

"AUNTIE.

"P.S.—I send you, *to guard against mistakes*, the exact proportions of the mixture—the *snuff* I mean, of course. I quite forgot a new collar for Psyche, *plated*. Make them engrave 'Mrs. Perfect, Gilroyd Hall,' upon it. Heaven bless you. We are all progressing upward. Amen! says your poor old Aunt Dinah, who loves you."

It was in his quiet college room by candlelight that William Maubray read this letter from his kind, wild, preposterous, old aunt, who had been to him as a mother from his early days.

Aunt Dinah! was it possible that he was about to lose that familiar friend and face, the only person on earth who cared about him.

He read the letter over again. A person who did not know Aunt Dinah so well as he, would have argued from the commissions about scents, dog-collars, and snuff, that the old lady had no honest intention of dying. But he knew that incongruous and volatile soul too well to infer reliable consolation from those levities.

"Yes, yes—I shall lose her—she's gone," said the young man in great distress, laying the letter, with the gentleness of despair, upon the table, and looking down upon it in pain and rumination.

It would certainly make a change—possibly a fatal one in his prospects. A sudden change. He read the letter through again, and then, with a sinking heart, he opened the window and looked out upon the moonlight prospect. There are times when in her sweetest moods nature seems unkind. Why all this smiling light—this cheer and serenity of sky and earth —when he was stricken only five minutes since, perhaps undone, by the message of that letter---that sorrow-laden burlesque?

This sort of suggestion, in such a moment, comes despairingly. The vastness of creation —the inflexibility of its laws, and "What is man, and what am I among men, that the great Projector of all this should look after ephemeral me and my concerns? The human sympathy that I could rely upon, and human power—frail and fleeting—but still enough— is gone, and in this solitary hour, as in the coming one of death, experience fails me, and I must rest all upon that which, according to my light is faith, or theory, or chance!"

With a great sigh, and a heavy heart, William Maubray turned away from the window, and a gush of very true affection flooded his heart as he thought of kind old Aunt Dinah. He read the letter once more, to make out what gleams of comfort he could.

A handsome fellow was William Maubray —nearly three-and-twenty by this time—good at cricket—great at football: three years ago, in the school days, now, so old, tall, and lithe. A studious man in his own way—a little pale, with broad forehead, good blue eyes, and delicately formed, but somewhat sad features.

He looked round his room. He had grown very fond of that homely apartment. His eyes wandered over his few shelves of beloved old books, in all manner of dingy and decayed bindings—some of them two centuries and a half old, very few of later birth than a hundred years ago. Delightful companions— ready at a moment's call—ready to open their minds, and say their best sayings on any subject he might choose—resenting no neglect, obtruding no counsel, always the same serene, cheerful, inalienable friends.

The idea of parting with them was insupportable, nearly. But if the break-up came, they *must* part company, and the world be a new one for him. The young man spent much of that night in dismal reveries and speculations over his future schemes and chances, all of which I spare the reader.

Good Dr. Sprague, whom he saw next day, heard the news with much concern. He had known Miss Perfect long ago, and was decorously sorry on her account. But his real regrets were for the young man.

"Well, you go, of course, and see your aunt, and I do trust it mayn't be quite so bad. Stay, you know, as long as she wants you, and don't despond. I could wish your reading had been in a more available direction: but rely on it, you'll find a way to make a start and get into a profession, and with your abilities, I've no doubt you'll make your way in the world."

And the doctor, who was a shrewd as well as a kindly little gentleman, having buttoned the last button of his gaiter, stood, cap in hand, erect, and smiling confidently, he shook his hand, with a "God bless you, Maubray," and a few minutes later William Maubray, with all his commissions stowed away in his portmanteau, had commenced his little journey to Gilroyd Hall.

The moon was up, and the little town of Saxton very quiet, as Her Majesty's mail, dropping a bag at the post office, whirled through it, and pulled up at the further end, at the gate of Gilroyd Hall, there to drop our friend, an outside passenger.

The tall, florid iron gate was already locked. William tugged at the bell, and drew back a little to reconnoitre the premises. One of the old brick gables overhangs the road, with only a couple of windows high up, and he saw that his summons had put a light in motion within them. So he rejoined his hat-case, and his portmanteau, awaiting him on its end, in front of the white iron gate that looked like lace-work in the moonlight.

"Ha! Tom; glad to see you."

"Welcome, Mr. William, sir; she a weary in to see ye, and scarce thought you'd a come to-night."

The wicket beside the great gate was now open, and William shook hands with the old retainer, and glancing anxiously up at the stone-faced windows, as it were to read the countenance of the old house, he asked, "And how *is* she, Tom, to-night?"

"Complainin' an' down-hearted a bit for *her*, that is now and again. She cried a good bout to-day wi' old Winnie, in the little parlour."

"She's up, then?"

"Ooh, ay; she's not a body to lay down while she's a leg to stan' on. But I do think she's nigh her endin'. Gie't to me," this referred to the portmanteau. "I do, poor old girl! and we's all be sorry, Master Willie."

William's heart sank.

"Where is she?" he inquired.

"In the drawing-room, I think."

By this time they were standing in the oak-pannelled hall, and some one looked over the banister from the lobby, upon them. It was old Winnie, the light of her candle shining pleasantly on her ruddy and kindly face.

"Oh! Master Willie. Thank God, you're come at last. Glad she'll be to see you."

Old Winnie ambled down the stairs with the corner of her apron to her eye, and shook him by both hands, and greeted him again very kindly, and even kissed him according to the tradition of a score of years.

"Is she *very* ill, Dobbs?" whispered he, looking pale.

"Well, not to say *very* to look at, you'd say, but she's 'ad a warnin', her and me sittin' in the bedroom, an' she's bin an' made a new will; the lawyer's bin up from Saxton. Don't ye say I said nothing, mind; 'twould only fret her, maybe."

---o---

CHAPTER III.

MISS DINAH PERFECT AND HER GUESTS.

"Is she alone?" he asked, postponing the trying moment of seeing her.

"No, the Doctor's with her still—Dr. Drake, and Miss Letty, his sister, you remember; they're drinkin' a cup o' tea, and some crumpets, and they'll all be right glad you're come."

"They ought to go away, don't you think?" mildly suggested William Maubray, a good deal shocked. "However, let me get to my room for two or thee minutes, and I shall be ready then."

They passed the drawing-room door, and Miss Letty Drake's deliberate tones were audible from within. When he had got to his room he asked Dobbs—

"What was the *warning* you spoke of?"

"Well, dear me! It was the table; she and me, she makes me sit before her, poor thing, and we—well, there *is* cracks, sure, on and off! And she puts this an' that together; and so one way or other—it puzzles my poor head, how—she does make out a deal."

William Maubray was an odd, rather solitary young man, and more given to reading and thinking than is usual at his years, and he detested these incantations to which his aunt, Miss Perfect, had addicted herself, of late years, with her usual capricious impetuosity; and he was very uncomfortable on hearing that she was occupying her last days with these questionable divinations.

When, in a few minutes, William ran down to the drawing-room, and with a chill of anticipation opened the door of that comfortable rather than imposing chamber, the tall slim figure of his aunt rose up from her arm-chair, beside the fire, for though it was early autumn, the fire was pleasant, and the night-air was frosty, and with light and wiry tread, stepped across the carpet to meet him. Her kind, energetic face was pale, and the smile she used to greet him with was nowhere, and she was arrayed from head to foot in deep mourning, in which, particularly as she abhorred the modern embellishment of crinoline, she looked more slim and tall even than she was.

The presence of her guests in no wise affected the greeting of the aunt and nephew, which was very affectionate, and even agitated, though silent.

"Good Willie, to come so quickly—I knew you would." Miss Perfect never wept, but she was very near tears at that moment, and there was a little silence, during which she held his hands, and then recollecting herself, dropt them, and continued more like herself.

"You did not expect to see me up and here; everything happens oddly with me. Here I am, you see, apparently, I dare say, much as usual. By half-past twelve o'clock to-morrow night I shall be dead! There, don't mind now—I'll tell you all by and by. This is my friend, Miss Drake, you know her."

They shook hands, Miss Drake smiling as brisk a smile as in a scene so awful she could hazard.

"And this, my kind friend Dr. Drake."

William had occasionally seen Dr. Drake in the streets of Saxton, and on the surrounding high roads at a distance, but he had never before had the honour of an interview.

The doctor was short and fat, a litle bald, and rather dusty, and somehow, William thought, resembled a jolly old sexton a good deal more than a physician He rose up, with his hands in his trowsers pockets, and some snuff in the wrinkles of his black cloth waistcoat, and bowed, with raised eyebrows and pursed mouth, gravely to his plate of crumpet.

William Maubray looked again on his aunt, who was adjusting her black draperies in her chair, and then once more at the doctor, whose little eye he caught for a second, with a curious and even cunning expression in it; but it was averted with a sudden accession of melancholy once more—and William asked—

"I—I hope, sir, there is nothing very imminent?"

The doctor cleared his voice, uneasily, and Aunt Dinah interposed with a nod, a little dryly—

"It is not quite in *his* department."

And whose department *is* it in? the student thought.

"I dare say Doctor Drake would tell you I'm very well—so perhaps, in a sense, I am; but—Doctor Drake has kindly come here as a friend."

Doctor Drake bowed, looking steadfastly into his cup.

"As a friend, dear Willie, just as you have come—an old friend." Miss Perfect spoke low, with a little tremor in her voice, and was, I believe, near crying, but braced her resolution. William drew near gently and sat down beside her, and placing her hand upon his, she proceeded,

"My dear friend Miss Drake, there, does not agree with me, I'am aware; but Doctor Drake who has read more, and perhaps, *thought* more, thinks otherwise—at least, so I'm led to suppose."

The Doctor coughed a little; Miss Drake raised her long chin, and with raised eyebrows, looked down on her finger tips which were drumming on the table, and my cousin William glanced from one to the other, not quite understanding her drift.

"But," she continued, "I've apprised them already, and I tell *you* of course; it is—you'll remember the name—an intimation from Henbane."

"Poison!" said William, under his breath, with a look of pale inquiry at Doctor Drake, who at the moment was swallowing his tea very fast, and was seized on a sudden with an explosion of couching, sneezing, and strangling which compelled him to jump to his feet, and stagger about the room with his face in his pocket-handkerchief and his back to the tea-table.

"When Dr. Henbane," said my aunt with severity, "I mean a—Doctor *Drake*—has quite done coughing, I'll go on."

There was a little pause.

"Confound it," thought William, who was half beside himself, "it's a very odd dying scene!"

The doctor blowing his nose, returned very red and solemn, and explained, still coughing at intervals, that it was a little tea in the trachea; it invariably occured to him when he drank tea in the evening; he *must* give it up; "*you* know, Letty."

Miss Drake did not deign to assist him.

"She does not seem to know so much about it as you do," observed Aunt Dinah with an irony.

"Owing to my not *thinking* so much," replied Miss Letty, sarcastically.

"Henbane!" murmured William again, in a puzzled horror.

"H'm!—yes!—Henbane? you seem to have forgotten; one of those—one of the spirits who have attached themselves to me," and Aunt Dinah shot a quick glance at the doctor who though looking again at his crumpet, seemed to cower awfully under it.

"Oh—ay—Henbane!" exclaimed William in a tone of familarity, which indicated anything but respect for that supernatural acquaintance. "Henbane, to be *sure*."

And he looked on his aunt with a half amused recognition, which seemed to say, "Well—and what about that humbug?"

But Aunt Dinah said decisively—

"So much for the present; you shall hear *more*—every thing by-and-bye."

And there followed a silence.

"Did you remember the snuff, dear William?" inquired the doomed lady, with rather an abrupt transition.

"Certainly; shall I fetch it?" said William, half rising.

Miss Perfect nodded, and away he went, somehow vastly relieved, and with his bedroom candle in his hand, mounted the oak stairs, which were broad and handsome in proportion to the other dimensions of that snug old house.

CHAPTER IV.

VIOLET DARKWELL.

At the head of the stairs, the topmost step of which had been their bench, there rose to him two female figures. He did not instantly recognise them, for one candle only was burning, and it was on the little table nearly behind them. One was old Winnie Dobbs, the other Violet Darkwell; she stood up slight and girlish still, but looking taller that he had expected, with an old faded silk quilted shawl of Aunt Dinah's about her shoulders, and hoodwise over her head, for the night was frosty.

"Ha! Vi—little Vi, I was going to say; dear me! how you have grown! So glad to see you."

He had a girl's slim hand in his, and was speaking as he felt, very kindly.

"We've been waiting here, Winnie and I, to hear what you thought of dear grannie,"—(grannie was merely a pet name in this case, defining no relationship)—"and what do you think, William?"

"I really don't understand it," he answered. "I—I hope it's all nonsense; I really think so. She says she is very well; and the doctor—Drake, you know—I really think he was laughing, and one thing I'm quite certain of—it is connected in her mind with that foolish spirit-rapping."

"And you don't believe in it?" inquired the young lady.

"All bosh and nonsence. Not a bit of it," he replied.

"Oh, William, I am so delighted to hear you say so!" she exclaimed, much relieved by the promulgation of so valuable an opinion. "And you're quite right, I *know*, about grannie. It *is*, really—is not it, Winnie?—all about that awful spirit-rapping. Grannie never speaks of it to me; I believe she's afraid of frightening me; but old Winnie, here—you must not tell of her—she tells me all about it—everything; and I *am* so afraid of it; and it is *entirely* that. Granny thinks she has got a message! fancy! How awful! And Winnie does not know what the words were; for grannie writes down the letters with a pencil, and tells her only what she thinks fit; and I am *so* delighted—you can't think."

"You good little Vi, I'm so glad to see you!" She laughed a low little laugh—the first for several days—as he shook her hand again; and he said—

"Winnie, do, like a dear old thing, open my portmanteau—here's the key—and fetch me a canister you'll see at the top, with a great paper label, blue and red, on it."

Away went Winnie Dobbs, with his key and candle, and he said to the pretty girl who stood leaning lightly against the banister—

"My old friend, Vi! When I went into the drawing-room just now, I looked all round for you, and could not think what had become of you, and was really afraid you had gone away to London. I don't think I should ever care to come to Gilroyd Hall again; I should prefer seeing my aunt anywhere else—it would not be like itself if you were gone."

"So you really missed me, William?" She laughed.

"I should think so. And another thing—you are not to call me William. Why don't you call me Willie, or old bear, as you used to do? If you change old names, I'll begin and call you Miss Darkwell."

"How awful!"

"Indeed I will, and be as formal as you please, and treat you like a young lady, and you'll never be 'wicked little Vi' any more."

She was laughing as she leaned back, and could see her small teeth, and he bethought him that she was looking really quite lovely; so with two fingers he picked up her little hand again, as it lay at her side, and he said—

"And we are always to be good friends you know—great friends; and although you've no more dolls to mend, I'll still be of use. I'm going to the bar, and I'll manage all your lawsuits, if you let me; and when you are going to be married, I'll draw your settlements, and you are to have me always for your counsel."

She was still smiling, but said nothing, and looked wonderfully pretty, with the old grey silk hood wrapped all about her, so that sober old William was on the very point of kissing the slender hand he held in his. But a new feeling of shyness prevented, and he only shook her hand gently once more, and laid it by her side again, as you replace some precious thing you have been admiring where you found it.

"And you really think we may be happy about dear old grannie again?" she said.

The sound of Winnie's footsteps was heard approaching.

"Yes; certainly. I'll try to get a word with Doctor Drake. I can't imagine anything serious. Won't you come to the drawing-room now?"

"No; not to-night; not while those people are there. I was so wretched about dear grannie, I could not bear to go in at first; and now it would be odd, I think, going down when tea is over."

"As if I had brought you down from the nursery, as I often did, Vi, on my back. Well, old Winnie, have you got it?"

"Here, I think, Master William," answered Winnie.

"Yes; all right. So you won't come, Vi?"

"No."

"Quite made up your mind?"

"Quite, Willie."

"Thats right—*Willie*," said he with a smile, and a nod of approbation. "I should so like to stay here a little longer, as you won't come, and here all the news, and tell you mine. But Aunt Dinah would lose patience—I'm afraid she *has*."

"Yes, indeed; you had better go. Good night, bear."

"Good night, wicked little Vi. Remember we meet at breakfast—shan't we?"

"Oh, certainly. Good night."

"Good night."

And so the gray silk hood vanished, with a smile, prettily, round the corner, and William Maubray descended with his snuff to the drawing-room, with the pretty oval portrait of that young face still hovering before him in the air.

Miss Letty Drake, whose countenance was unpleasantly long in proportion to her height, and pallid, and her small figure bony, and who was dressed on this sad occasion in her silk "half-mourning," a sad and, it was thought, a dyed garment, which had done duty during many periods of affliction, as William entered the room, was concluding a sentence with a low pointed asperity, thus—"which seems to me hardly compatible with Saint Paul's description of Christian charity," and a short silence followed these words.

"I was going to ring the bell William," said the doomed lady of the house. "One would have thought you were *making* that snuff. Let me see it—h'm. See, get off this cover. Ho! what is this? A lead wrapper!"

"You said, Aunt Dinah, you wished it."

"Did I? Well, no matter. Get it open. Thanks. Yes; that's it. Yes; very good. You take snuff, doctor, don't you?"

"A *yes*, certainly, nothing like it, I do believe—where a man is obliged to work his head—aw haw—a stimulus and a sedative."

The doctor, it was averred, "worked" his occasionally with brandy and water, and not a great deal of otherwise.

"No, many thanks; don't care for perfumes; high toast is my snuff." And Doctor Drake illustrated the fact by a huge pinch, which shed another brown shower over the wrinkles of his waistcoat.

"Letty, dear," said Aunt Dinah, turning suddenly to Miss Drake, "we won't quarrel; we can't agree, but I won't quarrel."

"Well, dear, I'm glad to hear you say so. I'm sure, for my part, I never quarrel. 'Be ye angry, and let not the sun go down on your wrath.'"

CHAPTER V.

AUNT DINAH IS IN THE HORRORS, AND DOCTOR DRAKE PUTS HIS NIGHT-CAP IN HIS POCKET.

"I WISH to say good-by to you very kindly," said Aunt Dinah, quite sadly and gently, and somehow not like herself, "and—I've tried to keep up; I know it must happen, and I'm sure it is for the best, but——"

"I hope and expect, my dear Dinah," interposed Miss Letty, sharply—she was pulling on her worsted "wrists"—"to see you in the enjoyment of many years of your accustomed health and spirits, and I have no doubt humanly speaking, that I shall."

Miss Letty was quiet and peremptory, but also a little excited. And the doctor for want of something better to do, cleared his voice, in a grand abstraction, and wound up his watch slowly, and held it to his ear, nobody knew exactly why.

"You won't believe me, but I know it, and so will you—too late; to-morrow night at twelve o'clock I shall be dead. I've tried to keep up—I have; I've tried it; but oh! Ho, ho, hoo, ooh," and poor Aunt Dinah quite broke down, and cried and hooted hysterically.

Dr. Drake had now before him an intelligible case, and took the command accordingly with desision. Up went the window; cold water was there, and spirit of hartshorn. And when she had a little recovered, the Doctor, who was a good-natured fellow said—

"Now Miss Perfect, ma'am, it won't do, I tell you; it's only right; you may want some assistance; and if as an old friend, you'll allow me to return and remain here for the night, a sofa, or an arm-chair, anything, I'll be most happy, I do assure you.

But Aunt Dinah, with many thanks, said, "No," peremptorily, and wilful man or woman, who will contend with?

So, like the awful banquet in Macbeth, Miss Dinah Perfect's tea-party broke down and up, and the guests, somewhat scared, got in to their walking wrappers, rather silently, and their entertainer remained behind unstrung and melancholic.

But William Maubray, who came down to assist in the rummage for cloaks and umbrellas, asked leave, in his blunt modest way, to accompany Miss Letty and her brother, the doctor, to Saxton.

Now there seemed something real and grisly in Aunt Dinah's terror, which a little infected William Maubray; and the little party marched in silence along the frost-hardened road, white in moonlight, with the bare switch-like shadows of the trees across it, on their way to the pretty old town of Saxton.

At last the doctor said—

"She won't miss you, do you think?"

"She told me she'd like to be quiet for half an hour and I should be so much obliged if you could tell me, whether you really, that is, *still* think that she ought to have a medical man in attendance to-night."

"Why, you know what hysteria is. "Well, she is in a highly hysterical state. She's a woman who resists; it would be safer, you see, if she gave way and cried a bit now and then, when nature prompts, but she won't, except under awful high pressure, and then it might be serious; those things sometimes run off into fits."

And so the doctor lectured William upon his aunt's nerves, until they had arrived at the door of his snug house in the High Street.

Here they shook hands; but William Maubray, who was unhappy about Aunt Dinah, after Miss Letty had mounted to her chamber, very urgently entreated the doctor to return, and see how it might end.

With a bottle of valerian, his slippers, and a night-cap in his packet. Docter Drake did consent to return, and he smuggled into Gilroyd Hall.

"I don't know what to make of that spirit-rapping quite," said the doctor, as side by side they approached the Hall. "There's a quantity of books published on it—very unaccountable if half what they say is true. I suppose you've read it all. You read a lot, Miss Perfect tells me."

"I've read very little about it, except in the papers. She fancies she has had a message, telling her she is to die sometime to-morrow. I can't believe there's really anything more than self-deceptioen · but is there not a danger ?"

"How ?" asked the doctor.

"I mean, being so nervous as you suppose, and quite convinced that she is to die at a particular time ; might not her own mind—you know Lord Lyttelton died in consequence of such a persuasion."

William paused, Doctor Drake lowered, between his fingers, the cigar he was smoking, and they came to a halt, with a little wheel to the left, and the doctor, with his head aside, blowing the smoke up in a thin stream, looked with a thoughtful scrutiny up at the clear bright moon; perhaps a not unsuitable source of inspiration upon their crazy theme.

"I forget *which* Lord Lyttelton that was," said the doctor, wisely. "Isn't it *Lyttleton*, you say ? But the thing is quite possible. There's a spirit you know she's always talking about. She calls him Henbane. Egad, sir, I was develish near laughing at tea when she named him so suddenly that time ; I'd have been up a tree if I had you know. You did not see what she was at, but I did. That Henbane's her gospel, egad, and she thinks it was he who told her—d'ye see ? Come along. She'll be wondering where you are."

So on they went towards Gilroyd Hall, whose outline, black and sharp, against the lumnious sky, was relieved at one point by the dull glow of candle-light through the red curtains, of what William Maubray knew to be Aunt Dinah's bedchamber window.

"She is in her room, I think—there's light in her window," said William. The doctor nodded, chucking his cigar stump far away, for he knew Aunt Dinah's antipathy to tobacco, and they were now on the door-step. He was thinking, if the case were to end tragically, what a capital paper he would make of it, beside the interesting letter he would send to the editor of the *Spatula*.

"Winnie's bin a callin' over the stairs for you, Master Willie. Misses wants ye to her room," said Tom, who awaited them on the door-steps.

"I'll sit by the fire in the study," whispered the doctor. "I don't mind sitting up a night now and then. Give me a cloak or something. There's a sofa, and I'll do very well."

The principle of life was strong in Aunt Dinah, and three hours later that active-minded lady was lying wide awake on her bed, with a variety of topics, not all consisting with the assumed shortness of her hours, drifting in succession through her head. The last idea that struck her was the most congruous, and up she jumped, made a wild toilet, whose sole principle was warmth, tied a faded silk handkerchief over her nightcap, across her ears, and with her long white flannel dressing gown about her, and a taper in her hand, issued, like the apparition of the Bleeding Nun, upon the gallery, and tapped sharply on William Maubray's door.

"William, William!" she called as she tapped, and from within William answered drowsily to the summons.

"Wait a moment," said the lady, and

"In glided Margaret's grimly ghost,
And stood at William's feet."

"We *must* have a *séance*, my dear boy ; I'm going to wake up old Winnie. It certainly has a connexion with your arrival ; but anything like the cracking, knocking, and creaking of *everything*, I've never yet heard. I have no doubt—so sure as you sit there"—(William was sitting up in his bed with glazed eyes, and senses only half awake)—"that your poor dear mother is here to-night. We're *sure* of Henbane ; and—just get your clothes on—I'm going for Winnie, and we meet in the study, mind, in five minutes."

And Aunt Dinah, having lighted William's candle, disappeared, leaving him with a fund of cheerful ideas to make his yawning and bewildered toilet.

——o——

CHAPTER VI.

IN WHICH THE WITCHES ASSEMBLE.

A FEW minutes later she glided into the study, overthrowing a small table, round which her little *séances* were accustomed to be made, and which the doctor had providently placed against the door.

Aunt Dinah held under her arm the 8vo "Revelations of Elihu Bung, the Pennsylvanian Prophet," a contribution to spiritual science which distanced all contemporary competition; and the chapter which shows that a table of a light, smart build, after having served a proper apprenticeship to "rapping," may acquire the faculty of locomotion and self-direction, flashed on her recollection as she recognised prostrate at her feet, in the glimmer of her taper, the altar of their mysteries, which she had with reverent hands herself placed that evening in its wonted corner, at the opposite end of the room.

Such a manifestation was new to her. She looked on it, a little paler than usual, and bethought her of that other terrible chapter in which Elihu Bung avers shat spirits, grown intimate by a long familiarity, will, in a properly regulated twilight—and her light at the moment was no more—made themselves visible to those whom they habitually favour with their advices.

Therefore she was strangely thrilled at sight of the indistinct and shadowy doctor, who awakened by the noise, rose at the opposite end of the room from the sofa on which he had fallen asleep. Tall and thin, and quite unrecognisable by him, was the white figure at the door, with a taper elevated above its head, and which whispered with a horrid distinctness the word "Henbane!"—the first heard on his awakening, the last in his fancy as he dropped asleep, and which sounded to him like the apparition's considerate announcement of its name on entering the room; he echoed "Henbane" in a suppressed diapason, and Aunt Dinah, with an awful ejaculation, repeated the word from the distance, and sank into a chair.

"Henbane!" cried the doctor briskly, having no other exclamation ready, and reassured by these evidences of timidity in the spectre, he exclaimed, "Hey, by Jove! what the plague!" and for some seconds he did not know distinctly where he was.

"Merciful goodness! Doctor Drake, why *will* you try to frighten people in this manner? Do you want to *kill* me, sir?"

"I? Ho! Ha, ha! ma'am," replied the learned gentleman, incoherently.

"What are you doing *here*, sir? I think you're mad!" exclaimed Aunt Dinah, fiercely.

The doctor cleared his voice, and addressed himself to explain, and before his first period was reached, William and old Winnie, wofully sleepy, had arrived.

Luckily the person who approaches such oracles as "Henbane," it is well known, must do so with a peaceful and charitable soul. So Miss Perfect was appeasable, and apologies being made and accepted, she thus opened her mind to the doctor—

"I don't complain, Doctor Drake—William, light the candles over the chimney-piece—although you terrified me a great deal more than in my circumstances I ought to have been capable of."

The candles were now lighted, and shone chearfully upon the short, fat figure, and ruddy, roguish face of Doctor Drake, and as he was taking one of his huge pinches of snuff, she added—

"And I won't deny that I *did* fancy for a moment you might be a spirit-form, and possibly that of Henbane."

William Maubray, who was looking at the doctor, as Miss Perfect reverently lowered her voice at these words, exploded into something so like a laugh, though he tried to pass it off for a cough, that his aunt looked sharply on him in silence for a moment.

"And I'm blowed but I was a bit frightened too, ma'am, when I saw you at the door there," said the doctor.

"Well, let us try," said Miss Perfect. "Come, we are four; let us try who are present—what spirits, and seek to communicate. You don't object Dr. Drake?"

"I? Ho! oh! dear no. I should not desire better—aw-haw—*instruction*, ma'am," answered the doctor.

I am afraid he was near saying "fun."

"Winnie, place the table as usual. There, yes. Now let us arrange ourselves."

The doctor sat down, still blinking, and with a great yawn inquired—

"Do we waw—haw—wa—w—want any particular information?"

"Let us first try whether they will communicate. We *always* want information," said Miss Perfect. "William, sit you there; Winnie, *there*. I'll take pencil and paper and record."

All being prepared, fingers extended, company intent, Aunt Dinah propounded the first question—

"Is there any spirit present?"

There was a long wait and no rejoinder.

"Didn't you hear something?" inquired the doctor.

William shook his head.

"I thought I *felt* it," persisted the doctor. "What do *you* say, ma'am?" addressing himself to Winnie, who looked, after her wont, towards her mistress for help.

"Did you feel anything?" demanded Miss Perfect sharply.

"Nothing but a little wind like on the back of my head, as I think," replied Winnie, driven to the wall.

"Wind on her head! That's odd," said Miss Perfect, looking in the air, as if she possessed the porcine gift of seeing it, "*very* odd!" she continued, with her small hand expanded in the air. "Not a breath stirring, and Winnie has no more imagination than that sofa pillow. You never fancy anything, Winnie?"

"Do I, ma'am?" inquired Winnie Dobbs, mildly.

"Well, *do* you, I say? No, you don't; of course you don't. You know you don't as well as I do."

"Well, I did think so, sure, ma'am," answered Winnie.

"Pity we can't get an answer," remarked the doctor, and at the same moment William felt the pressure of a large foot in a slipper—under the table. It had the air of an intentional squeeze, and he looked innocently at the doctor, who was, however, so entirely unconscious, that it must have been an accident.

"I say it is a pity, Mr. Maubray, isn't it? for we *might* hear something that might interest Miss Perfect very much, possibly, I say?"

"I don't know; I can't say, I've never heard anything," answered William, who would have liked to kick the table up to the ceiling and go off to his bed.

"Suppose, ma'am, we try again," inquired Dr. Drake.

"Certainly," replied Aunt Dinah, "we must have patience."

"Will you ask, ma'am, please, again if there's a spirit in the room?" solicited the doctor; and the question being put, there came an upward heave of the table.

"Well?" exclaimed the doctor, looking at Winnie, "did you feel that?"

"Tilt, ma'am," said Winnie, who knew the intelligence would be welcome.

"What do *you* say?" inquired Miss Perfect triumphantly of William.

Doctor Drake was changing his position just at the moment, and I perceived no other motion in the table—nothing but the little push he gave it," answered William.

"Oh, pooh! yes, of course, there was that," said the doctor a little crossly; "but I meant a sort of a start—a crack like, in the leaf of the table."

"I felt nothing of the kind," said William Maubray.

The doctor looking disgusted, and leaning back, took a large pinch of snuff. There was a silence. Aunt Dinah's lips were closed with a thoughtful frown as she looked down upon the top of the table,

"It is very strange. I certainly never witnessed in this house more unequivocal evidences—*preliminary* evidences, of course—of spiritual activity."

"I think, ma'am, I have read," said the doctor, with his hands in his pockets, "I *think*, somewhere, that if any one of the manipulators happens to be an unbeliever——"

"An unbeliever in the manifestations, of course the spirits won't communicate," interposed Miss Perfect, volubly laying down the law. "Winnie is a believer as much as I. We all know *that*. Nephew, how are you? Do you *believe?* You shake your head. Speak out. Yes or no?"

"Well, I don't," said he, a little sheepishly.

"You don't? And, not believing, you sit here with your fingers on the table, keeping Doctor Drake out of his—his——"

She could not say bed, and the doctor relieved her by saying, "Oh, as to me, ma'am, I'm only too happy; but you know it's a pity, all the same."

"Very true, doctor. Much obliged. We shall set it to rights, My dear William, you might have told us at starting; but we'll commence again. Sit by the fire, William, and I trust in a little time you may be convinced."

———o———

CHAPTER VII

THE FAMILIAR SPEAKS.

So the excommunicated William, with his feet upon the fender, leaning upon his elbow in the great chair, made himself comfortable by the fire, and heard his aunt propound the questions, and the answers by the previously appointed manifestations, duly noted down.

"Is there a spirit present?"

"Yes."

"Are there more than one?"

"No.'

"Is it a male or female spirit?"

No answer.

"Is it Henbane?"

"Yes" (emphatically).

William *was* surprised. All was now going smoothly, and he could not for a moment suspect a gentleman of Dr. Drake's respectability of participating in a trick. But there was a monotony in the matter of a quieting kind, and William grew too drowsy to keep his eyes long open.

"Did you give Miss Dinah Perfect a message on Monday last?"

"Yes."

"Did it concern her death?"

"Yes."

"Is her death to take place at the time then appointed?"

Here the table made a positive jump, and in spite of a grasp made at it by the doctor's fingers, it fell flat on the floor, and it must have been a very violent impulse, for Dr. Drake's slipper was off, and he, very red, no doubt from his effort to prevent the wilful fall of the table.

"Very extraordinary!" exclaimed he, standing up

"Most wonderful!" said my aunt.

Good old fat Winnie sat with her fingers raised in the air, looking at the postrate table with placid astonishment.

"That's a tilt," said the doctor, "that means *no*—a very *emphatic* tilt."

"I think it was a *jump*," said my aunt, sadly.

"No, ma'am, no—a tilt, a tilt, I'll take my oath. Besides, a *jump* has no meaning," urged he with energy.

"Pardon me; when a question is received with marked impatience a jump is no unfrequent consequence."

"Oh, oh!" groaned the doctor, reflectively. "Then it counts for nothing?"

"Nothing," said Miss Perfect in a low tone. "Winnie, get the table up again."

"Suppose, ma'am, to avoid mistakes," said the doctor, after reflection, "suppose we put it upon it to express itself in language. Just ask it what about Miss Dinah Perfect's death."

"I've no objection," said Miss Perfect; and in the terms prescribed by Dr. Drake the momentous question was put.

Hereupon the spelling commenced—

A-D-J-O-U-R-N-E-D."

"Postponed, put off, ma'am!" said the doctor, expounding eagerly.

"I know; good heaven! I understand," answered Aunt Dinah, faintly.

"Give her some water. *Here*, ma'am," said he, presenting a glass of water at her pale lips. She sipped a little.

"Now we'll ask, ma'am, please, for how long?" suggested the doctor.

And this question likewise having been propounded, the table proceeded once more to spell—

"S-I-N-E D-I-E."

"It ends with *die*," said my poor aunt, faintly.

"*Sine die*, ma'am. It means indefinitely, ma'am; your death is postponed without a day named—for ever, ma'am! It's all over; and I'm very happy it has ended so. What a marvellous thing, ma'am—give her some more water, please—those manifestations are. I hope, ma'am, your mind is quite relieved—perfectly, ma'am."

Miss Dinah Perfect was taken with a violent shivering, in which her very teeth chattered. Then she cried, and then she laughed; and finally Doctor Drake administered some of his ammonia and valerian, and she became, at last, composed.

With audible thanksgivings old Winnie accompanied her mistress upstairs to her room, where Aunt Dinah herself, who, notwithstanding her necromancy, was a well-intending, pious churchwoman, descended to her knees at her bedside, and poured forth her gratitude for the reprieve, and then in a loud and distinct voice read to old Winnie Dobbs the twentieth chapter of the Second Book of Kings, in which we read how the good king Hezekiah obtained by prayer ten years more of the light of life.

Then old Winnie persuaded her to have a glass of very hot port wine-negus, which agreed with her so well that she quickly fell asleep; and never did poor lady need repose more, or drink deeper and more tranquil draughts of that Lethe.

William Maubray was now wide awake, and he and the doctor, being a little chilly, sat before the study fire.

"It's jolly, isn't it?" exclaimed William, for the seventh time. "But is'nt it all very odd, sir, and very unaccountable—I—I think?"

"Very, very odd, to be sure," said the doctor, poking the corner of a lump of coal—"very, no doubt."

"I wish I had been awake. I should like to see one of those things—those *séances*. I had no idea there really was anything so coherent."

"Very lucky for her," replied the doctor, with a sly little wink to William.

William looked inquiringly at the doctor, who smiled on the poker's end, and pushed the embers gently with it.

"You don't believe in it, sir—do you?" inquired William, puzzled.

"I? Well, I don't know exactly what to say, you know. I put my foot in it on Sunday last, when I told her I did not believe a bit of it; nor more I *did*. Egad, you never saw a woman so angry, when I called it all bosh. You'd better not vex her that way, my boy—d'ye see? She lent me one of those wonderful queer books from America—very odd they are—and I read it to please her. So, you see, that's how we stand; very good friends again."

"And you are convinced it's true?" urged William, who, like other young men who sit up late, and read wild books, and drink strong coffee, was, under the rose, addicted to the supernatural.

"Why, you see, as Shakespeare says, there are more bubbles between heaven and earth than are dreamt of by the philosophers," observed the doctor, with a little paraphrase. "I wish to live at peace with my neighbours; and I advise you to think over this subject, old fellow, and not to tease the old lady upstairs about it—that's all.'

"'I wish he'd speak out, and tell me what happened to-night, and tell me his real opinion," thought William Maubray. "I've read in some old medical book," he continued aloud, "that the vital electricity escapes and diffuses itself at the finger-tips."

"Oh, to be sure! All sorts of theories. The hand's a very mysterious organ. The hand of glory, you may be certain, was not altogether a story. The electric light has been seen at the finger-tips in consumptive cases in the dark; and a patient convulsed, or in a state of extreme nervous exhaustion, will clench the hand so as to prevent the escape of this influence at the finger-points, and then joining hands, in love, you know, or friendship—and in fact it is, sir, a very mysterious organ; and I'm prepared to believe a great deal that's curious about its occult powers. Your aunt told you about the toad she saw climb over her coverlet one night, and turn into a hand and grasp her wrist."

"No," said William.

"Egad, she's ready to swear to it. Last winter she was so frightened, she was not fit to stand for a week after. She reads too much of those books. Egad, sir, she'll turn her head, and that will be the end of it. However, we've pulled her through this, and I hope she'll give it up, true or false. You see, there's no good in it; and if she goes on, sooner or later she'll frighten herself out of her wits."

"But that toad was a very curious idea," said William. "What does she make of it? Does she think it was a fancy only, or a real thing?"

"Pooh! A spirit of course. She calls it the key-spirit that unlocks the spirit world, you see; and from the time it touches you, you are in report with the invisible world, and subject, as she says she is, to their visitations you see— ha, ha, ha!"

William laughed too.

"Last winter?" he said. "She never told me."

"Pooh! All fancies," observed the doctor. "Better she should not talk of them. Those American people are all going mad. She'll get touched in the upper storey if she does not mind."

——o——

CHAPTER VIII.

WILLIAM MAUBRAY'S VISION.

After some more talk of this kind, they parted, and William Maubray, as he lay down again in his bed, wondered whether the doctor, whom he had heard described as a shrewd man, believed in the revelations at which he had assisted; or, was it possible—could he have been accessory to—Oh! no, it could not be!

The student, as I have said, had a sort of liking for the supernatural, and although now and then he had experienced a qualm in his solitary college chamber at dead of night, when, as he read a well-authenticated horror, the old press creaked suddenly, or the door of the inner room swung slowly open of itself, it yet was "a pleasing terror" that thrilled him; and now as he lay this night awake, with a patch of moonlight spread askance on the floor —for Aunt Dinah insisted on a curfew, and he, "preferring the light that heaven sheds" to no lamp at all, left the window-shutter a little open, and for a while allowed his eyes to wander over the old-fashioned and faded furniture of the apartment, and his fancy to wander among those dreams of superstition with which he rather liked to try his courage.

He conned over his aunt's story of the toad, recounted to him by Doctor Drake, and which he had never heard before, until the nodding shadow of the sprig of jessamine on the floor took the shape of the sprawling reptile, and seemed to swagger clumsily toward his bed and every noise in the curtains suggested, its slimy clamberings.

Youth, fatigue, pure country air, in a little while overpowered these whimsies, and William Maubray fell into a deep sleep.

I am now going to relate a very extraordinary incident; but upon my honour the narrative is true. William Maubray dreamed that he was in the room in which he actually lay; that he was in bed, and that the moonlight entered the room, just as he had seen it before going to sleep. He thought that he heard a heavy tread traverse the room over his head; he heard the same slow and ponderous step descend the narrow back stair, that was separated from him only by the wall at the back of his bed. He knew intuitively that the person thus approaching came in quest of him, and he lay expecting, in a state of unaccountable terror. The handle of his door turned, and it seemed that his intending visitor paused, having opened the door about a hand's breadth, and William knew that he had only suspended, not abandoned his purpose, be it what it might. Then the door swung slowly open, and in the deep shadow, a figure, of gigantic stature, entered, paused beside his bed, and seized his wrist with a tremendous gripe.

For a time, unable to stir, he remained passive under its pressure. Then with a horrified struggle he awoke. There was no figure visible, but his wrist was actually compressed in a cold grasp, and, with a ghastly ejaculation, he sprang from his bed and was released.

He had no means of lighting a candle; he had nothing for it but to bounce to the window, fling curtains and shutters wide, and admit the full flood of moonlight, which revealed the contents of the room, and showed that no figure but his own was there. But there were the marks of the grasp that had held him, still visible. He secured his door, and made search, in a state of horror, but was convinced. There was no visible intruder in the chamber.

Now William got back into his bed. For the first time in his life he had experienced a paroxysm of that wild fear with which it had been so often his delight to trifle. He heard the clock at the stair-head strike hour after hour, and at last, after having experienced every stage in the subsidence of such horrors, fairly overcome by fatigue, he sunk to sleep.

How welcome and how beautiful shone the morning! Slanting by his window, the sunbeam touched the quivering jessamine leaves and the clustering roses, and in the dewy air he heard the chirp and whistle of the happy birds. He threw up his window, and breathed the perfumed air, and welcomed all the pleasant sounds of morning in that pleasant season.

"The cock he crew,
Away then flew
The fiends from the church-door."

And so the uncomfortable and odious shadows of the night winged their foul flight before these cheerful influences, and William Maubray, though he felt the want of his accustomed sleep, ran down the well-known stairs, and heard with a happy heart from Winnie Dobbs that his kind old aunt was ever so much better.

Doctor Drake had withdrawn from his uncomfortable bivouac, carrying with him his night-cap and slippers, and hastening to his toilet in the pleasant town of Saxton, where, no doubt, Miss Letty cross-questioned him minutely upon the occurrences of the night.

I have said before that the resources of Gilroyd were nothing very remarkable; still, there was the Saxton Cricket Club, who practised zealously, and always welcomed William, whose hit to leg was famous, and even recorded as commendable in the annual volume of the great Mr. Lillywhite; where he was noted, in terms that perplexed Aunt Dinah, as a promising young bat, with a good defence. He fished a little; and he played at fives with young Trevor of Revington, whom nobody very much liked—the squire of Saxton, who assumed territorial and other airs that were oppressive, although Revington was only two thousand five hundred pounds a year; but, in that modest neighbourhood, he was a very important person, and knew that fact very well.

He had of late distinguished Violet with a slight admiration, that ought to have been gratifying. Once or twice he paid old Miss Perfect a little neighbourly, condescending visit, and loitered a good deal about the garden, and that acre and a half of shrubbery, which she called "the grounds." He sometimes joined in the walk home from church, and sometimes in other walks; and Aunt Perfect was pleased and favourable, and many of the Saxton mothers and daughters were moved to envy and malice.

"I played to-day," said William, giving an account of his hours at tea to the ladies, "two rubbers of fives; with whom do you think?"

He stopped, smiling slily on Violet, who was steadfastly looking down on Miss Perfect's crest on her tea-spoon.

"Well, I'm sure you know, by that unerring instinct that poets speak of," said William; "but it is hardly fair to ask you to name him."

Violet looked up, having blushed very prettily, but not very well pleased.

"Of course I mean Trevor—Vane Trevor—of Revington. It sounds very well. Trevor was two years my senior at school; he left at the end of the third half after I came; that makes him nearly twenty-five now. How old are you, Vi,—you'd make a very pretty mistress of Revington; yes, indeed, Vi, or anywhere else. Don't be vexed, but tell me exactly how old you are."

He tapped with his pencil on the table to hasten her answer, as he looked at her, smiling a little sadly.

"How old?" she repeated.

"Well?"

"Past seventeen. Why do you want to know?" she added, laughing.

"Well, he's not quite five-and-twenty yet; only twenty-four to your seventeen. Seven years is a very pretty difference."

"What *are* you talking about, William? This kind of thing is thought very funny: it is very disagreeable. If people will talk nonsense, do let it be amusing. You used to be sometimes amusing."

"That was long ago, when I told you 'Sinbad the Sailor,' and 'The Romance of the Forest;' before the romance of the shrubbery commenced."

"Folly" exclaimed Violet.

——o——

CHAPTER IX.

IN WHICH MISS VIOLET SAYS WHAT SHE THINKS OF MR. VANE TREVOR, AND IS VIOLET NO LONGER.

"Now, I tell you," continued William Maubray, and he glanced at Aunt Dinah; but she was reading, with her gold spectacles on, the second of a series of old letters, which she had in an old stamped letter box beside her, and had forgotten all else. "You really must tell me what you think of Vane Trevor?"

Miss Vi fixed her glowing eyes full upon his for a moment, and then dropped them suddenly. His were full of their old, gentle, good-natured mirth.

There was a little pause, and, suddenly looking up, she said, rather petulantly:

"Think of him? Why, I suppose I think what every one else does. I think him handsome; I think him agreeable; I think he has an estate; I think he looks like a gentleman; and I think he is the only man who ever appears in this neighbourhood that is not in one way or other a bore. Shall I sing you a song?"

And with heightened colour and bright eyes, this handsome girl sat down to the piano, which had a cracked and ancient voice, like the reedy thrum of a hurdy-gurdy, contrasting quaintly with her own mellow tones, and she sang—nothing to the purpose, nothing with a sly, allegoric satire in it, but the first thing that came into her head—sweet and sad as a song of old times; and ancient Miss Perfect, for a verse or so, lowered her letter, and listened, smiling, with a little sigh; and William, listening also, fell into a brown study, as he looked on the pretty songstress, and her warblings mingled with his dreams.

"Thank you, little Vi," said he, rising with a sudden smile, and standing beside her as the music ceased. "Very pretty—very sweet."

"I am glad you like it, William," she said, kindly.

"*William*, again!" he repeated.

"Well—*yes*."

"And why not *Willie*, as it used to be?" he persisted.

"Because it sounds foolish, somehow. I'm sure you think so. I do."

It seemed to him, as, with a sad smile, he looked at her, thinking over the words that sounded so like a farewell, so light and cruel, too, that there yet was wisdom—that precocious wisdom with which nature accomplishes the weaker sex—in her decision; and something of approval lighted up his sad smile, and he said, with a little nod:

"I believe the young lady says wisely; yes, you are a wise little woman, and I submit."

Perhaps, she was a little disappointed at his ready acquiescence; at all events, she wound up with a loud chord on the piano, and standing up, said:

"Yes, it sounds foolish, and so, indeed, I think, does *William;* and people can't go on being children always, and talking nonsense; and you know we are no relations—at least, that I know of—and I'll call you—yes, I *will*—*Mr. Maubray*. People may be just as friendly, and yet—and yet call one another by their right names. And now, Mr. Maubray, will you have some tea?"

"No, thanks; no more tea to-night. I'm sure it has lost its flavour. It would not taste like tea."

"What's the matter with the tea?" asked Miss Perfect, over the edge of her letter. "You don't like your tea, William? Is not it strong enough?"

"Quite; too much; almost bitter, and a little cold."

"Fancy, child," said Aunt Dinah, who apprehended a new attack on her tea-chest, and hated waste. "I think it particularly *good* this evening," and she sipped a little in evidence of her liking, and once more relapsed into reading.

"I can add water," said Violet, touching the little ivory handle of the tea-urn with the tip of her finger, and not choosing to apprehend William's allegory.

"No, thank you, Vi—Violet, I mean—Miss

Darkwell; indeed, I forgot. What shall I read to-night?" and he strode listlessly to the little book case, whose polished surface flashed pleasantly to the flicker of the wood fire. "'Boswell's Johnson,' 'Sir Charles Grandison, "Bishop Horsley's Sermons,' 'Trimmer's Works,' 'A Simple Story,' 'Watts' Sacred Songs,' 'Rasselas,' 'Poems, by Alfred Tennyson.'"

His quiet voice as he read the names on the backs of Aunt Dinah's miscellaneous collection, sounded changed and older, ever so much, in Violet's ear. All on a sudden for both, a part of their lives had been cut off, and a very pleasant time changed irrevocably to a retrospect.

"I think 'Tennyson.' What do you?" he asked, turning a smile that seemed faded now, but kindly as ever, upon her.

As the old name was gone, and the new intolerable, he compounded by calling her by none; and she, likewise, in her answer:

"Oh! yes, Tennyson, Tennyson, by all means; that is, if Miss Perfect wishes."

"Yes—oh! to be sure; but haven't you read it before?" acquiesced Miss Perfect.

William smiled at Violet, and said to Miss Dinah, "I think—and don't you?"—this was to Vi, parenthetically, "that poetry is never heard fairly on a first reading. It resembles music—you must know it a little to enjoy it."

"That's just what I think," said Violet, eagerly.

"Very good, young people," said my aunt, with a little toss of her head. "For my part, I think there's but one Book will bear repeated reading, and that is the Bible."

"Not even 'Elihu Bung?'" suggested William.

"There—read your poetry," said Miss Perfect. "I shan't interrupt; I'm reading these, looking back for the date of a family event."

This was an exercise not unfrequently imposed on her by Henbane, who now and then made a slip in such matters, and thus perplexed and troubled Aunt Dinah, who had sometimes her secret misgivings about his accuracy and morality.

"What shall I read?" asked William in a lower tone.

"Anything, 'Mariana,'" she answered.

"The 'Moated Grange,'" repeated William, and smiled. "'The poetry of monotony.' I could fancy, if a few pleasant faces were gone, this Gilroyd Hall, much as I like it, very like the Moated Grange."

And without more preface he read that exquisite little poem through, and then leaned back in his chair, the book open upon the table, pretty Violet sat opposite, working at her crochet, in a reverie, as was he as he gazed on her.

"Where did she learn all that? How much wiser they are than we. What a jolly ass *I* was at seventeen, and all the fellows. What fools—weren't they?—in things like that; and by Jove! she's quite right, I could not go on *Vi*-ing her all my days, just because when she was a child she used to be here. They are certainly awfully wise in that sort of thing. Pretty head she has—busy, busy—quite a little world within it now, I dare say. What a wonder of wonders, that little casket! Pretty hair, awfully pretty, and the shape of her head, so pretty, and yet the oval reminds me, right or wrong, of a serpent's head; but she has nothing of that in her, only the wisdom, and, perhaps the fascination. She'll make some fellow's heart sore yet; she'll make some great match, I dare say; but that's a long way off, eight years; yes, she'll be twenty-four then; time enough before her."

"Is there any cricket for to-morrow?" asked Vi on a sudden.

"No match, no. I'm going up to look at Revington. Trevor said he'd call for me early—eleven o'clock—for *me*, mind; and you know I begin to feel an interest in Revington."

"Oh! it's very pretty, great old timber," she said, "and a handsome place, and a good estate—three thousand a year, only it owes some money. What an ambitious, audacious person I must be. I'm certain you think so, because it is quite plain I covet my neighbour's house, and his ox, and his ass, and everything that is his; and coveting, Dr. Mainwaring tells us, is the fountain-head of all iniquity, for how could a person so poor as I ever obtain all these fine things without fraud and chicanery?"

Miss Violet was talking a little recklessly and angrily, but she looked unusually handsome, her colour was so beautiful and there was so strange a fire in her vexed eyes. What was the meaning of this half-suppressed scorn, and who its real object? How enigmatical they grow so soon as the summer hours of fascination, and of passion with its disguises and sorrows, in all their transient glow and beauty, approach—the season of hope, of triumph, and of aching hearts.

CHAPTER X.

VANE TREVOR IS DISCUSSED AND APPEARS.

It was in this mysterous turbulent frame of mind that old Winnie Dobbs, bearing the Bible and book of family prayers, surprised Miss Violet Darkwell, and recalled Aunt Dinah from the sound and fury of forty years ago, now signifying no more than the discoloured paper on which they were recorded.

"Dear me! can it be a quarter to ten already?" exclaimed Miss Perfect, plucking her watch from her side and inspecting it. "So it is; come in."

And fat Mrs. Podgers, the cook, and Tom, with his grimmest countenance, and the little girl with a cap on, looking mild and frightened.

So, according to the ancient usage of Gilroyd Hall, to William's lot fell the reading of the

Bible, and to Aunt Dinah's that of the prayers, and then the little congregation broke up, and away went Vi to her bed-room, with old Winnie.

William was not worse, nor, I dare say, much better than other young Cambridge men of his day and College; but he liked these little "services" in which he officiated, and they entered into his serene and pleasant recollections of that sequestered habitation.!

"Well, William dear, I thank God I am spared to be with you a little longer."

"Amen," he said, "you dear Aunt, dear dear, old Aunt Dinah."

And they kissed very lovingly, and tnere was a silence, which Aunt Dinah in a few minutes broke by mentioning the very subject at that moment in his mind.

"You saw Violet a good deal grown—very pretty figure—in fact, I think her lovely; but we must not tell her so, you know. She has been very much admired, and a good, affectionate, amiable little soul she is. There's young Mr. Trevor. I can tell you people are beginning to talk about it. What do *you* think?"

William sat down his bedroom candle on the tea table, rubbed the apex of its extinguisher with the tip of his finger, and returned an answer answerless.

"He's very good-looking; isn't he? But he thinks a lot of himself; and don't you think it would be an awful pity little Vi should be married so soon?'

"Then you think he means to ask her?" said Miss Perfect, her silver-pencil case to her chin, her head a little aside, and looking very curiously into her nephew's eyes.

"I don't know; I haven't a notion. He said yesterday he thought her very pretty; but Trevor always talks like no end of a swell, and I really think he fancies a prnicess, or something of the sort, would hardly be good enough for him."

"It would, of course, be a very good match for Vi," said Miss Perfect, dropping her eyes, perhaps a little disappointed, and running her pencil-case back and forward slowly on the edge of William's plated candlestick, from which they both seemed to look for inspiration; "but a girl so pretty as she may look higher than Mr Trevor without presumption."

"Yes, indeed, and there's no hurry, Heaven knows. I don't think Trevor half good enough for her," said William.

"Oh, I don't say that; but—but more unlikely things have happened."

"Does he—does he make love to her?" said William who drew altogether upon the circulating library for his wisdom in those matters.

"He certainly admires her very much; he has been very attentive. I'm sure he likes her, and I can't hear that he is anything but a straightforward, honourable young man."

"I suppose he is," said William; "I'm sure he's that. And what does Violet—Miss Darkwell—say?"

"Say! Why of course I can't ask her to say anything till he speaks. I dare say she likes him, as why should she not? But that's only conjecture, you know; and you are not to hint it to him, mind, if he should question or poke you on the subject."

"Oh, no certainly," answered William, and there came a long pause. "But indeed, aunt, I don't think Vane Trevor half good enough for her."

"Oh! that's for *them*, my dear, to settle. There's nothing, in point of prudence, against it."

"No—oh, no. Everything *very* well. Lucky fellow, to be able to marry when he likes."

"And—but I forgot you don't mind. You think there's nothing in it. Still I may tell you. I have had—old Winnie and I—some answers."

"Table-rapping?" said William.

"A little *séance*. We sit down together, Winnie and I; and some responses, in my mind, can hardly refer to anything else, and most sweet and comforting they have been."

Once on this subject, my aunt was soon deep in it, and told her story of the toad which turned into a hand; whereupon William related his dream, and the evidences afforded by his waking senses of the reality of the visitation. My aunt was at once awe-struck and delighted.

"*Now*, William, you'll read, I've no doubt, the wonderful experiences of others, having had such remarkable ones of your own. Since my hand was held in that spirit-hand—no doubt the same which seized yours—I have become accessible to impressions from the invisible world, such as I had no idea of before. You need not be uncomfortable or nervous. It is all benevolent—or, at worst, just. I've never seen or felt that hand but once; the relation is established for ever by a single pressure. I have satisfied Dr. Drake—a very intelligent man, and reasonable—convinced him, he admits. And now, dear William, there is another link between us; and if, in the mysterious ways of Providence, you should after all be taken first, I shall have the happiness of communion with you. Good night, dear, and God bless you, and be careful to put out your candle."

So William departed, and notwithstanding Miss Perfect's grisly conversation, he slept soundly, and did not dream of the shadowy giant, nor even of Trevor and Violet.

Pleasant, listless Gilroyd Hall! thought William, as, after breakfast, he loitered up and down before the rich, red-brick front of the old gabled house, with its profusion of small windows, with such thick, white sashes, and casings of white stone; and the pointed gables, with stone cornice and glittering weather-vane on the summit. That house, somehow, bore a rude resemblance to the old world dandyism which reigned in its younger days, and reminded William of the crimson coats, the bars of lace and quaint, gable-like cocked hats, which had, no doubt, for many a year passed in and out at its deep-porched door; where I could fancy lovers loitering in a charmed murmur, in summer shade, for an enchanted hour, till old Sir Harry's voice and whistle, and the pound of his crutch-handled cane, and the scamper and yelp of the dogs, were heard in the oak hall approaching.

Under the old chestnuts, clustered with ivy, Violet joined him.

"Well, how are we to-day? I think we were a little cross last night, weren't we?" said William, with his old trick of lecturing little Vi.

"We! One of us may have been, but it was not I," she answered.

"I think my watch is wrong. Did you happen to look at the clock as you passed?"

"Half-past eleven."

"Ah! so I thought. How many hours long, Miss——" (Vi he was going to say)—"Darkwell, are contained in half an hour's waiting? The spirit of Mariana has come upon me:

'She only said, "My life is dreary,"
"He cometh not," she said;
She said "I am a-weary, a-weary,
I would that I were dead!"'

Can't you a little understand it, too?—not, of course, quite like me, but a little?"

Vi was not going to answer, but suddenly she changed her mind, and said—

"I don't know, but I think you were a great deal more agreeable when you were a schoolboy. I assure you, I'm serious. I think you've grown so tiresome and conceited. I suppose all young men in the universities are. 'A little learning is a dangerous thing,' you used to tell me, and I think I can now agree with you—at least, it seems to make people vain and disagreeable."

Maubray answered looking on her gently, but speaking as if in a pensive soliloquy, and wondering as he went along whether he had really turned into a coxcomb; for he was one of those sensitive, because diffident souls on whom the lightest reproof tells, and induces self-examination.

"I don't know," he said, "that I've even got the little learning that qualifies for danger. I don't think I am vain—that is, not a bit vainer than I used to be; but I'm sure I'm more disagreeable—that is, to you. My babble and dull jokes were very well for a child, but the child has grown up, and left childish things behind; and a young lady in her teens is more fastidious, and—and, in fact, is a sort of an angel whom I am not formed to talk to with a chance of being anything but a bore. Very unlearned, and yet a book-worm; very young, and yet not very merry; not a bad fellow, I think, and yet, with hardly a friend on earth, and—by Jove! here comes Trevor at last."

And Trevor entered the gate, and approachd them.

—o—

CHAPTER XI.

UNDER THE CHESTNUTS.

Vane Trevor was rather good-looking; a young gentleman of the slender and delicate type; his dark hair curled, and on his small forehead one of those tresses, twisted, barber-fashion, into a neat little Ionic volute, and his glossy whiskers were curled on each cheek into little rolls like pistol barrels. There was in his toilet something of elaboration and precision which was uncomfortable, and made one fear to shake hands with him, and wish him back safely again in his band-box.

He approached simpering. There was a general air of May Fair—cameo studs, varnished boots, and lavender gloves—that had nothing of the rough and careless country in it.

"How do, Miss Darkwell—charming day, is not it? Everything really so fresh; you can't imagine—as I came along, and a—this, now really this little—a—*place*, it looks quite charming---quite, really, now—a—as you turn off the road, there's *every* thing you know to *make* it charming."

This latter period was delivered in a low tone, and with a gracious significance.

"How d'ye do, Maubray?"

"Quite well, thank you," said William, with a smile that had a flicker of unconscious amusement in it. Perhaps without knowing it, he was envying him at that moment. "He's a worse fool, by Jove! than I thought he was," was his mental criticism; but he felt more conscious of his clumsy shoes, and careless get-up. "That's the sort of thing they admire—why should a fellow be vexed—they can't help it—it's pure instinct."

"What delicious ground for croquet; positively I never say anything so beautiful in my life. Do you play, Miss Darkwell?"

"Sometimes, at the Rectory—not here. The Miss Mainwarings play, and once or twice I've joined their party."

"But they have no ground there," insisted Mr. Trevor; "it's all on a slope. I happen to know it very well, because, in fact, it belongs to me. Old Mainwaring pays me a pretty smart rent for it, at least he thinks so. Ha! ha! ha!" and Vane Trevor cackled gaily over his joke, such as it was.

"Do you play?" demanded Violet of William.

"Croquet?—no, not much—just a little—once or twice—I'll do to fill a place if you want a very bad player."

"Oh, never mind, we'll pull you through, or push you—ha, ha, ha!—we will, indeed. You'll learn it a---in no time, it's so simple—isn't it, Miss Darkwell? And then if you can get up one of those Miss Mainwarings—awfully slow girls, I'm told, but they'll do to play with *you*, Maubray, just by way of ballast, he's such a fast fellow—ha, ha, ha! You'll want a—a slow partner, eh?"

"Yes, and *you'll* want a clever one, so I surrender Miss Darkwell, just to—to balance the game," answered William, who was a little combative that morning.

"Egad, I should like uncommonly to be balanced that way, I can tell you; much better, I assure you, Miss Darkwell, than the sort of balancing I've been at the last two days, with my Steward's books—ha, ha, ha! Awful slow work, figures. A regular dose of arithmetic. Upon my honour you'd pity me if you knew; you really would."

"You really would," echoed William, "if you knew how little he knows of it."

"Come, now, old fellow, none of your chaff, but get the balls and hoops, if Miss Darkwell will allow you, and we will choose the ground."

"Lots of ground—I'll choose that if you like—only *you'll* just run and get the hoops and balls, for we have none here," answered Maubray.

"No croquet!" ejaculated Mr. Trevor, expanding his lavender kid fingers, and elevating his eyebrows. "I thought every one had croquet now—I mean, you know, the mallet-things, and hoops, and balls,—and—and those little painted sticks, you know—and what are we to do, Miss Darkwell?"

"I really don't know. It's quite true; and besides we have not got Miss Mainwaring, you forget."

"Oh! you'll send Maubray, won't you, to fetch her?"

"Yes," said Maubray, "I'll go with great pleasure, if Miss Darkwell wishes; but as I never saw the young lady before, I'm not quite sure that she'll come away with me."

"Well, no—ha, ha, ha!—I don't think she'd run away with Maubray at *first sight*."

"Particularly to come to *you*," replied Maubray.

"There now, let's be serious—there's a little fellow I saw at your gate—yes, there he is, Miss Darkwell. Suppose you let me send him to Revington. I've no end of those things there; and I'll give him a note to Sparks, and we shall have them in no time."

"A long time, I'm afraid," objected Violet.

"No, I assure you; a mere nothing; not twenty minutes. Do, pray, allow me."

And he wrote with a pencil on the back of a card, an order to Sparks for the croquet apparatus, and away trotted the messenger.

"Three can play, you know, or two for that matter, as well as twenty, and so we can do quite well without troubling Miss Mainwaring."

There was now a knocking at the drawing-room window, where William had seen dimly through the glass, the form of Aunt Dinah at her knitting, with Psyche in her new collar, seated by her. All looked towards the signal, and Miss Perfect threw up the window and said:

"How do you do, Mr. Trevor? what a sweet morning."

"Perfectly charming," responded the master of Revington, with a tender emphasis which Violet could not fail to understand, and smiling toward Miss Perfect with his hat in his hand; and Aunt Dinah smiled and nodded again in return.

"William, I want you for a moment—here, dear, you need not come in."

The instinct which makes old ladies afford a dole now and then of a few minutes to lovers, is in harmony with the general rule of mercy and mitigation which alleviates every human situation.

As soon as Miss Dinah raised the window, William saw standing in the chiaroscuro of the apartment, a tall and rather handsome old clergyman. A little rusty was his black suit—a little dust was on his gaiters. It must have been he whom William had mistaken for the attorney who was to have visited his aunt that morning. He had seen him walk his nag up to the door about an hour ago and dismount.

The old clergyman was looking observantly and kindly on William; and, nodding to him, and with her thin hand extended toward her nephew, she said, "This is he!" with a proud smile in her old eyes, for she thought William the handsomest fellow alive.

"Happy to make your acquaintance, sir," said the cleric, stepping forward and shaking William's hand. "I knew your father, and grandfather, and your aunt and I are very old friends; and I've just been telling her how happy I shall be"——

"This is Doctor Waggett, my very good and kind old friend; you may have heard me speak of him often, I dare say," interposed my aunt.

"And your reading, sir, has been rather desultory, your aunt tells me, like my own, sir—ha, ha, ha! We had rather give our time than pay it; read what is not exacted of us than what is. But I don't know, Miss Perfect," continued the Doctor, turning to that lady, as if they were in consultation upon William's case, "reading—that is in the case of a man who thinks, and I am sure our young friend here thinks for himself—resembles the browsing of cattle; they choose their own herbage, and the particular flowers and grasses that answer their special conditions best, eh? and so they thrive. Instinct directs us creatures, in the one as in the other; and so we read, he and I—ha, ha! what best nourishes, you see—what we can assimilate and enjoy. For plodding fellows, that devour the curriculum set before them—neither more nor less—are, you see, stall-fed, bulkier fellows; higher priced in the market; but they haven't our flavour and texture. Oh, no, ha, ha! eh?"

The ecclesiastic was cheery and kindly, and in his manner was a curious mixture of energy and simplicity, which William Maubray liked.

The conclusion of this little harangue he had addressed to William Maubray; and I am afraid that Miss Perfect was more interested by the picture on the lawn, for, without reference to the doctor's subject, she desired to know, looking with a pleased inquisitiveness at the young people, whether they were going to take a walk, or *what?* And prolonged her little *tête-à-tête* with William over the window-stool.

When William Maubray looked up again at

Doctor Wagget, that divine had picked up a book, a trick of his, like that of the cattle from whom his illustration was borrowed, and who employ every moment's pause at the wayside, in a pluck at the nearest foliage or tuft of grass; and with the intimation, "you may as well join them," Miss Perfect dismissed her nephew.

—o—

CHAPTER XII.

CROQUET.

While William Maubray was thus employed, Mr. Trevor agreeably accosted Miss Violet.

"Now we are to choose the ground, you know Miss Darkwell—you are to choose it, in fact. I think, don't you, it looks particularly smooth just there. By Jove it does!—really, now, just like a billiard-table, behind those a—those a — what-d'ye-call-em's — the evergreens there."

"I think it does, really," said Miss Vi, gliding very contentedly into his ambuscade. "There's a little shade too."

"Yes, lots of shade; I hate the sun. I'm afraid my deeds are darkness as Dr. Mainwaring says. There's only one sort of light I really like, no w upon my honour—the light—the light you—you know, the light that comes from Miss Darkwell's eyes—ha, ha! upon my honour."

The idea was not quite original perhaps, but Miss Darkwell blushed a little, and smiled as it were, on the leaves, and wondered how soon the messenger with the croquet things would return. And Mr. Trevor consulted his watch, and, said he would allow him a quarter of an hour more, and added that he would willingly allow the poor little beggar an hour, or any time; for his part, the—the time, in fact, went only too fast for him.

Miss Perfect, looking over her spectacles, and then with elevated chin through them, said:

"Where have they gone to? can you see?"

"Yes—that is, I don't know—I suppose sauntering about—they can't be very far," answered William, looking a little uneasily. And somehow forgetting that he was in the midst of a dialogue with Aunt Dinah, he strode away, whistling a little air, anxiously, in the direction in which he had left them.

"We have such a charming piece of ground here," exclaimed Violet, on whose cheeks was a flush, and in whose beautiful eyes a light which Maubray did not like.

"First rate; capital, by Jove! it is," exclaimed Trevor in corroboration.

"I don't see anything very wonderful about it. I think the ground on the other side of these trees better, decidedly; and this is out of sight of the windows," said William, a little drily.

"We don't want a view of the windows—do we?" asked Mr. Trevor, with an agreeable simplicity, of Miss Darkwell. "The windows? I really did not think of them; but, perhaps, Mr. Maubray wishes to be within call for lunch."

Mr. Trevor laughed pleasantly at this cruel sally.

"Well, yes, that, of course," said William, and, beside, "my aunt might want to speak to me again, as she did just now; and I don't want to be out of sight, in case she should."

This was very bitter of William; and, perhaps, Miss Violet was a little put out, as she certainly was a little more flushed, and a short silence followed, during which, looking and walking slowly toward the gate, she asked, "Is that the boy with the croquet?"

"Yes—no—*yes*, by Jove, it *is!* What wonderful eyes yours are, Miss Darkwell?"

The latter remark was in a tender undertone, the music of which was accompanied by the long-drawn screak of the iron gate, as the boy entered with a holland bag, mallets, and hoops.

The hoops were hardly placed, when Miss Perfect once more knocked at the window and beckoned.

"Aunt Dinah wants me again," said William, and he ran to the window, mallet in hand.

The old clergyman had gone away, and I think Aunt Dinah only wanted to give the lovers a few minutes.

"Vilikens and his Dinah," said Mr. Trevor, and exploded in repeated cachinations over his joke. "I vote we call him Villikens—capital names, isn't it—I really do. But, by Jove, I hope the old lady won't go on calling him up from his game every minute. We'd have been a great deal better at the the other side of the trees, where we were going to play, don't you think?"

"He is coming at last," said Miss Violet.

"Shall we be partners, you and S? Do let us, and give him two balls," urged Mr. Trevor, graciously, and a little archly.

"Well, I think that's dull, rather, isn't it? one playing with two balls," remonstrated Miss Darkwell.

And before the debate could proceed William Maubray had arrived.

"Every one for himself, eh?" said Trevor; and so the game set in, Trevor and William Maubray playing rather acrimoniously, and making savage roquets upon one another; and Miss Darkwell—though William dealt tenderly with her—was hard upon him, and, so far as her slender force would go, knocked him about inconveniently. "Capital croquet, Miss Darkwell," Trevor would cry, as William's ball bounded away into perspective, and his heart felt sore, as if her ungrateful mallet had smitten it; and his reprisals on Trevor were terrific.

Thus, amid laughter, a little hypocritical, and honest hard knocks, the game proceeded, and Miss Darkwell, at its close, was the winner.

William Maubray could lose as good

humouredly as any fellow at other games, but he was somehow sore and angry here. He was spited by Violet's partial dealing. Violet, how unnatural! Little Vi! his bird! his property, it seemed, leagued with that coxcomb to whack him about—to make a butt and a fool of him.

"I'm not going to play any more. I'll sit down here, if you like, and do"—*gooseberry*, he was on the point of saying, for he was very angry, and young enough, in his wrath, to talk away like a schoolboy—"and do audience, or rather spectator; or, if you choose, Trevor, to take that walk over the Warran you promised me, I'm ready. I'll do exactly whatever Miss Darkwell prefers. If she wishes to play on with you, I'll remain, and if she has had enough of us, I'll go."

"I can't play—there is not time for another game," said Miss Vi, peeping at her watch. "My aunt will want me in a few minutes about that old women—old Widow Grey. I—I'm afraid I must go. Good-bye."

"Awfully sorry! But, perhaps you can? Well, I suppose, no help for it," said Trevor.

And they walked slowly to the door, where Miss Vi pronounced the conventional invitation to enter, which was, however, wistfully declined, and Trevor and William Maubray set out upon their walk, and Miss Vi, in the drawing-room, sat down on the old-fashioned window-seat, and looked out, silent, and a little sulkily, after them.

Miss Perfect glanced over her spectacles, with a stealthy and grave inquisitiveness, at the pretty girl.

"Well, dear, they went away?" she said, after a silence.

"Oh! yes; I was tired playing, and, I think, William wanted to go for a walk."

"There seemed to be a great deal of fun over the game," said Aunt Dinah, who wanted to hear everything.

"Yes, I believe so; but one tires of it. I do, I know," and saying this, Miss Violet took up her novel, and Aunt Dinah scrutinized her, from time to time, obliquely, over her crochet needles, and silence reigned in the drawing room,

"Very pretty Miss Darkwell is. I quite envy you. Your cousin, isn't she?" said Trevor, graciously. He felt that William would be flattered by the envy, even playful, of Vane Trevor, Esq., of Revington.

"Cousin, or something, someway or other connected or related, I don't know exactly. Yes, I believe she is very well. She was prettier as a child, though. Isn't there a short way to the Warren?"

"Yes, I'll take you right. She looks, I'd say, about seventeen."

"Yes, I dare say," answered William. "Do you know those Miss Mainwarings—Doctor Mainwaring's daughters?"

But it would not do. Vane Trevor would go on talking of Violet Darkwell, in spite of William's dry answers and repeated divergences, unaccountably to that philosophical young gentleman's annoyance.

CHAPTER XIII.

UNSOCIABLE.

At dinner, in the parlour of Gilroyd Hall, there was silence for some time. William looked a little gloomy, Violet rather fierce and stately, and Aunt Dinah eyed her two guests covertly, without remark, but curiously. At last she said to William—

"You took a walk with Mr. Trevor?"

"Yes, a tiresome one," he answered.

"Where?"

"All about and round that stupid Warren—six or seven miles," answered William.

"How very fatiguing!" exclaimed Violet, compassionately, as if to herself.

"No, not the exercise; that was the only thing that made it endurable," answered William, a little crossly. "But the place is uglier than I fancied, and Trevor *is* such a donkey."

Aunt Dinah, with her eyes fixed on William's, made a nod and a frown, to arrest that line of remark, which, she felt, might possibly prejudice Vi, and could do no possible good. And Miss Vi, looking all the time on the wing of the chicken on her plate, said, "The salt, please," and nothing more.

"Vi, my dear," said Miss Perfect, endeavouring to be cheery, "he asked my leave last Sunday to send you an Italian greyhound. He has two, he says, at Revington. Did he mention it to-day?"

"I—I—perhaps he did. I really forget," said Miss Vi, carelessly, laying down her fork, and leaning back, with a languid defiance, for as she raised her eyes, she perceived that William was smiling.

"I know what you mean," she said, with a sudden directness to William. "You want me—that is, I *think* you want me to think *you* think—"

"Oh! do stop one moment. There are so many 'thinks' there, I'm quite bewildered among them all. Let's breathe an instant. You think I want to make you think that I think. Yes, now I have it, I *think*. Pray go on."

"Polite!" said Miss Vi, and turned toward Aunt Dinah.

"Well, no," said William, for the first time laughing a little like himself; "it was not polite, but very rude and ill-bred, and I'm very sorry; and I assure you," he continued more earnestly, "I should be very angry, if any one else had made the stupid speech that I have just made; and, really, I believe it is just this—you have been too patient with me, and allowed me to go on lecturing you like an old tutor—and—and—really, I'm certain I've been a horrid bore."

Vi made no reply, but looked, and, no doubt, thought herself more ill-used for his apologies.

After tea she played industriously, having avowed a little cold, which prevented her singing. William had asked her. He turned over the leaves of a book, as he sat back in an elbow-chair, and Aunt Dinah was once more deep in her old box of letters, with her gold spectacles on.

They were as silent a party as could be fancied; more silent than at dinner. Still, the pleasant light of fire and candle—the handsome young faces and the kindly old one—and the general air of old-fashioned comfort that pervaded the apartment, made the picture pleasant; and the valses and the nigger ditties, with snatches of Verdi, and who knows what composer beside, made the air ring with a merry medley, which supplied the lack of conversation.

To William, with nothing but his book to amuse him, time moved slowly enough. But Miss Violet had many things to think of; and one could see that her eyes saw other scenes, and shapes far away, perhaps, from the music and that she was reading to herself the romance that was unrolled within her pretty girlish head.

So prayers came, and William read the chapter; and I am afraid his thoughts wandered, and he felt a little sore and affronted, he could not tell why, for no one had ill-used him; and when their devotions were over, Miss Vi took her candle, and bid Grannie good night, with an embrace and a kiss, and William with a nod and a cold little smile, as he stood beside the door, having opened it for her.

He was growing formal in spite of himself, and she quite changed. What heartless, cruel, creatures these pretty girls are!

She had quite vanished up the stairs, and he still held the door handle in his fingers, and stood looking up the vacant steps, and, as it were, listening to distant music. Then, with a little sigh, he suddenly closed the door, and sat down drowsily before the fire, and began to think that he ought to return to his Cambridge chambers, his books, and monastic life; and he thought how fortunate those fellow were—who like Trevor!—were born to idleness, respect, and admiration.

"Money!—d—n money—curse it! I wish I had a lot of it" and William clutched the poker, but the fire did not want poking, and he gave it a rather vicious knock upon the bar, which startled Miss Perfect, and recalled his own thoughts from unprofitable speculations upon the preposterous injustice of Fate, and some ultimate state of poetical compensation, in which scholars and men of mind, who played all sorts of games excellently, and noodles, who never did anything decently—in fact, he and Trevor—would be dealt with discriminately, and with common fairness.

"Don't, dear William, pray, make such a clatter I'm *so* nervous."

"I beg a thousand pardons. I'm so stupid."

"Well, it does not signify—an accident—but don't mind touching the fire-irons," said Miss Perfect; "and how did your walk with Mr. Trevor—a—a—proceed? Did he—a—talk of anything?"

"Oh! didn't he? Fifty things, He's a wonderful fellow to talk, is Trevor," said William, looking with half-closed eyes into the fire.

"Oh, yes," persisted Aunt Dinah; "but was there anything—anything particular—anything that could interest us?"

"Next to nothing that could interest any one," said William; uncommunicatively

"Well, it would interest *me*, if he talked of Violet," said Aunt Dinah, coming directly to the point. "*Did* he?"

"Of Violet? Yes, I believe he did," answered William, rather reluctantly.

"Well, and why did not you say so? Of course, you knew that's what I meant," said Miss Perfect.

"How could I know, Auntie?"

"I think, William Maubray, you are a little disagreeable to-night."

William at. these words, recollected that there was truth in the reproof. His mood was disagreeable to himself, and, therefore, to others.

"My dear Auutie, I'm very sorry. I'm sure I have been—not a little, but *very*—and I beg your pardon. What was it? Yes—about Violet. He did a great deal. He—in fact—he talked about her untill he quite tired me."

"He admires her, evidently! Did he—a—talk of her good looks? She *is*, you know, extremely pretty," said Aunt Dinah.

"Yes, he thinks her very pretty. She *is* very pretty. In fact, I don't think—judging by the women who come to church—there is a good-looking girl, except herself, in this part of the world; and she would be considered pretty anywhere—*very* pretty."

"Revington is a very nice place, and the Trevors a good old family. The—the—connection would be a very desirable one; and I—though, of course, not knowing, in the least, whether the young man had any serious intentions—I never alluded to the possibility to Vi herself. Yet, I do think she likes him.

"I should not wonder," said William.

"And—and—he talked pretty frankly?" continued Aunt Dinah.

"I suppose so. He did not seem to have anything to conceal; and he always talks a great deal, an enormous quantity;" and William yawned, as it seemed, over the recollection.

—o—

CHAPTER XIV.

A SUNNY MORNING.

"I SUPPOSE, if he likes her, there's nothing to conceal in that?" challenged Miss Perfect.

"No, of course," replied William, spiritedly; "I think she's a thousand times too good for him, *every* way—that's what I think; and

I wonder, young as she is, Vi can be such a fool. What can she see in him? He has got two thousand a-year, and that's all you can say for him."

"I don't know that—I can't see—in fact, he strikes me as a very pretty young man, quite apart from his property," said Aunt Dinah, resolutely; "and I could quite understand a young girl's falling in love with him."

William, leaning with his elbow on the chimney-piece, smiled a little bitterly, and said, quietly, "I dare say."

"I don't say, mind, that she *is*. I don't, upon my life, know the least, whether she cares twopence about him," said Aunt Dinah.

"I hope she doesn't," rejoined William.

"And why so?" asked Aunt Dinah.

"Because, I'm perfectly certain he has not the least notion of ever asking her to marry him. He's *not* thinking seriously about her, and never *will*," replied he.

"Well, it's nothing to vaunt of. You need not talk as if you wished her to be mortified," said Aunt Dinah.

"*I!*—I wish no such thing, I assure you; but, even if she admires and adores the fellow all you say, still I can't wish her his wife—because—because I'm sure he's not the least worthy of her. I assure you he's no better than a goose. You don't know him—you *can't*—as the fellows in the same school did—and Violet ought to do fifty times better."

"You said he does not think seriously about her," said Miss Perfect. "Remember, we are only talking, you and I, together, and —and I assure you I never asked her whether she liked him or not, nor hinted a possibility of anything, as you say, serious coming of it; but what makes you think the young man disposed to trifle?"

"I didn't say to trifle," answered William; "but every fellow will go on like that where there's a pretty girl, and no one supposes they mean anything. And from what he said today, I would gather that he's thinking of some swell, whenever he marries, which he talks of like a thing so far away as to be nearly out of sight; in fact, nothing could be more contrary to any sign of there being any such notion in his head—and there isn't. I assure you he has no more idea, at present, of marrying than I have."

"H'm!" was the only sign of attention which Aunt Dinah emitted, with closed lips, as she looked gloomily into her work-basket, I believe for nothing.

William whistled "Rule Britannia," in a low key, to the little oval portrait of the Very Rev. Simeon Lewis Perfect, Dean of Crutch Friars, the sainted and ascetic parent of the eccentric old lady, who was poking in her work-basket, his own maternal grandfather; and a silence ensued, and the conversation expired.

Next morning, William, returning from his early saunter in the fields, saw the graceful head of Miss Violet peeping through the open window of the parlour, through the jessamine and roses that clustered round it. Her eyes glanced on him, and she smiled and nodded.

"Uncertain as the weather!" thought he, as he smiled and kissed his hand, approaching, "a lowering evening yesterday, and now so sunny a morning."

"How do you do, Miss Violet? you said you wanted a water-lily, so I found two in my morning's ramble, and here they are."

How beautiful. Thank you very much. Where did you find them?" said Miss Vi quite glowing.

"In the Miller's Tarn," he answered. "I'm so glad you like them."

"Quite beautiful! The Miller's Tarn?" She remembered that she had mentioned it yesterday as a likely place, but it was two miles away; four miles there and back, for a flower. It deserved her thanks, and she did thank him; and reminded him in tone and look of that little Vi of other years, very pleasantly yet somehow sadly.

"I mean to return to Cambridge to-morrow," said William, a little regretfully; he had glanced round at the familiar scene; "and I am sorry to leave so soon."

"And *must* you go?" asked Violet.

"Not quite *must*, but I think I ought. If I had brought with me some papers I have been transcribing for Doctor Sprague, I might have stayed a little longer, but they are locked up, and he wants the copy on Tuesday, and so I can't help it."

"It was hardly worth while coming. Poor Grannie will miss you very much."

"And you, not at all."

"I? Oh, yes, of course we shall all miss you."

"Some, but not you, Vi."

The old "Vi" passed quite unnoticed.

"I, and *why* not I?"

"Because your time is so pleasantly occupied."

"I don't know what you mean," said the young lady coldly, with a little toss of her head. "More riddles I suppose."

"Mine are poor riddles; very easily found out. Are we to have croquet to-day?"

"I'm sure I can't tell," replied she.

"Did not Trevor tell you he was coming here at eleven?" asked William.

"I don't recollect that he said anything about coming to-day," she answered carelessly.

"I did not say *to-day*," said William provokingly.

"You did. I'm nearly certain. At all events I *understood* it, and really it does not the least signify."

"Don't be vexed — but he told me he had settled with you to come here to-day, at eleven, to play as he did yesterday," said William.

"Ho! Then I suppose I have been telling fibs as usual? I remark I never do anything right when *you* are here. You can't think how pleasant it is to have some one by you always insinuating that you are about something shabby."

"You put it in a very inexcusable light,"

said William, laughing. It may have been a vaunt of Trevor's, for I think he's addicted to boasting a little; or a misapprehension, or —or an indistinctness; there are fibs logical and fibs ethical, and fibs logical *and* ethical; but you don't read logic, nor care for metaphysics."

"Nor metaphysicians," she acquiesced with cruel scorn.

"Well," said William, "he says he's coming at eleven, and——"

"I think we are going to have prayers," interrupted Miss Violet, turning coldly from the window, through which William saw the little congregation of Gilroyd Hall assembling at the row of chairs by the parlour door, and Aunt Dinah's slight figure gliding to the corner of the chimney-piece, to the right of the Very Rev. Simeon Lewis Perfect, sometime Dean of Crutch Friars, where the bible and prayer-book lay, and in the shadow her golden spectacles glimmered like a saintly glory round her chaste head.

So William hastened to do his office of deacon, and read the appointed chapter; and their serene devotions over, the little party of three, with the windows open, and the fragrance and twitterings of that summer-like morning entering through those leafy apertures, sat down to breakfast, and William did his best to entertain the ladies with recollections lively and awful of his college life.

"Half-past nine, Miss Violet; don't forget eleven," said William, leaning by the window-frame, and looking out upon the bright and beautiful landscape. "I'll go out just now and put down the hoops."

"Going to play again to-day," enquired Miss Perfect briskly; "charming morning for a game—is he coming, William?"

"Yes, at eleven."

"H'm!" murmured Aunt Dinah, in satisfactory rumination.

And William, not caring to be drawn into another discussion of this interesting situation, jumped from the window upon the sward, and kissing his hand to Aunt Dinah, strolled away toward the river.

——o——

CHAPTER XV.

DINNER AT REVINGTON.

Trevor did appear, and was received smilingly; and Aunt Dinah came out and sat a little apart on the rustic seat, and looked on cheerfully; the day was so very charming. Perhaps she fancied it a case for a Chaperone, and being a little more in evidence, than a seat in the drawing-room window would make her, and with her work, and with Psyche at her feet, she presided very cheerily.

When, after two or three games, Trevor was taking his leave, Miss Violet Darkwell having, notwithstanding various nods and small frowns from Grannie, persisted in announcing that she was tired, and had beside a long letter to write before Tom left for the town, the master of Revington said—(he and Maubray were knocking the balls about at random)—

"I say, Maubray, you must come over to Revington and have a mutton chop, or something. You really must; an old schoolfellow, you know, and I want to talk to you a bit, upon my honour I do. I'm totally alone, you know, at present, and you must come."

"But I'm going to-morrow, and this is my last evening here," said William, who felt unaccountably queer and reluctant.

What could Trevor want to talk to him about? There was something in Trevor's look and manner a little odd and serious—he fancied even embarrassed. Perhaps it is some nonsense about little Vi.

"I want him to come and dine with me, Miss Perfect, and he says you can't spare him," said Trevor, addressing that lady. "I really do. I've no one to talk to. Do tell him to come."

"Certainly," said Aunt Dinah, with an imperious little nod to William Maubray. "*Go*, William, my dear, we shall see you to-night, and to-morrow morning. He'll be very happy I'm sure," said Aunt Dinah, who, like William Maubray, possibly anticipated a revelation.

So William, having no excuses, did walk over to Revington to dine. There was almost a pain at his heart as he paused for a moment at the stile, only one field away, and saw pretty Vi on the dark green grass, looking at the flowers, with little Psyche frisking beside her, and the kindly old front of Gilroyd Hall, and its lofty chestnuts in the sad evening light, and he sighed, thinking—"Why won't things stay as they are, as they *were?* What is the drift of this perpetual mutation? Is it really progress? Do we improve? Don't we" (he would have said Violet?) "grow more selfish and less high-minded? It is all a beautiful decay, and the end is death."

Violet was plainly intent on her flowers, she had her hoe and her rake, and her movements somehow were so pretty that, unseen, he paused for another moment.

"It is a blessed thing to have so little affection [illegible] that pretty creature; old times are nothing for her, and I, like a fool, yearn after them. The future for her no doubt looks all brilliant; for me it is a story, to the end of which I dare not look, and the pleasant past is a volume shut up and over; she is little Vi and Violet no longer, and even Miss Darkwell will very soon be like the song of a dead bird —a note only remembered; and—and I suppose I shall bring back the news to-night, a message from Mr. Vane Trevor, of Revington, to say that he lays his heart and his title-deeds at her feet. It's all over; I look on it as all settled."

Just at these words the edge of the red sun sank behind the hills, and the last level beams of sunset gave place to the tender gray of twilight, except in the uplands of Revington, where they lingered for a few seconds.

"Ay," said William, allegorizing; "the shade for William Maubray; the golden light of life for Vane Trevor! Vane Trevor of Revington! William Maubray of—nothing at all!—charming contrast."

And looking still on Gilroyd Hill, and the fading image of Violet Darkwell and Psyche frisking about, no longer white, but a moving gray spot on the sloping grass, he said, touching his finger-tips to his lip and waving them lightly towards her, "Good-by, little Vi; good-by, wicked little Vi; good-by, dear, old, wicked little Vi, and may God bless you, you darling!"

So with a sigh and a sad smile he turned and walked up to Revington. It is a good ancestral looking place, only a little too large for the estate as it now is. The Trevors had parted from time to time with many acres, and a house upon a scale which would have corresponded with three times their income, was rather a tax upon what remained.

"I never liked this place," thought William, as the iron gate clanged behind him; "I always thought it gloomy, and stingy, and pompous. I wish he had let this dinner alone, I'd have been pleasanter at home, though it's as well, perhaps, to hear what he has to say. I think he *has* something to say; but, hang it, why could not he tell it as well at Gilroyd, and to the people it concerns? why need he bring *me* this stupid walk up his hill?" And William as he talked was switchthe laurel leaves at his side with his cane, and leaving here and there half a leaf or a whole one on the gravel, and sometimes half a dozen—not quite unconsciously; there was something of defiance, I am afraid, in this trespass.

William came in; the hall was not lighted; he was received in the dusk by a serious and rather broad gentleman in black, who took his hat and cane with a bow, led him through an anteroom, illuminated dismally by a single lamp, and announced his name at the drawing room, where Vane Trevor received him, advancing from the hearth-rug to the middle of the room, in an unexceptionable evening toilet, and in French boots, and shook hands with just a little inclination which implied something of state, though smilingly performed.

Mr. Trevor was very conscious of the extent of the mansion of Revington, of the scale of the rooms, of the pictures, and in short of everything that was grand about him.

William was a little disgusted and rather uncomfortable, and eat his soup, and cutlets, and kickshaws, gloomily, while Trevor, leaning on his elbow, talked away, with a conscious superiority that was at once depressing and irritating.

They had a jug of claret—not the best even in Trevor's cellar, I am afraid—after dinner, and sat facing the fire, and sipping that nectar.

"Snug little room this," said Trevor, looking along the ceiling, with his napkin over his knee, and his claret glass in his fingers. "It isn't a parlour, only a sort of breakfast-room. The parlour, you know, is a—it's considered a handsome room. Thirty-five feet by twenty."

"Yes, I know," said William, with a dry carelessness.

"Ah! well, yes—I dare say. A good many people—it's an old place, rather—do know something about Rivengton."

"Especially those who have lived the greater part of their lives within half a mile of it," rejoined William.

"Ah, ha!—yes; to be sure; I forgot you have been so constantly at Gilroyd. What a nice little bit of a thing it is. I could fancy growing quite in love with it—isn't it?"

"Yes," said William, shortly, and filled his glass, and drank it in a hurry. He fancied that Trevor was about to come to the point.

——o——

CHAPTER XVI.

OVER THEIR CLARET.

"Great fun, croquet, isn't it? Awful fun with pretty girls," exclaimed Vane Trevor, rising, and standing on the hearthrug, with his back to the fire, and his glass in his hand, and simpering agreeably, with his chin in the air. "I think it capital fun, I know. There's so much cheating—ha, ha!—isn't there?—and such lots of—of—whispering and conspiring—and—and —all that sort of thing, you know; and the girls like it awfully. At Torhampton we had capital games, and such glorious ground. Do you know the Torhamptons?"

"The Marquess?—ha—ha!—no, of course I don't; how should I?" said William with a little laugh of disgust.

"Oh! well I—I thought a—but Lady Louisa, she is so sweetly pretty, I was told off pretty often to play with her, and we *had* such fun knocking the fellows about. Capital player and awfully clever—they're all clever—one of the cleverest families in England they're thought; the old lady is *so* witty—you can't imagine—and such a pleasant party staying there. I was almost the only fellow not a swell, by Jove, among them," and he ran his eye along his handsome cornices, with a sort of smile that seemed to say something different. "I fancy they wish to be civil, however, I—from something Lady Fanny said—I rather fancy they have an idea of putting up Lord Edward —you know, for the county, but don't let that go further, and I suppose they thought I might be of use. Won't you have some more claret?"

"I don't know them—I don't understand these things; I don't care if all the Marquesses in England were up the chimney," said William, cynically, throwing himself back in his chair, with his hands in his pockets, and looking sulkily into the fire.

"Well—ha, ha!—that need not prevent

your filling your glass, eh?" laughed Trevor, graciously and indulgently, as though he belonged himself to that order of Marquesses of whom Maubray spoke so slightly, and forgave him.

"Thanks; I will," and so he did, and sipped a little; and after a little silence he asked with a surly quietude, "And why don't you marry that lady—what's her name—*Louisa*—if she liked you?"

"It doesn't *follow* that she likes me, and you know there are difficulties; and even if she did, it does not follow that *I* like *her;* don't you see?" and he cackled in gay self-complacency; "that is, of course, I mean liking in the way you mean."

Again this desultory conversation flagged for a little time, and Trevor, leaning on the chimney-piece, and looking down on William, remarked profoundly—

"It's odd—isn't it?" when you come to think of it, how few things follow from one another; I've observed it in conversation—almost nothing, by Jove!"

"Nothing from nothing, and nothing remains," said William drowsily, to the fire, repeating his old arithmetical formula.

"And about marrying and that sort of thing; seriously, you know—your glass is empty again; do have some more."

So William poured a little into his glass and his heart seemed to stop and listen, although he looked as if he only half heard, and was weary of the subject.

"And as we were saying, about marrying—and by-the-bye, Maubray, it's the sort of thing would just answer you, a quiet fellow—why don't you think about it, old fellow, eh?"

It was a way Trevor had of always forgetting those little differences of circumstance which, in contrast, redounded to his importance, and he asked such questions, of course, quite innocently.

"You know very well I couldn't," said William, poking the fire, unbidden, with a few angry stabs. "How the devil can a fellow marry in —— college, and without a shilling?"

"Ah, ah, it isn't *quite* so bad; come! But, of course, there is a difference, and, as you say, there's lots of time to look about—only if a fellow is really spooney on a girl—I mean awfully spooney, the big wigs say—don't they? The best thing a fellow going to the bar can do is to marry, and have a wife and lots of babbies---it makes them work so hard ---doesn't it? You're going to the bar, you say, and that is the way to get on, eh?"

"I'm glad there's any way, but I don't mean to try that," murmured William, a little bitterly, and after a little pause, during which who knows what a dance his fancy led him, "I know that sort of talk very well; but I never could see what right a fellow has to carry off a poor girl to his den, merely that her hunger, and misery, and cries may stimulate him to get on at the bar; and the fact is, some fellows are slaves, and some can do just as they please; and life is damnably bitter for some, and very pleasant for others, and that's the whole story; you can marry whenever you please, and I can't."

"I' m afraid it's a true bill," said Trevor, complacently; whereupon there issued a sience, and twice and again was William Maubray moved to break it with a question, and as often his voice seemed to fail him. At last, however, he did say, quite quietly—

"And why don't you marry, if you think it so good a thing?"

Was it something in William's tone and air, although he was trying his best to seem quite unconcerned, that elicited the quick, and somewhat cunning glance that Trevor shot on him?

At all events Trevor's manner became a little diplomatic and reserved.

"Why don't I? Oh! fifty reasons—a hundred. There are all sorts of difficulties; I don't mean, of course, anything mysterious—or—or that sort of bosh; and—and this house and the property, every one knows, are very well. I've been four years in possession, and I've no fault to find with Revington—either tenants or *this,*" and he nodded towards the ceiling, indicating that he meant the house.

"But—but you know, for a fellow like me; we've been here, you know, a long time; there was a Trevor here in Henry the Fifth's time; but you know more history than I do."

Trevor considered his family and his domicile as a part of English history, and William, who was in an unpleasant mood just then, said—

"And the estate was larger, wasn't it?"

"Ah, ha; *yes, certainly;* that is, there was another estate," acquiesced Trevor, eagerly, but looking a little put out. "The Torhamptons, by-the-bye, have got it now; a marriage or something."

"A purchase, I thought," insisted Maubray.

"A *purchase!* very likely. It does not signify sixpence if the thing's gone, and gone it is. But you see, having been here for a longer time, I'm afraid, than you or I are likely to live; and—and having a sort of place among the people, you understand; a kind of a—quite undeserved—only because we have been here so long, that sort of an *influence*, or what, ever it is, a fellew isn't as free as you'd fancy. By Jove! he's tied up, I can tell you; horribly tied up. A poor devil like me. Egad, he's not like a man with an income out of the funds; there's that sort of thing, I suppose it is the shadow, don't you see, of the old feudal thing, but so it is. There's a sort of rural opinion, a kind of loyalty, in a very small way, of course; but it *is* that sort of feeling, and there's no use, you know, in blinking it; and a fellow has to consider, you know, how his tenants and people would receive it; and, ask any one, you can't conceive how a fellow's hampered, really hampered, now."

"Do you really think they care a farthing?" asked Maubray.

"Care! You've no idea," exclaimed his friend.

"Well, when I make my fortune, I'll keep it in the funds," said Maubray.

"I *strongly* advise you," said Trevor, with admirable solemnity. "Have some coffee? And—and here's curacoa."

"When will we talk about Vi," thought William, as he set down his coffee cup; "he can't have brought me here to dinner merely to hear that pompous lecture."

And, indeed, it seemed to William that Trevor had something more to say, but did not know how to begin it.

——o——

CHAPTER XVII.

MOON-SHINE.

AND now, for they kept early hours at Gilroyd, William, with a peep at his watch, declared he must go, and Trevor popped on his fez and produced his cigars, and he set out with Maubray, in the moonlight, to see his friend out of the grounds.

As they walked down the slope, with the thick chestnuts of Gilroyd Hall and two of its chimneys full in view—the misty lights and impenetrable shadows of moonlight—and all the familiar distances translated into such soft and airy outline—the landscape threw them, I dare say, somewhat into musing, and that sort of sympathy with the pensive moods of nature which has, time out of mind, made moonlight the lamp of lovers. And some special associations of the scenery induced them to smoke on in silence for some time, insensibly slackening their pace, the night scene was so well worth lingering over.

"And—and your cousin—isn't she?—down there, how awfully pretty she is," said Trevor, at last, lowering his cigar between his fingers.

"Cousin; I suppose we're all cousins in some roundabout way related—I don't know how. Yes, she is—she's very pretty."

"Darkwell; connected, are they, with the Darkwells of Shropshire?" asked Trevor.

"Perhaps—I really don't know—I never knew there were Darkwells in Shropshire," said William.

"Oh, dear, yes! I thought every one knew that. Darkwell's the name of the place, too. A very old family," said Trevor.

"I did not know; but her father is a barrister, and lives in London, and has some sons, but I never saw them," answered William.

Trevor sighed. He was thinking what low fellows these sons might possibly be. A barrister! He remembered "young Boles's" father visiting Rugby once, a barrister, making fifteen hundred a year, a shabby, lean-looking fellow, with a stoop, and a seedy black frock coat, and grizzled whiskers, who talked in a sharp, dry way, with sometimes a little browbeating tendency—not a bit like a gentleman. On the other hand, to be sure, there were lots of swells among them. But still there was the image of old Boles's father intruding into the moonlight, and poking about the old trees of Gilroyd. They had come to a halt under the mighty clump of beech trees that you can see against the sky from the distant road to Audminton, and, after a silence, Trevor said—

"I remember a thing I saw in a play in London, about a fellow that married a mermaid, or something of the sort; and—and, egad, they got on capitally till her family began to appear, and—and the situation began to grow too—too fishy, in fact, for him; so, by Jove, he cut and ran; and—and I forget how the play ends; but it was awfully funny."

"Yes," said William, "they ought to come to us like Aphrodite, from the foam of the sea, and have no kindred—in utter isolation."

"Who?" asked Trevor.

"Our beautiful brides!" exclaimed Maubray, a little mockingly.

"It's a confounded world we live in," resumed Trevor, after a little silence. "Look at me, now, for instance, how we are, and all this belongs to me, and has been ours for—goodness knows how many centuries; and I assure you I sometimes feel I'd rather be a simple fellow with a few hundreds a-year, and my way to make in the world, and my liberty along with it—than—than all this."

"Suppose we exchange," said William, "I'll take the estate off your hands, and allow you three hundred a-year, and your liberty, and wish you joy of the pleasant excitement of making your way in the world, and applaud when you get on a bit, and condole when you're in the mud."

Trevor only smiled grandly, and shook his head at William's waggery.

"But seriously, just consider. You know I'm telling you things, old fellow, that I wouldn't say to every one, and this won't, I know, go further." He resumed after a little interval spent in smoking, "But just think now: here's everything, as you see; but the estate owes some money; and I give you my honour, it does not bring me in, net, when everything's paid, three thousand a-year."

"Oh, no!" said William, in a tone which unconsciously implied, "a great deal less, as we all know."

"No, not three thousand—I wish it was," said Trevor, with an eager frankness, that savoured of annoyance. He had not intended to be quite believed. "And there's the—the position. You're expected to take a lead in things, you see, as if you had your six thousand a-year, egad, or whatever it is; and how the devil are you to manage it? Don't you see. And you tumble in love with a girl; and—and you find yourself encumbered with a pedigree—a confounded family tree, by Jove! and every one expects you to—to marry accordingly. And I don't say they're not right, mind, for, by Jove! on the whole, I belive they are. So here I am with—with all this about me, and not a soul on earth to bully me, and yet I can't do as I like. I don't say, by Jove, that I do want to marry. I dare say it would not answer at all, at least for a jolly good number of years, and then, I suppose, I must do as the rest of the world does. I must, you see, have some money, and I must have something of—of, you know, a—a *family;* and that's how I stand. Come along, it's growing awfully late, and—and it's very likely—ha—ha—ha!—I may die an old bachelor."

"Well, you know," said William, who thought that Trevor had spoken with extraordinary good sense, "there's no such hurry. Fellows wait, as you say, and look about them; and it's a very serious thing—and, by Jove! here we are at the gate; and I've had a very pleasant evening—*jolly!* I did not think two fellows by themselves, could be so jolly, and—and that capital claret!" Poor William was no great judge, nor, for that matter, indeed, was his great friend, Mr. Trevor, who, however, knew its price, and laying his hand on William's arm, said—

"Well, old fellow, I'm glad—I really am—you enjoyed yourself; and I hope when next you come, you'll have another glass or two with me. There's one thing I say about wine, be it what it may—hang it, let it be real, and get it from a good house; and give my respects to your ladies—don't forget; and when you come again, we must have more croquet. Let the balls and mallets stay where they are, you know, till then; and God bless you, Maubray, old boy, and if I can give you a lift, you know, any way, tell me, and I dare say, my solicitor *can* give you a lift when you get to the bar. Sends out a lot of briefs, you know. I'll speak to him, if you wish."

"A good time before that," laughed William. "Many thanks, though; I suppose I shall turn up in a few weeks again, and I'm beginning to take to the croquet rather, and we can have lots of play; but, by Jove! I'm keeping you all night—good bye."

So they shook hands, each thinking more highly of the other. I'm afraid our mutual estimates are seldom metaphysically justifiable.

"Well," thought Trevor, as he smoked his way up hill to the house, "no one can say I have not spoken plain enough. I should not like to have to give up that little acquaintance. It's an awfully slow part of the world. And now they know everything. If the old woman was thinking about anything, this will put it quite out of her head; and I can be careful, poor little thing! It would be a devil of a thing if she did grow to like me."

And with a lazy smile he let himself in, and had a little sherry and water, and *Bell's Life* in a drawing-room.

William Maubray experienced an unaccountable expansion of spirits and sympathies, as he strode along the pathway that debouches close upon the gate of Gilroyd Hall. Everything looked so beautiful, and so interesting, and so serene. He loitered for a moment to gaze on the moon; and, recollecting how late it was, he rang at the bell fiercely, hoping to find Violet Darkwell still in the drawing-room.

"Well, Tom, my aunt in the drawing-room?" said William, as he confided his coat and hat to that faithful domestic.

"Ay, sir, she be."

"And Miss Darkwell!"

"Gone up wi' Mrs. Winnie some time."

"Oh, that's all right, nothing like early sleep for young heads, Tom; and it's rather late," said William Maubray, disappointed, in a cheerful tone.

So he opened the door, and found Aunt Dinah in the drawing-room.

CHAPTER XVIII.

SUPPER.

"Elihu Bung" was open upon the table, also the Bible; and in the latter volume, it is but fair to say, she had been reading as William rang the bell. With her pleasant smile of welcome Miss Perfect greeted him.

"Now, sit down, William, and warm yourself at the fire—you are very cold, I dare say."

"Oh, no: it's quite a summer night."

"And, Thomas, tell Mrs. Podgers to send up something for Master William's supper."

Vainly William protested he could eat nothing; but Mrs. Podgers had been kept out of her bed—an allusion which was meant to make him feel, too, his late return—for the express purpose of broiling the bones with which he was to refresh himself; and Aunt Dinah, who had the military qualities strong within her, ordered Tom to obey her promptly.

"Well, dear William, how did you like your dinner. Everything very nice, I dare say. Had he any one to meet you?"

"No, quite alone; everything very good and very pleasant—a very jolly evening, and Trevor very chatty, chiefly about himself, of course.

Aunt Dinah looked at him with expectation, and William, who understood her, was not one of those agreeable persons who love to tantalize their neighbours, and force them to put their questions broadly.

"Violet has gone to bed?" said William.

"Oh, yes, some time."

"Yes, so Tom said," pursued William. "Well, I've no great news about Trevor's suit; in fact, I'm quite certain there's nothing in it." Aunt Dinah's countenance fell.

"And why?" she enquired.

"He mentioned her. He admires her—he thinks her very pretty, and all that," said William.

"I should think so," interposes Miss Perfect, with the scorn of one who hears that Queen Ann is dead.

"But he made quite a long speech, at the same time—I mean in continuation—and there's nothing—nothing *serious*—nothing whatever—nothing on earth in it," concluded he.

"But what did he say? Come, try and remember. You are young, and don't know how reserved, and—and how hypocritical—all lovers are; they affect indifference often merely to conceal their feelings.

"I hope she does not like him," began William.

"I'm very sure she doesn't," interpolated Aunt Dinah rapidly; "no girl likes a man till she first knows that he likes her."

"Because he took care to make it perfectly clear that he could not think of marrying her," added William.

"Upon my life," exclaimed the old lady briskly, "remarkably civil! To invite her cousin to dinner in order to entertain him with such an uncalled-for impertinence. And what did you say, pray?"

"He did not mention her, you see, in connection with all this," said William.

"Oh! pooh! then I dare say there's nothing in it," exclaimed Aunt Dinah, vigorously grasping at this straw.

"Oh! But there is, I assure you. He made a long speech about his—his circumstances," commenced William.

"Well, surely he can afford to keep a wife," interrupted Dinah, again.

"And the upshot of it was just this—that he could not afford to marry without money—a lot of money and rank."

"Money and rank! Pretty well for a young coxcomb like Mr. Vane Trevor, upon my word."

This was perhaps a little inconsistent, for Aunt Dinah had of late been in the habit of speaking very highly of the young gentleman.

"Yes, I assure you, and he said it all in a very pointed way. It was, you see, a kind of explanation of his position, and although there was nothing—no—no actual connecting of it at all with Violet's name, you know he couldn't do that; yet there was no mistaking what he meant."

Aunt Dinah looked with compressed lips on a verse of the Bible which lay open before her.

"Well, and what did he mean?" she resumed defiantly. "That he can't marry Violet! And pray who ever asked him? I, for one, never encouraged him? and I can answer for Violet. And *you* always thought it would be a very disadvantageous thing for her, so young and so extremely beautiful as she unquestionably is; and I really don't know any one here who has the smallest reason to look foolish on the occasion." "Well, I thought I'd tell you," said William, "tell what he said, I mean."

"Of course—quite right!" exclaimed she. "And there could be no mistake as to his intention. I know there isn't, and—and really, as it is so, I thought it rather honourable his being so explicit. Don't you?" said William.

"That's as it may be," said Aunt Dinah, oracularly shutting the Bible and "Elihu Bung. and putting that volume on the top of the other; "young people now-a-days are fuller a great deal of duplicity and—and worldliness, than old people used to be in my time. That's my opinion, and home goes his croquet in the morning. I've no notion of his coming about here, with his simpering airs and graces, getting my child, I may call her, talked about and sneered at."

"But," said William, who instinctively saw humiliation in anything that savoured of resentment, "don't you think any haste like that might connect in his view with what he said to me this evening?"

"At seven o'clock to-morrow morning, that's precisely what I wish," exclaimed Aunt Dinah.

At this moment Tom entered with the bones and other good things, and William, with the accommodating appetite of youth on second thoughts accepted and honoured the repast.

"And, Thomas, mind, at seven o'clock to-morrow morning, let little Billy Willocks bring over those great hammers, and wooden balls, and—and iron things; they're horribly in the way in the hall, with my compliments, to Revington, to Mr. Trevor, and—and don't fail. He'll say—Billy Willocks—that they were forgotten at Gilroyd. At seven o'clock, mind, with Miss Perfect's compliments."

"And I'm very glad, on the whole," said Miss Perfect, after about a minute had elapsed "that that matter is quite off my mind."

William, who was eating his broiled drumstick, with diligence and in a genial mood, was agreeably abstracted, and made no effort to keep the conversation alive.

"He talks very grandly, no doubt, of his family. But he'll hardly venture his high and mighty airs with you or me. The Maubrays are older than the Trevors; and, for my part, I would not change the name of Perfect with any in England. We are Athelstanes, and took the name of Perfect in the civil wars, as I've told you. As to family, William, you could not stand higher. You have, thank God, splendid talents, and, as I am satisfied, excellent—indeed, magnificent prospects. Do you see much of your cousin Winston at Cambridge?"

"Nothing," said William, who was, it must be confessed, a little surprised at his aunt's glowing testimony to his genius, and particularly to "his prospects," which he knew to be of a dismal character, and he conjectured that a supernatural light had been thrown upon both by Henbane.

"Do you mean to say that Winston Maubray has not sought you out or showed you any kindness?"

"I don't need his kindness, thank goodness. He could not be, in fact, of the least use to me; and I think he's ashamed of me rather."

"Ha!" ejaculated Aunt Dinah, with scorn.

"I spoke to him but once in my life—when Sir Richard came to Cambridge, and he and Winston called on Dr. Sprague, who presented me to my uncle," and William laughed.

"Well?"

"Well, he gave me two fingers to shake, and that sort of thing, and he said, 'Winston, here's your cousin,' and Winston smiled, and just took my hand, with a sort of slight bow."

"A bow! Well, a first cousin, and a *bow!*"

"Yes, and he pretended not to know me next day at cricket. I wish he was anywhere else, or that no one knew we were connected."

"Well, never mind. They'll be of use—of immense use to you. I'll tell you how," said Aunt Dinah, nodding resolutely to William.

———o———

CHAPTER XIX.

DEBATE.

"I'd rather work my own way, auntie. It would be intolerable to owe them anything," said William Maubray.

"I don't say *Winston*, but Sir Richard—*he* can be of the most immense use to you, and without placing you or me under the slightest obligation."

This seemed one of Aunt Dinah's paradoxes, or of her scampish table's promises, and made a commensurate impression on William's mind.

"You saw Doctor Waggett here yesterday?"

"I know—yes—the old clergyman, isn't he who paid you a visit?"

"Just so; he is a very old friend, *very*, and thinks it a most desirable arrangement."

"What arrangement? I don't quite——"

"You shall see," interrupted Aunt Dinah. "One moment's patience. I must first show you a—a paper to read." She walked over to a little japanned cabinet, and as she fumbled at the lock, continued, "And—and when you —when you have read it—you—ah! *that's* it—when you have read it, I'll tell you exactly what I mean."

So saying, she presented a large, official-looking envelope to William, who found that it contained a letter and a paper, headed, "Extract from the will and testament of the late Sir Nathaniel Maubray, of Queen's Maubray, bearing date ——, and proved, &c., on ——, 1831."

The letter was simply a courteous attorney's intimation that he enclosed herewith a copy, extract of the will, &c., as requested, together with a note of the expenses.

The extract was to the following effect:

"And I bequeath to my said son, Richard, the advowson of, and right of perpetual presentation to the living and vicarage of St. Maudlen of Caudley, otherwise Maudlin, in the diocese of Shovel-on-Headley, now absolutely vested in me, and to his heirs for ever, but upon the following conditions, namely, that if there be a kinsman, not being a son or step-son, of my said son or of his heir, &c., in possession, then, provided the said kimsman shall bear the name of Maubray, his father's name having been Maubray, and provided the same kinsman shall be in holy orders at the time of the said living becoming vacant, and shall be a good and religious man, and a proper person to be the incumbent of the said living, he shall appoint and nominate the said kinsman; and if there be two or more kinsmen so qualified, then him that is nearest of kin; and if there be two of equal consanguinity, then the elder of them; and if they be of the same age, then either, at the election of the bishop."

Then there was a provision that in case there were no such kinsman the Dean and Chapter of the Cathedral of Dawdle-cum-Drone should elect a cleric, being of the said diocese, but not of the said chapter, or of kin to any one of the said chapter; and that the said Richard, or his heir, should nominate the person so elected. And it was also conditioned that his son Richard should procure, if practicable, a private Act of Parliament to make these conditions permanent.

"He must have been a precious odd old fellow, my grand-uncle, observed William, as he sheathed the document again in the envelope.

"A conscientious man, anxious—with due regard to his family—to secure a good incumbent, and to prevent simony. The living is fifteen hundred a year, and there is this fact about it, that out of the seven last incumbents, three were made bishops. *Three!*"

"That's a great many," said William with a yawn.

"And *you'll* make the fourth," said Aunt Dinah, spiritedly, and took a pinch of her famous snuff.

"*I?*" repeated William, not quite believing his ears. "I am going to the bar."

"Into the Church you mean, dear William."

"But," remonstrated William, "but, I assure you, I, without a feeling of fitness—I—in fact, I could not think of it."

"Into the Church, sir." Aunt Dinah rose up, and, as it were, mounted guard over him, as she sternly spoke these words.

William looked rather puzzled, and very much annoyed.

"Into—the—*Church!*" she repeated, with a terrible deliberation.

"My dear Aunt," William began.

"Yes, the *Church!*, Listen to me. I—I have reason to—to know you'll be a bishop. Now mind, William I'll hear no nonsense on this subject. *Henbane!* Is that what you mutter?"

"Well, speak out. *What* of Henbane? Suppose I have been favoured with a—a communication; suppose I have tried to learn by that most beautiful and innocent communion, something of the—the expediency of the course I proposed, and have succeeded. then?"

William did not answer the challenge, and after a brief pause she continued—

"Come, come, my dear William, you know your poor old aunt loves you; you have been her first, and very nearly her only object, and you won't begin to vex her now, and after all, to—to break her heart about nothing."

"But I assure you," William began.

"A moment's patience," broke in Aunt Dinah, "you won't let me speak. Of course you may argue till doomsday, if you keep all the talk to yourself I say, William, there are not six peers in England can show as good blood as you, and I'll not hear of your being shut up in a beggarly garret in Westminster Hall, or the Temple, or wherever it is they put the—the paltry young barristers, when you might and *must* have a bishopric if you choose it, and marry a peer's daughter. And choose what you will, *I* choose that, and into the Church you go; yes, into the *Church*, the Church, sir, the *Church!* and that's enough, I hope."

William was stunned, and looked helplessly at his aunt, whom he loved very much. But the idea of going into the Church, the image of his old friend Dykes turned into a demure curate as he had seen him three weeks ago. The form of stout Doctor Dalrymple, with his pimples and shovel hat, and a general sense of simony and blasphemy came sickenly over him; his likings, his conscience, his fears his whole nature rose up against it in one abhorrent protest, and he said, very pale and in the voice of a sick man, gently placing his hand upon his aunt's arm, and looking with entreating eyes into hers:

"My dear aunt, to go into the Church without any kind of suitability, is a tremendous thing, for mere gain, a dreadful kind of sin. I know I'm quite unfit. I *could* not."

William did not know for how many years his aunt had been brooding over this one idea, how she had lived in this air-built castle, and what a crash of hopes and darkness of despair was in its downfall. But if he had, he could not help it. Down it must go. Orders were not for him. Deacon, priest, or bishop, William Maubray never could be.

Miss Perfect stared at him with pallid face.

"I tell you what, William," she exclaimed, "you had better think twice—you had better——"

"I *have* thought—indeed I have—for Doctor Sprague suggested the Church as a profession long ago; but I can't I'm not fit."

"You had better grow fit, then, and give up your sins, sir, and save both your soul and your prospects. It *can* be nothing but wickedness that prevents your taking orders—holy orders. Mercy on us! A blasphemy and a sin to take holy orders! What sort of state *can* you be in?"

"I wish to heaven I *were* good enough, but I'm not. I may be no worse than many who do go into the Church. Others may, but I couldn't."

"*You* couldn't! You conceited, young, provoking coxcomb! As if all the world were looking for miracles of piety from *you! Who* on earth expects you to be one bit more pious than other curates who do their best? Who are you, pray, that anything more should be expected from you? Do your duty in that state of life to which it shall please God to call you. *That's* simple. We expect no more."

"But that's everything," said William, with a hopeless shake of his head.

"What's everything? I can't see. I don't comprehend you. Of course there's a pleasure in crossing and thwarting me, But of let or hindrance to your entering the Church, there is and can be none, except your secret resolution to lead a wicked life."

"I'm not worse than other fellows. I'm better, I believe, than many who do get ordained; but I do assure you, I have thought of it before now, often, and it is quite out of the question."

"You *won't?*" said Aunt Dinah, aghast, in a low tone, and she gaped at him with flashing eyes, her gold spectacles shut up, and tightly grasped like a weapon in her hand. He had never seen her, or any one, look so pallid. And after a pause, she said slowly, in a very low tone—

"Once more, William—yes or no."

"My dear aunt, forgive me; don't be vexed, but I must say no," moaned poor William Maubray thus sorely pressed.

Aunt Dinah Perfect looked at him in silence; the same white, bright stare. William was afraid that she was on the point of having a fit. Who could have imagined the discussion of his profession so convulsive and frightful an ordeal?

——o——

CHAPTER XX.

FAREWELL.

For a minute or two, I think she could not speak; she closed her lips tightly, and pressed two of her fingers on them, perhaps to hide some tremor there; and she went and placed one of her slender feet on the fender, and looked steadfastly on the macerated countenance of the Very Rev. the Dean of Crutch Friars, who, in his oval frame, over the chimney-piece, seemed to hear and endure William's perversities with the meekness of a good, sad, suffering Christian.

Aunt Dinah sighed twice, two deep, long, laborious sighs, and tapped the steel of her stays ferociously with her finger tips. In his distress and confusion, William rose irresolutely. He would have approached her, but he feared that his doing so would but precipitate an explosion, and he remained standing, with his fingers extended on the table as if on the keys of a piano, and looking wan and sad over his shoulder on the back of Aunt Dinah's natty old-fashioned cap.

"Well, young gentleman, you have made up your mind, and so have I," said Aunt Dinah, abruptly returning to the table. "You go your own way. I shall not interfere in your concerns. I shall see your face *no more—never!* I have done with you, and depend upon it I shan't change. I never change. I put you away from me. I wash my hands of you. I have *done* with you. I shall send a hundred pounds to Dr. Sprague, when you leave to-morrow, first, to pay college expenses, and the balance *you* may take, and that ends all between us. I hate the world, ungrateful, stiff-necked, rebellious, *heartless*. All I have been to you, you know. What you would have been without me, you also know, a beggar—simply a beggar. I shall now find other objects. You are free, sir, henceforward. I hope you may enjoy your liberty, and that you may never have reason to repent your perversity and ingratitude as bitterly as I now see my folly. Go, sir, good night, and let me see your face no more."

William stood looking on his transformed aunt; he felt his ears tingle with the insult of her speech, and a great ball seemed rising in his throat.

Her face was darkened by a dismal anger; her look was hard and cold, and it seemed to him that the gates of reconciliation were closed against him for ever, and that he had come into that place of exclusion at whose entrance hope is left behind.

William was proud, too, and sensitive. It was no equal battle. His obligations had never before been weighed against his claims, and he felt the cruel truth of Aunt Dinah's words beating him down into the dust.

With her chin in the air, and averted gaze, she sat stiff and upright in her accustomed chair by the fire. William stood looking at her for a time, his thoughts not very clear, and a great vague pain throbbing at his heart. There was that in her countenance which indicated something different from anger—a cold alienation.

William Maubray silently and softly left the room.

"He thinks it will be all over in the morning, but he does not know *me*." So thought Aunt Dinah, folding her cold hands together. "Gone to bed; his last night at Gilroyd."

Holding her mind stiffly in this attitude, with a corresponding pose and look she sate, and in a minute more William Maubray entered the room very pale, his outside coat was on, and his hat in his hand. His lip trembled a little, and he walked very quickly to the side of her chair, laid his hand softly on her shoulder, and stooping down kissed her cheek, and without a word left the room.

She heard the hall door open, and Tom's voice talking with him as their steps traversed the gravel, and the jarring sound of the iron gate on its hinges. "Good night," said the well-known voice, so long beloved; and "Good night, Mr. William, good night, sir," in Tom's gruff voice, and a little more time the gate clanged, and Tom's lonely step came back.

"He had no business to open the gate without my order," said Miss Perfect.

She was thinking of blowing Tom up, but her pride prevented; and, as Tom entered in reply to her bell, she asked as nearly as she could in her usual way—

"My nephew did not take away his trunk?"

"No, mum."

"He gave directions about his things, of course?"

"Yes, they're to follow, mum, by the mornin' coach to Cambridge."

"H'm! very good; that's all. You had better get to your bed now. Good night."

And thus, with a dry and stately air, dismissed, he withdrew, and Aunt Dinah said, "I'm glad that's off my mind; I've done right; I know I have. Who'd have thought? But there's no help, and I'm glad it's over."

Aunt Dinah sat for a long time in the drawing-room, uttering short sentences like these, from time to time. Then she read some verses in the Bible; and I don't think she could have told you, when she closed the book, what they were about. She had thoughts of a *séance* with old Winnie Dobbs, but somehow she was not exactly in the mood.

"Master William is not in his room yet," observed that ancient domestic.

"Master William has gone to Cambridge to-night," said Miss Perfect, drily and coldly, "and his luggage follows in the morning. I can't find my night-cap."

So old Winnie, though surprised, was nothing wiser that night respecting the real character of the movement. And Aunt Dinah said her prayers stiffly; and, bidding old Winnie a peremptory good-night, put out her candle, and re-stated to herself the fact she had already frequently mentioned: "I have acted rightly; I have nothing to regret. William will, I dare say, come to his senses, and recollect all he owes me."

"In the mean time, William, with no very distinct ideas, and only his huge pain and humiliation at his heart, trudged along the solitary road to Saxton. He sat down on the stile, under the great ash tree by the roadside, to gather up his thoughts. Little more than half an hour before, he had been so unusually happy, and now, here he sat shipwrecked, wounded, and forlorn.

He looked at his watch again. A dreadful three-quarters of an hour must elapse before the Cambridge coach would draw up at the Golden Posts, in High Street. Had he not better go on, and await its arrival there? Yet what need he care? What was it to him whether he were late or not? In his outcast desperation he fancied he would rather like to wear out his shoes and his strength in a long march to Cambridge. He would have liked to lift his dusty hat grimly to Violet, as he strode footsore and cheerless on his way. But alas! he was leaving Violet *there*, among those dark-tufted outlines, and under the high steep roof whose edge he could just discern. There could be no chance meeting. Farewell! Back to Cambridge he was going, and through Cambridge into space, where by those who once liked him he should be found no more; on that he was resolved.

So up he got again, without a plan, without a reason, as he had sat down; and he lifted his hat, and, with extended arm, waved his farewell toward Gilroyd. And the old ash tree looked down sadly, murmuring, in the fickle night breeze, over his folly.

CHAPTER XXI.

WILLIAM CONSULTS A SAGE.

STARTING afresh, at a pace wholly uncalled for by time or distance, William Maubray was soon in the silent street of Saxton, with the bright moonlight on one side of it, and the houses and half the road black in shadow on the other.

There was a light in Doctor Drake's front parlour, which he called his study. The doctor himself was in evidence, leaning upon the sash of the window, which he had lowered, and smoking dreamily from a "churchwarden" toward the brilliant moon. It was plain that Miss Letty had retired, and, in his desolation, human sympathy, some one to talk to, ever so little, on his sudden calamity—a frienly soul, who knew Aunt Dinah long and well, and was even half as wise as Doctor Drake was reputed to be, would be a Godsend. He yearned to shake the honest fellow's hand, and his haste was less, and subsided to a loitering pace, as he approached the window, from which he was hailed, but not in a way to make it quite clear what the learned physician exactly wanted.

"I shay—shizzy—shizhte—shizh-shizh-shizhte—V—V—Viator, I shay," said the Doctor—playfully meaning, I believe, *Siste Viator*.

And Doctor Drake's long pipe, like a shepherd's crook, was hospitably extended, so that the embers fell out on the highway, to arrest the wayfarer. So William stopped and said:

"What a sweet night—how beautiful, and I'm so glad to find you still up, Doctor Drake."

"Alwayzh—all—alwayzh up," said the Doctor, oracularly, smiling rather at one side of his cheek, and with his eyes pretty nearly closed, and his long pipe swaying gently, horizontally, over the trottoir; "you'll look—insth'r pleashure—acquaintensh."

By this time the doctor, with his disengaged hand, had seized William's, and his pipe had dropped on the pavement, and was smashed.

"Bl—bloke—bl—boke!" murmured the doctor, smiling celestially, with a little vague wave of his fingers toward the fragments of his churchwarden, from the bowl of which the sparks were flitting lightly along High Street. "Blo—boke—my—p—p—phife!"

"I—shay, ole boy, you—come—in," and he beckoned William, grandly, through the window.

William glanced at the door, and the doctor, comprehending, said, with awful solemnity:

"All—thingsh deeshenly—in an—in or—or—orrer, I shay. Come—ole fellow—wone ye?—tooth th'—th' door sh'r—an'—an' you'll norr regresh—no—never."

William, though not very sharp on such points, perceived that Doctor Darke had been making merry in his study; and the learned gentleman received him at the hall-door, laying his hand lovingly and grandly on his arm.

"Howzhe th'—th' ladle—th' admir'bl' womr, over there, Mish Perfek?"

"My aunt is very well—perfectly well, thanks," answered William.

"No thangs—I thang *you*, sh'r—I thang Prover'l!" and the doctor sank with a comfortable sigh, and his back against the wall, shaking William's hand slowly, and looking piously up at the cornice.

"She's quite well, but—but I've something to tell you," said William.

"Comle—comle—ong!" said the doctor, encouragingly, and led the way unsteadily into his study.

There was a jug of cold water, a "tumbler," and a large black bottle on the table, to which the doctor waved a gracious introduction.

"Ole Tom, ole Tom, an' w—wawr hizh dring the chryshle brook!"

The doctor was given to quotation in his cups, and this was his paraphrase of "The Hermit."

"Thanks, no," said William; "I have had my glass long ago. I—I'm going back to Cambridge, sir; I'm going to make a push in life. I've been too long a burden on my aunt."

"Admiral wom'le sh'r? Wurle—worry—no wurrier—ladle!" (worthier lady! I believe he meant) exclaimed the doctor, with growing enthusiasm.

Contented with these evidences of mental vigour, William, who must have spoken to the roadside trees, rather than refrain himself, proceeded to tell his woeful story—to which Doctor Drake listened, clinging rather to the chimney-piece with his right hand, and in his left sustaining a large glass of his favourite "Old Tom" and water, a little of which occasionally poured upon the hearth-rug.

"And, Doctor Drake, you won't mention what I'm going to say?"

The doctor intended to say, "silent as the sepulchre," but broke down, and merely nodded, funereally pointing his finger perpendicularly toward the hearthstone; and having let go his hold on the chimney, he made an involuntary wheel backward, and sat down quite unexpectedly, and rather violently, in an elbow-chair.

"You promise, really and truly, sir?" pressed William.

"Reel-reel-reelan'-*tooral*," repeated the doctor as nearly as he could.

And upon this assurance William Maubay proceeded to state his case, and feeling relieved as he poured forth his wrongs, waxed voluble; and the doctor sat and heard, looking like Solomon, and refreshing his lips now and again, as if William's oration parched them.

"And what, sir, do you think I had best do?" said William, not very wisely it must be owned, applying to Philip, certainly not sober—for judgment.

"Return to my duty?" repeated William, interpreting as well as he could the doctor's somewhat vague articulation. "Why, I am certain I never left it. I have done all I could to please her; but this you know is what no one on earth could be expected to do—what no one *ought* to do."

"*Wrong*, sh'r!" exclaimed the doctor with

decision. "Thersh—r—r—*right*, and th'rsh wrong—r—*ry*—an' *wrong*—moshe admira'l ladle, Mish Perfeck!—moshe amiable; we all appresheay—sheniorib—bush pie—ri—pie—oribush—ole Latt'n, you know. I 'preshiay an' *love* Mish Perfey."

Senioribus prioribus. There was a want of clearness, William felt, in the doctor's views; still it weighed on him that such as they were they were against him.

"The principle on which I have acted, sir, can't be shaken. If I were, at my aunt's desire, now to enter the Church, I should do so entirely from worldly motives, which I know would be an impiety such as I could not endure to practise."

"Conn'ry toop—toop—prinsh'p'l—*conn'ry*—conn'ry," murmured the doctor, with an awful shake to his head.

The coach was now seen to pass the windows, with a couple of outside passengers, and a pile of luggage on top, and pulled up some sixty yards lower down the street, at the Golden Posts. With a hasty shake of the hand, William Maubray took his leave, and mounted to his elevated seat, as the horses, with their looped traces hanging by them, emerged from the inn-yard gate, like shadows, by the rapid sleight-of-hand of groom and hostler—to replace the wayworn team, now snorting and shaking their flanks, with drooping necks, and emitting a white steam in the moonlight, as they waited to be led off to rest and comfort in the stables of the Golden Posts.

——o——

CHAPTER XXII.

AN ADVERTISEMENT.

CHILL was the night. The slight motion of the air was against them, and made a cutting breeze as they drove on. The gentleman who sat beside him in a huge cloak and fur cap, with several yards of cashmere swathing his throat and chin and chops, was taciturn, except when he offered William a cigar. The cold, dark and solitude helped his depression—and longing to see Dr. Sprague, to whom, in his helplessness he looked for practical counsel. The way seemed more than usually long. There was one conclusion clearly fixed in the chaos of his thoughts. He had done with dependence. No matter to what level it might reduce him, he would earn his own bread. He was leaving Gilroyd Hall behind him, and all its dreams, to be dreamed no more. Perhaps there was in the surrounding gloom that romantic vista, which youth in its irrepressible hepefullness will open for itself, and William Maubray in the filmy perspective saw a shadow of himself as he would be a few years hence—wealthy, famous, the outcast restored, with the lawn and the chestnuts about him, and pretty old Gilroyd spreading its faint crimson gables and glittering window-frames behind, and old Aunt Dinah, and another form in the foreground, all smiles and tears, and welcome.

Poor fellow! He knows not how few succeed—how long it takes to make a fortune—how the process transforms, and how seldom that kind of gilding touches any but white heads, and when the sun is near its setting, and all the old things past or passing away.

In the morning William Maubray presented himself before Dr. Sprague, who asked him briskly—"How is Miss Perfect?

"Quite well sir, thank you; but—but something very serious has happened—very serious sir, and I am very anxious to ask your advice."

"Eh!" said the doctor; "wait a moment," and he quaffed what remained of his cup of tea, for William had surprised him at breakfast. "Hey?—Nothing very bad, I hope?" and the doctor put on his spectacles and looked in William's face, as a physician does into that of a patient, to read something of his case in his countenance.

So William reported the great debate, and alas! the division on the question of holy orders, to all which the good little man listened, leaning back in his chair, with his leg crossed and his chin raised.

"You're in the right, sir," he said, so soon as he had heard the young man out—"*perfectly*. What do you wish me to do? I'll write to Miss Perfect if you wish it."

"Very kind of you, sir; but I'd rather not, on that sub'ect, at least till I'm quite out of the way. I should not wish her to suppose that I could seek to return to my old position of—of obligation. I must never cost her a farthing more."

So William explained his feelings fully and very candidly, and Doctor Sprague listened, and looked pleased though grave; and, said he—

"You haven't been writing for any of the Magazines, or that sort of thing?"

No, he had no resource of that kind. He had a good deal of loose manuscript, he confessed with a blush, but he had no introduction.

"Well, no," said Doctor Sprague, "you'd probably have a long wait, too long for your purpose. You have, you know, a trifle of your own, about twenty-three pounds a year, isn't it?" and he looked in the direction of his desk, where the memorandum was; "something thereabout, that I received for you. There's a money order for eleven pounds and something in my desk since yesterday."

"Don't you think, sir, that I should apply that little annuity to pay back all I can to my anut, who has been so good to me."

"Tut-tut, your aunt would not accept a guinea, and would mistake your motive; don't talk of any such thing. Her past affection is a matter of kindly recollection. You could not reduce it to money—no, no; but on the whole I think you have resolved wisely. You must undertake, for a little, something in the way of tuition; I don't mean here. You're hardly well enough up in the business for that; but we'll find out something *here*," and he tapped the *Times*, which lay open on the table beside him. "I dare say, to suit you—not a school, that would not do either—a tutor in a country house. You need not stay away more than six months, and you'll have something to go on with then; and in the mean time you can send your manuscripts round, and try if you can't get into some of the periodicals.

"It is very odd, sir, but some months since I spoke of such a plan when I was at Gilroyd, and my aunt was positively horrified; she is full of fancies, you know, and she told me that none of my family had ever done anything of the kind."

"I don't know about *that;* but I've done it, I can tell you, and better men than I," said the doctor.

"I only mean that she made such a point of it; she would think I had done it expressly to vex her, or she might come wherever I was, and try to make me leave it."

"So she might," said the cleric, and laughed a little to himself, for he knew her, and fancied a scene, "but what can you do? I think you *must* in fact, and the best way will be to tell her nothing about it. She has cut you, you know, for the present, and—and you need not, if you think it would vex her, go in your own name, do you see? We'll call you Mr. Herbert, you're descended maternally, you know, from Herberts; now—not for a moment, now, just hear me out; there shall be no deception, of course. *I'll* tell them that for certain family reasons I have advised you to take that measure. I'll take it all on myself, and say all I think of you, and know of you, and I saw, just now, in this very paper, something that I think would answer very nicely. Yes, yes, I'll make it all quite straight and easy. But you must do as I say."

The kind little gentleman was thinking that eccentric and fierce Miss Perfect might never forgive his engaging himself as a tutor, without at least that disguise, and he looked forward as he murmured *varium et mutabile semper*, to a much earrier, *redintegratio amoris* than William dreamed of.

"It's unlucky her having made a point of it. But what is the poor fellow to do? She must not, however, be offended more than we can help, and that will show a wish as far as was practicable, to consult her feelings."

Doctor Sprague looked along a column in the *Times*, and said he, after his scrutiny—

"I think there's just one of these you'll like—say which you prefer, and I'll tell you if it's the one I think."

So William conned over the advertisements, and, in Aunt Dinah's phrase, put on his considering cap, and having pondered a good while, "This one, I think?" he half decided and half inquired.

"The very thing!" said Dr. Sprague, cheerily. "One boy—country-house—just the thing; he'll be in his bed early, you know, and you can take your books and write away till twelve at night; and now you had better drop them a line—or stay, I'll do it; you can't sign your name, you know."

So, communications being opened, in a day or two it turned out that Doctor Sprague knew the gentleman who advertised. It was a very old and long interrupted acquaintance.

"He's a quiet, kind fellow, and Kincton Hall, they say, a pretty place and old. I'll write to Knox."

The Knoxes of Kincton Hall William had heard Trevor occasionally mention, but tried in vain to recollect what he used to say of them; six months, however, was no great venture, and the experiment could hardly break down very badly in that time.

"Maubray, your cousin, has quarrelled with his father, you heard?"

"No."

"Oh, yes, just about the time when you left this—a few days ago. Young Maubray has some little property from his mother, and chooses to take his own way; and Sir Richard was in here with me yesterday, very angry and violent, poor man, and vows (the doctor would not say "swears" which would have described the procedure more accurately) he'll cut him off with a shilling; but that's all moonshine. The estates are under settlement, and the young fellow knows it, and that's at the bottom of his independence; and he's gone abroad, I believe, to amuse himself: and he has been no credit to his college, from all I hear."

CHAPTER XXIII.

KINCTON HALL.

In the parlour of Kincton Hall the family were assembled at breakfast; Mrs. Kincton Knox dispensed tea and coffee in a queenlike way, hardly called for, seeing that her husband, daughter, and little son, formed the entire party.

Mrs. Kincton Knox was what some people call a clever woman—that is, she did nearly everything with an object, but somehow she had not succeeded. Mr. Kincton Knox was not Deputy Lieutenant or a Member for his county. Her daughter Clara—with blue eyes and golden hair—a handsome girl, now leaning back in her chair and looking listlessly through the window across the table—was admitted confidentially to be near five-and-twenty, and was in fact past eight-and-twenty, and unmarried still. There was not that intimacy between the Croydon family and the Kincton Knoxes for which she had laboured so cleverly and industriously. She was not among the patronesses, and only one of the committee, of the great county ball, at which the Prince figured, and which, on the plea of illness, she had with proper dignity declined attending. She blamed her daughter, she blamed her husband, she blamed the envy and combination of neighbours, for her failures. There was nothing that the wit and industry of woman could do she had not done. She was the best bred and most far-seeing woman in the country round, radiant with a grave sort of fascination, always in supreme command, never for a moment losing sight of her object, yet, great or small, somehow never compassing it—a Vanderdecken, thwarted invisibly, and her crew growing old around her. Was ever admirable woman so persecuted by fortune?

Perhaps if the accomplished Mrs. Kincton Knox had been some twenty years before bereft of her brilliant intellect and shut up in a remote mad-house, or consigned under an unexceptionable epitaph to the family vault in Smolderton Church, the afflicted family might have prospered; for Miss Clara was really pretty, and could draw and sing better than most well-married young ladies of her rank in life. And, though he was not very bright, no man was more inoffensive and genial than portly old Kincton Knox, if only she had permitted his popularity to grow, and had left him and his belongings a little to nature.

"Hollo! what are those fellows doing?" exclaimed Kincton Knox, attracted by a sound of chopping from without. "Hollo! ho!" and with his arms extended, he made a rush at the window, which he threw up, shouting, "Hollo there! stop that."

A man stood erect with an axe in his hand, by the trunk of one of the great walnut trees.

"What the devil are you doing, sir, cutting down my tree?" cried the old gentleman, his handsome face flushed with wrath, and his silver fork, with a bit of ham on the end of it, grasped fiercely in his left hand. "Who the devil ordered you, sir, to—to how—pow—cut down my trees, sir?"

"I've spoken to you till I'm tired, Kincton, about that tree; it buries us in perfect damp and darkness, and I"—began the dignified lady in purple silk, and lace coif.

"Don't you presume, sir, to cut down a tree of mine without my orders; don't you dare, sir; don't—don't attempt it, sir, or it will be worse for you; take that hatchet away, sir, and send Wall the gardener here this moment, sir, to see what can be done, and I've a mind to send you about your business, and egad if I find you've injured the tree, I *will* too, sir; send him this moment; get out of my sight, sir.

It was not more than once in two years that Mr. Kincton Knox broke out in that way, and only on extraordinary and sudden provocation. He returned to the table and sat down in his chair, having shut the windows with an unnecessary display of physical force. His countenance was red and lowering, and his eyes still staring and blinking rapidly, and his white waistcoat heaving, and even the brass buttons of his blue coat uneasy. You might have observed the tremulous shuffle of his fingers as his fist rested on the tablecloth, while he gazed through the window and muttered and puffed to the agitation of his chops. Upon such unusual occasions Mrs. Kincton Knox was a little alarmed and even crestfallen. It was a sudden accession of mania in an animal usually perfectly docile, and therefore it was startling, and called not for chastisement so much as management.

"I may be permitted to mention, now that there's a little quiet, that it was I who ordered that tree to be removed—of course if it makes you violent to take it down, let it stand; let the house be darkened and the inhabitants take the ague. I've simply endeavoured to do what I thought right. I'm never thanked; I don't expect thanks; I hope I know my duty, and do it from higher motives. But this I know, and you'll see it when I'm in my grave, that if it were not for me, every single individual thing connected with you and yours would be in a state of the most inextricable neglect and confusion, and I may say ruin."

"I object to the place being denuded. There is not much in that," blustered Mr. Kincton Knox, plaintively.

He was now subsiding; and she, availing herself of this frame of mind, proceeded with even more force, and dignity, till interrupted by Miss Clara, who observed serenely—

"Mamma, that greedy little pig will choke himself with apricot-stones, if you allow him."

Master Howard Seymore Knox—a stunted and billious boy—scowled at Miss Clara, with muddy eyes, his mouth being too full for convenient articulation, and clutched his plate with both hands.

"My precious rosebud, be careful," remonstrated his mamma with gentle fervour.

Stooping over his plate, a clatter of fruit-stones was heard upon it, and Master Howard ejaculated—

"You lie, you do, you tell-tale-tit!"

"Oh! my love," remonstrated Mrs. Kincton.

"Briggs shall box your ears for that, my fine fellow," said Miss Clara.

"There's another cram! I'd like to see her," retorted the youth.

"Greedy little beast!" observed Clara.

"Clara, my love!" suggested her mamma.

"Not half so greedy as you. Who took the woodcock pie up to her bedroom? Ah-ha!" vociferated the young gentleman.

"Now I'll do it myself!" exclaimed the languid young lady, rising with sudden energy.

"I'll fling these in your ugly face, if you come near me," cried he, jumping up, and behind his mamma's chair, with a knife and fork in his right hand, covered with Savory pie.

"I won't have this; I won't have it," said Mrs. Kincton Knox with peremptory dignity. "Howard, be quiet, my love; Clara, sit down."

"The *imp!* he'll never stop till he murders some one," exclaimed Miss Clara, with intense feeling, as she sat down with brilliant cheeks and flashing eyes. "Look at him, mamma; he's saying ha-ha, and shaking his knife and fork at me, the little murderer; and the liar!"

"Clara, I *insist*," interposed Mrs. Kincton Knox.

"Yes, I do believe he's an actual devil," persisted the young lady.

"I *won't* have this," continued the *mater familias*, peremptorily.

"Ha, ha!" whispered the imp obliquely, from the other side, wagging his head, and clutching his knife and fork, while he touched the points of the fork, with a horrid significance, with the finger tip of his disengaged hand.

Miss Clara raised her hand, and opened her mouth to exclaim; but at this moment the servant entered with the letters, and the current of conversation was diverted.

CHAPTER XXIV.

WILLIAM IS SUMMONED.

Mrs. Kincton Knox had no less than seven notes and letters, her husband one, and Miss Clara two crossed manuscripts, which engrossed her speedily; and, possibly, these figures would have indicated pretty accurately their relative influence in the household.

The matron deigned no account of her letters to mortal, and exacted from all others an habitual candour in this respect, and so much had it grown to be a matter of conscience with her husband, that I don't think he could have slept in his bed if he had failed to submit any one such communication to her inspection.

Her own were now neatly arranged, one over the other, like the discarded cards in piquet, beside her plate.

"Well, my dear, what is it?" she said to her husband, accompanying the inquiry with a little motion, like a minature beckoning, of her fore-finger.

"Something about the *Times*—the tutor," he began.

"Oh!" said Mrs. Kincton Knox, interrupting, with a warning nod and an awful look, and a glance at Master Howard, who was fortunately so busy in tying bits of paper, in imitation of a kite-tail, on the string of the window-blind, that he had heard nothing.

"Oh!" murmured Mr. Kincton Knox, prolonging the interjection softly—he was accustomed, with a guilty and abject submission, every now and then, to receive that sort of awful signal—"I did not know." And he whistled a little through his round mouth, and looked a little frightened, and ashamed of his clumsiness, though he seldom knew in what exactly the danger consisted.

"Howard, my precious rosebud, I've told Rogers he may fire the pistol for you three times this morning; he says he has powder, and you may go now."

So away ran Master Howard to plague Roger the footman; and Mrs. Kincton Knox said with a nod—

"*Now.*"

"Here," said he, mildly pushing the letter towards her, "*you'll* understand it better;" and she read aloud—

"My dear Sir,—I venture to renew an old acquaintance at the instance of a young friend of mine, who has seen your advertisement in the *Times*, for a tutor, and desires to accept that office. He is capitally qualified, as your advertisement says, 'to prepare a boy of twelve for school.' He is a fair scholar, and a gentleman, and for his character, I can undertake to answer almost as for my own. I feel pretty certain that you will like him. There is but one condition, to which I am sure you will not object."

"He shan't smoke or sit up all night, if that's it," said the lady loftily, by way of gloss.

"He and I agree," she read on, "that he should be received under the name of William Herbert." This paragraph she read twice over very deliberately. "As I have pressed upon him, for reasons which, you will readily believe, are not dishonourable—what strikes me as a strong objection to his accepting the position you offer under his own name."

"That's very odd, it strikes me. Why shouldn't he tell his name?" observed Mrs. Kincton Knox, with grim curiosity.

"I dare say he's a low person, and his name is not pretty," sneered Miss Clara, carelessly.

"Who is that Mr. Edmund—Edward Sprague?" inquired the matron.

Mr. Kincton Knox testified to his character.

"But, just stop a moment—it is very odd. Why should he be, if he is a fit person to be received at Kincton — why should he be ashamed of his name?" repeated Mrs. Kincton Knox, grandly.

"Perhaps it may be as well to let it drop," suggested Kincton Knox, in the hope that he was enticipating his wife's wishes. But that grave lady raised her nose at his remark, and turned away, not vouchsafing an answer.

"Of course; I don't say it is not all quite proper; but say what you may, and take it how you please, it is a very odd condition."

There was a pause here. Clara did not care enough to engage in the discussion, and old Kincton Knox rumpled his *Times* uneasily, not knowing whether he was called on for a solution, and not caring to hazard one, for he was seldom lucky.

"Well, and what do you propose to do?" demanded his wife, who thus sometimes cruelly forced the peaceable old gentleman into debate.

"Why," said he, cautiously, "whatever you think best, my dear."

"I'm not likely to receive much assistance from you, Mr. Kincton Knox. However, provided I'm not *blamed* for doing my best, and my servants stormed at for obeying me——"

Mr. Kincton Knox glanced unconsciously and penitently at the walnut tree.

"I suppose, as something *must* be done, and nothing will be done otherwise, I may as well take *this* trouble and responsibility upon myself."

"And what am I to say to Sprague?" murmured Mr. Kincton Knox.

"I suppose the young man had better come. Mr. Sprague, you say, is a proper person, and I suppose we may rely upon what he says. I *hope* so, I'm sure, and if he does not answer, why he can go about his business."

In due course, therefore, Mr. Kincton Knox's reply, which he had previougly read aloud to his wife, was despatched.

So Fate had resolved that William Maubray should visit Kincton Hall, while Aunt Dinah was daily expecting the return of her prodigal to Gilroyd.

"If I don't hear from William Maubray before Sunday, I shall write on Monday morning to Doctor Sprague" said she, after a long silence at breakfast.

She looked at Miss Violet, but the young lady was looking on the cloth, and with her finger-tips stirring hither and thither some flowers that lay there—not her eyes, only her long eyelashes were visible—and the invitation to say something conveyed in Aunt Dinah's glance, miscarried.

"And I think it very strange—not what I should have expected from William—that he has not written. I don't mean an apology, that's a matter between his own conscience and his Maker. I mean some little inquiry. Affection of course we cannot command, but respect and courtesy we may."

"I had thought better of William. I think Doctor Sprague will be surprised," she resumed. "I did not think he could have parted on the terms he did, and never written a line after, for nearly a week. He seems to me quite a—a changed person."

"Just at that age," said Miss Violet, in a low tone, looking nearer to her flowers, and growing interested in a rose whose rumpled leaves she was adjusting with her finger-tips, "some one says—I read it lately somewhere—I forget who—they grow weary of home, and home faces, and want change and adventure, that is action and danger, of one kind or another, what they are sent into the world for, I suppose—that and liberty." She spoke very low, as if to her flowers, and when she ceased, Miss Perfect listened still, and finding she had no more to say, Aunt Dinah added—

"And a wise business they make of it—fifty blunders in as many days, and begin looking out for wives before they know how to earn a guinea."

Miss Violet looked up and smiled, and popped her nose gently into the water glass beside her, and went on adjusting her flowers.

"Wives, indeed! Yes—just what his poor father did before him, and his grandfather, old Sir Everard, he was married privately, at twenty! It runs in the blood, my dear, like gaming or drinking; and the next I shall hear of William, I dare say, will be a note to ask my blessing on his marriage!"

Again Miss Violet laughed softly, and smiling for a moment, with a pretty slip of verbena in her fingers, she added it to the growing bouquet in the glass.

"You may laugh, my dear, but it is what I'm afraid of. I assure you I am serious."

"But it may turn out very happy, or very splendid, you know; he may meet with a young lady more foolish than himself, and with a great dot."

"No, my dear, he's a soft romantic goose, and I really think if it were not imprudent, the romance would lose all its attraction. I tell you, it runs in the family, and he's not a bit wiser than his father, or his grandfather before him."

"This will never do without a bit of blue. May I run out to the flowers?"

"Certainly, dear;" and Aunt Dinah peered through her spectacles at the half made-up bouquet in the glass. "Yes, it does—it wants blue. Isn't there blue verbena?"

And away ran Violet, and her pretty figure and gay face flitted before the windows in the early sun among the flowers. And Aunt Dinah looked for a moment with a smile and a sigh. Perhaps she was thinking of the time when it was morning sun and opening flowers for her, and young fellows—one of whom, long dead in India, was still a dream for her—used to talk their foolish flatteries, that sounded now like muffled music in the distant air; and she looked down dreamily on the back of her slim wrinkled hand that lay on the table.

CHAPTER XXV.

W. MAUBRAY ARRIVES.

When, a few days later, Maubray, who was a shy man, stepped down from his fly, as the vehicle which conveyed him from the neighbouring railway station, though it more resembled a snail, was called, and found himself under the cold, grey, Ionic colonnade which received people at Kincton with a dismal and exclusive hospitality, his heart sank, a chilly shadow descended upon him, and in the silent panic of the moment he felt tempted to re-enter the vehicle, return to Dr. Sprague, and confess that he wanted nerve to fulfil his engagement.

William was conducted through the hall, up the great stairs, over a sombre lobby and up a second and narrower stair, to a gallery cold and dim, from which his room-door opened. Upon this floor the quietude of desertion reigned. He looked from his low window into a small court-yard, formed on three sides by the house itself, and on the fourth by a rear of the offices, behind which a thick mass of autumnal foliage showed itself in the distance. The circumscribed view was dreary and formal. How different from homely, genial old Gilroyd! But that was a dream, and this reality; and so his toilet proceeded rapidly, and he descended, looking by no means like a threadbare domine, but handsome and presentable, and with the refinement of his good birth and breeding in his features.

"Can I see Mr. Kincton Knox?" inquired William of the servant in the hall.

"I'll inquire, sir."

And William was left in that tesselated and pillared apartment, while the servant entered his master's study, and speedily returning, informed him with a superciliousness which was new to William, and decidedly uncomfortable, that he might enter.

It was a handsome study, stored with handsome books and sundry busts, one of the deceased Horace Kincton Knox, in porphyry, received William on a pedestal near the door, and looked alarmingly like a case of smallpox.

The present master of Kincton, portly, handsome, though threescore years had not passed over him in vain, with a bald forehead, and a sort of simple dignity, as William fancied, rose smiling, and came to meet him with his hand extended, and with a cordial glow about him, as though he had known him for years.

"You are very welcome, sir—very happy to see you—very happy to make your acquaintance; and how is my good friend, Sprague? a very old friend of mine, though we have dropped out of sight a good deal; and I correspond very little—so—so we loose sight of one another; but he's well, and doing well too? I'm very happy to see you."

There was something homely and reassuring in this kind old man, which was very pleasant to William.

"Dr. Sprague was very well when I left him, and gave me this note, sir, for you," replied William, presenting it to his host, who took it, and glanced at it as they stood on the hearthrug together; and as he read it he observed:

"Very cold the weather is. I don't remember—very cold—at this time of year. You've had a cold drive. Not had luncheon yet? Two o'clock, you know: yes, about a quarter to two now, in a quarter of an hour."

He had by this time laid Doctor Sprague's note on the table.

"And the little boy, sir, where is he?" suggested William.

"Oh, oh! little Howard! I—I suppose we shall see him at lunch."

"I should wish very much to hear any directions or suggestions, and to know something as to what he has been doing," said William.

"Very true—very right, Mr.—Mr.," and old Kincton Knox groped towards the note, intending to refresh his memory.

"*Herbert*," interposed William, colouring a little. "Doctor Sprague made a point of the name, and I believe, sir, wrote particularly about it."

"Quite so—very right, sir. It is *Herbert*. I quite approve—quite, sir. He did—perfectly explicit; and about the boy. The fact is, Mr. Herbert, I leave him very much to his mother. She can tell you much more what he has been doing—very young, you know, still—and—and she'll tell you all about him; and I hope you will be happy, I'm sure; and don't fail to tell the people whatever you want, you know; I live very much to myself—quiet room this—fond of books, I suppose? Well, I shall be always very happy to see you here; in fact it will be a great pleasure. We may as well sit down, do, pray; for you know ladies don't care very much for this sort of reading;" and he waved his short white hand towards the bookcases; "and sometimes one feels a little lonely; and Sprague tells me you have a turn for reading."

The door opened, and a servant announced that Mrs. Kincton Knox wished to see Mr. Herbert in the schoolroom.

"Ho!" exclaimed the master of Kincton, with a grave countenance and a promptitude which savoured of discipline. "Well, at lunch I shall see you, Mr. Herbert; we'll meet in ten minutes or so; and, Edward, you'll show Mr.—a—Herbert to the schoolroom."

Across the hall was he conducted, to a room in which were some sporting prints and two dingy oil paintings of "sometime," favourite hunters who sniffed and heard their last of field and bugle a century ago. There were also some guns and fishing rods; and, through this to the school-room, where Mrs. Kincton Knox, in purple silk, with a turban on her head, loomed awfully before him as he entered, and made him a slight and rustling courtesy, which rather warned him off than greeted him.

"Mr.—a—a—Herbert?' said the lady of the prominent black eyes, with a lofty inquiry.

"I—a—Doctor Sprague—told me he had written very fully about the—the," stammered William, who began to feel like a concealed ticket-of-leave man.

"The *name, yes*," said Mrs. Kincton Knox, looking steadily on him, and then ensued a silence.

"He informed me that having explained the circumstances fully, and also that it was *his* not *my* particular wish, you had seen no difficulty in it," said William.

"Difficulty—none—there can be no difficulty when there's no constraint," replied Mrs. Kincton Knox, laying down a metaphysical axiom, as she sometimes did, which William could not quite clearly understand; "and although I have always maintained the position that where there's mystery there is guilt; yet feeling a confidence in Doctor Sprague's character and profession—of both of which Mr. Kincton Knox happened to know something—we have endeavoured to overcome our objection."

"I understood there was *no* objection," interposed William, flushing

"Pray allow me. An objection satisfied is

not necessarily an objection foregone; in this case, however, you are at liberty to treat it in that light. We waive our objection, and we have every reasonable confidence that we shall not have occasion to repent having done so."

This was spoken graciously and condescendingly, for she thought that a person who looked so decidedly like a gentleman would rather conduce to the dignity of the Kincton "household." But it did not seem to strike the young man at all in that light.

"You are about, Mr.—a—sir, to undertake the charge of my precious child—sensitive, delicate—too delicate and too impressionable to have permitted his making all the progress I could have wished in the rudiments—you understand—of future—a—a—education and accomplishment; a little wild, but full of affection, and—and of natural docility—but still unused—from the causes I have mentioned—to restraint or coercion. Your duty will therefore be a delicate one. I need not say that nothing of the nature of punishment will be permitted or endured. You will bear in mind the illustration of the sacred writer—the sun and the tempest, and the traveller's cloak" At this point William coughed slightly into his handkerchief. "Mild influences, in my mind, effect more than ever was accomplished by harshness; and such is the system under which our precious Howard must learn. Am I understood?"

"Quite," said William. "I should not myself undertake the task of punishing any child; but I'm afraid, unless the parents are prepared to pull him up now and then, for idleness or inattention, you will find his progress far from satisfactory."

"That is a question quite for *them*," said Mrs. Kincton Knox, in her queen-like way.

William bowed.

"What I want chiefly in a person—in a gentlemen in your capacity—is that he shall begin to—a—my precious child shall begin to associate with a superior mind, and imbibe rather by contact than task-work. Do I make myself clear? The—a—the—you know, of course the kind of thing."

William did not apprehend quite so clearly the nature of his duties as he would have wished, but said nothing.

"You and he will breakfast with us at half-past nine. I regret I cannot ask you to lunch. But you and Howard will dine at three o'clock in this room, and have tea—and—and any little thing that Mrs. Ridgeway, the housekeeper, may send you at six. The boy goes to his bed at half-past nine, and I conclude you already know your own room."

"And where is your—my pupil?" inquired William.

Mrs. Kincton Knox rang the bell. "He shall be with you presently, Mr. *Herbert*, and you will please to bear in mind that the dear boy's health is just at present our first object, and that he must not be pressed to study more than he wishes."

Master Howard Seymour Knox entered, eyeing the tutor suspiciously andloweringly. He had, perhaps, heard confidently of possible canings, and viewed William Maubray with a sheepish kind of malevolence.

———o———

CHAPTER XXVI.

WILLIAM MAUBRAY BEGINS TO EXCITE AN INTEREST.

There was positively nothing to interest William Maubray in his pupil, and a great deal to irritate and disgust him. What can be more sterile than the nature of a selfish child spoiled by indulgence. It was one comfort, however, that he was not expected to accomplish a miracle, that is, to teach a boy who had the option of learning nothing, and often for two hours or more at a time he was relieved altogether of his company, when he went out to drive Mrs. Kincton Knox, or to have a ride on his pony with the groom

But the monotony and solitude grew dreadful. At breakfast he sat with, but not of, the party. Except, indeed, the kindly old gentleman, who lived in a monastic seclusion among his books and trees and flowers, and to whom William's occasional company was a cheer and a happiness, no one at the breakfast table seemed, after the first slight and silent salutation was over, conscious of his presence.

Miss Clara and her mamma talked of matters that interested them—their neighbours, and the fashions, and the peerage, and even the furniture, as if William were a picture, or nothing at all.

He could not fail, notwithstanding his exclusion, to perceive that Clara was handsome—very handsome, indeed—quite a brilliant blonde, and with that confident and haughty air of—was it fashion—was it blood—was it the habit of being adored with incense and all sorts of worship—he could not tell. He only knew that it became her, and helped to overpower him.

We are not to suppose that all this time female curiosity at Kincton slumbered and slept over such a problem as William Maubray. Treat him how they might in his presence, he was a topic both of interest and inquiry in his absence. The few letters that reached him afforded no clue; they were addressed with uniform exactitude to "W. Herbert, Esq." The books he had brought with him to Kincton contributed no light; for William had not inscribed his name in his books. Miss Clara's maid, who was intensely interested in the investigation, brought a pocket handkerchief of the tutor's to her young mistress's room, where both she and her mamma conned over the initials "W.M." in a small but florid arabesque in the corner. It was, no doubt, a condescension such as William ought to have been proud of.

"There's five on 'em so, Miss—the rest

unmarked, and nothing else marked, except three old shirts."

"Why, you goose, what can I care?" laughed Miss Clara. "I'm not his nurse, or his seamstress. Take it away this moment. What a pretty discussion!"

This "W.M.," however, was not without its interest, and two days later the maid exhibited an old copy of Feltham's "Resolves," abstracted from William's little file of books, with "William Martin" neatly inscribed on the fly-leaf, but in a hand so quaint and ancient, and with ink so brown, that even Miss Clara "pooh-poohed" the discovery.

Now, the young lady could not help in some sort requiting William's secret estimate of her good looks. She thought the young tutor decidedly handsome; in fact, there could be no question about it. He was well formed, too; and with that undefinable grace which people are apt to refer to gentle blood. There was, moreover, a certain refinement and sensitiveness in his countenance utterly incompatible with the idea of vulgarity of any kind. Now, a tutor might be anything—a decayed nobleman or a chandler's son. Was not Louis Philippe an usher in a school? All you were to assume was that he could teach Latin grammar, and was in want of money.

There were some little signs of superfluity, too, in William's valuables. The butler, who was a native of Geneva, presuming on William's tutorship, had, on a fitting opportunity, begged leave to inspect his watch, and appraised it at twenty guineas among his fellow-servants. This and the massive gold chain, which also excited his admiration, were gifts from Miss Perfect, as was also that glorious dressing-case, presented on his attaining his twenty-first year, resplendent with gold and mother-o' pearl, and which the same competent authority valued at seventy guineas at least. Now, those things, though little, and some not at all seen outside the walls of his own little bedroom, emitted, like the concealed relics of a saint, so to speak, a glory and a fragrance which permeated the house. It was quite impossible, then, that want of money had driven this Mr. Herbert, or whoever he was, into his present position.

On the plate on top of this resplendent dressing-case the maid, who, fired by Monsieur Drouet's report, had visited the treasure clandestinely, were inscribed, as she reported to Miss Clara, the same mysterious characters "W.M."

"I like the old gentleman—kind old man. What wonderful things books are; nourishment for all sorts and sizes of minds—poor old Mr. Kincton Knox. How he reads and positively enjoys them. Yet the best things in them might just as well never have been written or thought, for any real perception he has of them! A kind man; I like him so much; I feel so obliged to him. And what ill-bred, insupportable persons the ladies are; that pompous, strong-willed, stupid old woman; her magnificence positively stifles me; and the young lady, how disagreeably handsome she is, and how impertinent. It must be a love of inflicting pain and degradation—how cruel, how shabby, how low!"

Such was William's review of the adult members of the family among whom he had come to reside, as he lay down with his fair hair on the pillow, and his sad eyes long open in the dark, looking at scenes and forms of the past, crossed and troubled by coming sorrows and apprehensions.

The ice and snow spread crisp and hard, and the frosty sun has little heat, but yet the thaw will come. And the radiance emitted by William's dressing-case, watch and other glories, began imperceptibly to tell upon the frozen rigour of his first reception. There was a word now and then about the weather, he was asked more graciously to take some more tea. The ladies sometimes smiled when they thus invited him, and Miss Clara began to take an interest in her brother, and even one day in her riding habit, in which she looked particularly well, looked into the school-room for a moment, just to give Howard a little box of bon-bons she had promised him before she went out.

"May I, Mr. Herbert?" asked Miss Clara, with that smile which no one could resist.

"Certainly," said William, bowing very low, and she thought there was something haughty in his grave humility.

So she thanked him, smiling more, and made her present to Howard, who broke out with—

"This ain't the one you said. You've been and eat it, you greedy!"

"*Now!*" pleaded Miss Clara, whose fingers tingled to box his ears, though she prolonged the word in her most coaxing tone, "Howard! Howard! could you? your own poor Clara! You shall come up and have any two others you like best, when I come back, if Mr. Herbert allows it," and with a smile, and a light kiss on the boy's forehead, who plunged away from her muttering, that brilliant vision vanished, leaving William standing for a moment wondering, and thinking how graceful and pretty she looked in that becoming get-up.

"Well," thought William, that night compunctiously and pleased, "I believe I have done them an injustice. I forgot that I was a total stranger, and expected a reception different perhaps from what I was entitled to. But this perhaps is better; people whose likings and confidence move slowly, and whose friendship bestowed gradually is not suddenly withdrawn."

And so he went to sleep more happily.

———o———

CHAPTER XXVII.

FROM KINCTON TO GILROYD.

A MONTH passed away with little change. Thanks to the every explicit injunction, constantly repeated, to teach his pupil no more than his pupil wished to learn, William Maubray got on wonderfully well with that ill-conditioned brat, who was "the hope of the house of Kincton Knox." Still, notwithstanding this, and all those flattering evidences of growing favour vouchsafed by the ladies of the mansion, the weeks were very long. Miss Clara, although now and then she beamed on him with a transient light, yet never actually conversed; and magnificent and dreary Mrs. Kincton Knox, whether gracious or repellant, was nearly equally insupportable.

Every time he walked out, and pausing on the upland, looked long and mournfully in the direction in which he fancied lay Gilroyd, with its sunset blush of old red brick, its roses, deep green sward, and chestnut shadows, a sort of home sickness overcame him. Beyond that horizon there was affection, and in old times the never-failing welcome, the smile, the cordial sympathy, and the liberty that knew not Kincton. And with a pain and swelling at his heart came the scene of his expulsion—a mute, hurried leave-taking; the clang of the iron gate, never to open more for him; and Aunt Dinah's fierce and cruel gaze, like the sword of fire in the way, forbidding his return.

How was it with fierce and cruel Aunt Dinah all this time? "The boy will come to his senses," she was constantly repeating to herself, as she closed her book from which her thoughts had been straying, upon her finger, with a short sigh and a proud look. Or when she looked up from her work, with the same little sigh, on the pretty flower landscape, with its back ground of foliage, seen so sunnily through the jessamine and rose clusters, "Time will bring him to reason; a little time, a very little time."

But when a little time passed away, and no signs came with the next week of returning reason, Aunt Dinah grew fiercer and more warlike. "Sulky and obstinate! Ungrateful young man! Well, so be it. We'll see who can maintain silence longest. Let him cool; let him take his own time. *I* won't hurry him, I promise him," and so forth.

But another week passed, still in silence, and Miss Perfect "presented her compliments to Dr. Sprague, and begged to inquire whether her nephew, William Maubray, had returned to Cambridge a little more than a fortnight since. Not that she had the least right or *wish* to enquire minutely henceforward into his plans, place of residence, pursuits, or associates; but simply that having for so long a time taken an interest in him, and, as she hoped, been of some little use to him—if supporting and educating him entirely might so be deemed—she thought she had a claim to be informed how he was, whether well or ill. Beyond that—she begged to be excused from asking, and requested that Doctor Sprague would be so good as to confine himself to answering that simple inquiry, and abstain from mentioning anything further about William Maubray."

In reply to this, Doctor Sprague "begged to inform Miss Perfect that when he last saw him, about ten days since, when he left Cambridge, her nephew, William Maubray, was very well. On his return from his recent visit to Gilroyd, he had remained but a week in his rooms, and had then left to prosecute a plan by which he hoped to succeed in laying a foundation for future efforts and success. Doctor Sprague was not very well, and had been ordered to take a little exceptional holiday abroad, and Miss Perfect's letter had reached him just on the eve of his departure for the Continent.

Unobserved, almost to herself, there had been before Aunt Dinah's eyes, as she read her book, or worked at her crochet, or looked out wearied on the lawn, a little vignette, representing a college tutor's chamber, Gothic in character, and a high-backed oaken chair, antiquated and carved, in which like Faust philosophising to the respectful Vagner, sat Doctor Sprague, with his finger on the open letter she had sent him, exhorting and reproving the contumacious William Maubray, and in the act of despatching him, in a suit of sackcloth, with peas in his shoes, on a penitential pilgrimage to Gilroyd.

This pleasing shadow, like an illusion of the magic lantern, vanished in pitch darkness, as Miss Perfect read the good doctor's answer. With a pallid, patient smile, and feeling suddenly cold from her head to her feet, she continued to gaze in sore distress upon the letter. Had William enlisted, or had he embarked as steward on board an American steamer? Was he about working his passage to New Zealand, or had he turned billiard marker?

Neighbours dropped in now and then to pay a visit, and Violet had such conversation as the vicinity afforded, and chatted and laughed all she could. But Miss Perfect was very silent for some days after the arrival of Dr. Sprague's letter. She was more gentle, and smiled a good deal, but was wan, and sighed from time to time, and her dinner was a mere make belief. And looking out of her bedroom window in the evening, toward Saxton, she did not hear old Winnie Dobbs who had thrice accosted her. But after a little she turned to the patient old handmaid, and said—

"Pretty the old church looks in the sun; I sometimes wish I were there."

Old Winnie followed the direction of her eyes, and gazed also, saying mildly—

"Good sermons, indeed, ma'am, and a good parson, kind to the poor; and very comfortable it is, sure, if they did not raise the stove so high. I think 'twas warmer before they raised it."

"For a hundred and fifty years the Gilroyd people have been all buried there," continued Aunt Dinah, talking more to the old church than to Winnie.

"Well, I should not wonder," said Winnie, "there is a deal o' them lies there. My grandmother minded the time old Lady Maubray was buried yonder, with that fine marble thing outside o' the church. The rails is gone very rusty now, and that coat of arms, and the writing, it's wearing out—it is worn, the rain or something, and indeed I sometimes do think where is the good of grandeur, when we die it's all equal, the time being so short as it is. Master Willie asked me show it him last Sunday three weeks coming out o' church, and even his young eyes——"

"Don't name him, don't mention him," said Aunt Dinah suddenly in a tone of cold decision.

Winnie's guileless light blue eyes looked up in helpless wonder in her mistress' face.

"Don't name his name, Winnie Dobbs. He's *gone*," said she in the same severe tone.

"Gone!" repeated Winnie. "Yes, sure! but—but he'll come back."

"No, he shan't, Winnie; he'll darken my doors no more. Come what may, *that* shan't be. I—I'll, perhaps, I may *assist* him occasionally still, but see him, never! He—he has renounced me, and I—I wash my hands of him." She was answering Winnie's look of consternation. "Let him go his own way as he chooses it—I've *done* with him."

There was a long pause here, during which ancient Winnie Dobbs stared with an imbecile incredulity at her mistress, who was looking still at the old church. Then old Winnie sighed. Then she shook her head, touching the tip of her tongue with a piteous little "tick, tick, tick," to the back of her teeth.

And Aunt Dinah continued drearily—

"And Miss Violet must find this very dull—very. I've no right to keep her here. She would be happier in some other home, poor child. I'm but a dismal companion—very; and how long is it since young Mr. Trevor was here? You don't remember—there, don't try, but it must be three weeks or more, and—and I do think he was very attentive. I mean Winnie, but you are to say nothing below stairs, you know—I mean, I really think he was in love with Miss Vi."

"Well, indeed, they did talk about it—the neighbours; there was talk, a deal o' talk, and I don't know, but I often thought she liked him."

"Well, *that's* off too, *quite*, I think; you know it is very rude, impertinent, in fact, his never having called here once, or done more than just raise his hat to us in the church door on Sundays, ever since William Maubray went away. I look upon his conduct as altogether outrageous, and being the kind of person he is, I'm very glad he disclosed himself so early, and certainly it would have been a thousand pities the girl should have ever thought of him. So that's over too, and all the better it is, and I begin to grow tired of the whole thing—very tired, Winnie; and I believe the people over there," and she nodded toward the churchyard, "are best provided for, and it's time, Winnie, I should be thinking of joining them where the wicked cease from troubling, and the weary are at rest."

"God forbid, ma'am!" remonstrated old Winnie, mildly, and they turned together from the window to accomplish Aunt Dinah's toilet.

CHAPTER XXVIII.

THE PIPING BULLFINCH.

NEXT Sunday Mr. Vane Trevor, after church, happened to be carried in one of the converging currents of decently-dressed Christianity into the main channel through the porch, almost side by side with the two Gilroyd ladies then emerging.

Mr. Vane Trevor, in pursuance of his prudent reserve, would have avoided this meeting. But so it was. In the crowded church porch, out of which the congregation emerges so slowly, with a sort of decent crush, almost pressed inconveniently against good Miss Perfect, the young gentleman found himself, and in a becoming manner, with a chastened simper, inquiring after their health, and making the proper remarks about the weather.

Aunt Dinah received these attentions very drily; but Miss Vi, in such an arch, becoming little shell-like bonnet, looked perfectly lovely; and to do her justice, was just as friendly as usual.

It was no contrivance of his, the meeting with this bewitching little bonnet where he did. How could he help the strange little thrill with which he found himself so near—and was it in human nature, or even in good manners, to deny himself a very little walk, perhaps only to the church-yard gate, beside Miss Violet Darkwell?

"How is my friend Maubray?" inquired Trevor of Miss Perfect, whom he found himself next.

"I really don't know—I have not heard—I suppose he is very well," she answered, with an icy severity that rather surprised the young man, who had heard nothing of the quarrel.

"I must write. I ought to have asked him when he meant to return. I am so anxious for an excuse to renew our croquet on the lawn at Gilroyd."

This little speech was accompanied with a look which Violet could hardly mistake.

"I don't think it likely," said Miss Perfect, in the same dry tone.

"Any time within the next three weeks. The weather will answer charmingly," continued Trevor, addressing Miss Darkwell.

"But I rather think Miss Darkwell will have to make her papa a little visit. He's to return on the eighteenth, you remember, my dear; and he says, you know, you are to meet him at Richmond."

So said Aunt Dinah, who had no notion of this kind of trifling.

Trevor again saw the vision of a lean, vulgar, hard-voiced barrister, trudging beside him with a stoop, and a seedy black frock coat; and for a minute was silent. But he looked across at pretty Miss Vi, so naturally elegant, and in another moment the barrister had melted into air, and he saw only that beautiful nymph.

"I want to look at old Lady Maubray's monument round the east end here, of the church. You would not dislike, dear, to come—only a step. I must have any repairs done that may be needed. Good morning, Mr. Trevor."

But Mr. Trevor begged leave to be of the party, knowing exactly where the monument stood.

There is a vein of love-making with which a country church-yard somehow harmonizes very tenderly. Among the grass-grown graves the pretty small feet, stepping lightly and reverently, the hues and outlines of beauty and young life; the gay faces shadowed with a passing sadness—nothing ghastly, nothing desolate—only a sentiment of the solemn and the melancholy, and underlying that tender sadness, the trembling fountains of life and gladness, the pulses of youth and hope.

"Yes; very, very much neglected," said Miss Perfect. "We can do nothing with that marble, of course," she observed, nodding toward the arched cornice at top, which time and weather had sadly worn and furrowed. "It was her wish, my dear father often told me; she *would* have it outside, not in the church; but the rails, and this masonry—we must have that set to rights—*yes*."

And so, stepping lightly among weeds and long grass, and by humble headstones and time-worn tombs, they came forth under the shadow of the tall elms by the church-yard gate, and again Miss Perfect intimated a farewell to Trevor, who, however, said he would go home by the stile—a path which would lead him by the gate of Gilroyd; and before he had quite reached that he had begun to make quite a favourable impression once more on the old lady; insomuch that, in her forgetfulness, she asked him at the gate of Gilroyd to come in, which very readily he did; and the little party sat down together in the drawing-room of Gilroyd, and chatted in a very kindly and agreeable way; and Vane Trevor, who like Aunt Dinah, was a connoisseur in birds, persuaded her to accept a bullfinch, which he would send her next morning in a new sort of cage, which had just come out.

He waited in vain, however, for one of those little momentary absences which, at other times, had left him and Violet alone. Miss Perfect, though mollified, sat him out very determinedly. So at last, having paid a very long visit, Mr. Vane Trevor could decently prolong it no further, and he went away with an unsatisfactory and disappointed feeling, not quite reasonable, considering the inflexible rule he had imposed upon himself in the matter of Gilroyd Hall and its inhabitants.

"Maubray has told her all I said," thought Vane Trevor, as he pursued the solitary path along the uplands of Revington. "The old woman—what a bore she is—was quite plainly vexed at first; but—but that jolly little creature—Violet—Violet, it *is* a pretty name—she was exactly as usual. By Jove! I thought *she'd* have been a bit vexed; but she's an angel," he dreamed on, disappointed. "I don't think she can have even begun to care for me the least bit in the world—I really *don't*." He was looking down on the path, his hands in his pockets, and his cane under his arm; and he kicked a little stone out of his way at the emphatic word, rather fiercely. "And so much the better; there's no need of all that caution. Stuff! They know quite well I've no idea of marrying; and what more? And there's no danger of her, for she is plainly quite content with those terms, and does not care for me—now, that's all right."

It is not always easy to analyze one's own motives; but beneath that satisfaction, there was very considerable soreness, and something like a resolution to make her like him, in spite of her coldness. The pretty, little, impertinent, cold, bewitching gipsy. It was so absurd. She did not seem the least flattered by the distinction of his admiration.

Next morning, after breakfast, he drove down in his dog-cart, instead of sending the bird as he had proposed. There were some ingenious contrivances in this model cage which required explanation. The oddest thing about the present was that the piping bullfinch sang two of Miss Violet's favourite airs. Trevor had no small difficulty, and a diffuse correspondence, in his search for one so particularly accomplished.

When in the drawing-room at Gilroyd, he waved a feather before its eyes, and the little songster displayed his acquirements. Trevor stole a glance at Miss Vi; but she looked perfectly innocent, and smiled with a provoking simplicity on the bird. Miss Perfect was, however, charmed, and fancied she knew the airs, but was, honestly, a little uncertain.

"It is really too good of you, Mr. Trevor," she exclaimed.

"On the contrary, I'm much obliged by your accepting the charge. I'm a sort of—of wandering Arab, you know, and I shall be making the tour of my friends' country houses; so poor little Pipe would have been very lonely, perhaps neglected; and I should very likely have had a letter some day announcing his death, and that, for fifty reasons, would have half broken my heart;" whereat he laughed a little, for Aunt Dinah, and glanced one very meaning and tender ogle on Miss Violet.

"Well, Mr. Trevor, disguise it how you may, you are very good-natured," said Miss Perfect, much pleased with her new pet; "and I'm very much obliged."

CHAPTER XXIX.

A MESSAGE IN THE "TIMES."

With this little speech, Aunt Dinah, thinking for the moment of nothing but her bird, and very much pleased with Mr. Trevor, carried the little songster away to her room, leaving the young people together at the open parlour window.

"I hope *you* like him?" Trevor said, in a a low tone.

"Oh, *charming!*" replied Miss Vi.

"I should not for all the world—you'll never know the reason why, perhaps—have let him go to any place else, but here—upon my honour," said Mr. Vane Trevor, speaking very much in earnest.

"Miss Perfect, I can see, is charmed," said Miss Violet.

"Ah, *yes* you think so—very happy, I'm sure; but—but I shall miss him very much. I—I—you've no idea what company he has been to me; and—and what a lot of trouble I had in finding one to—in fact, the sort of one I wanted."

"They are very pretty, very sweet; but, after all, don't you think the natural song the best. I should be afraid of the repetition; I should tire of the same airs," said Miss Darkwell.

"Of others—yes, perhaps, I should, but of those, *never*," said Mr. Vane Trevor eloquently.

No romantic young gentleman, who means to walk in the straight and narrow path of prudence, does well in falling into such a dialogue of covert-meanings with so very pretty a girl as Miss Violet Darkwell. It is like going up in a baloon, among invisible and irresistible currents, and the prince of the powers of the air alone can tell how long a voyage you are in for, and in what direction you may come down.

The flattering tongues of men! sweet airy music atuned to love and vanity, to woman's pride and weakness, half despised, half cherished. Long after—a phrase—a fragment of a sentence, like a broken bar or half-remembered cadence of some sweet old air, that sounded in your young ears, in dances and merry-makings, now far and filmy as bye-gone dreams, turns up unbidden—comes back upon rememberance, and is told with a saddened smile, to another generation. Drink in the sweet music at your pretty ears; it will not last always. There is a day for enjoyment, and a day for rememberance, and then the days of darkness.

A little blush—the glory, too, of ever so faint a smile! the beautiful flush of beauty's happy triumph was on the fair face of the girl, as she listened for a moment, with downcast eyes; and Vane Trevor, conceited young man as he was, had never felt so elated as when he saw that transient, but beautiful glow, answering to his folly.

I may look on her with different eyes, like the Choragus of an old play, and wonder and speculate which it is she likes—the flattery or the lover—or each for sake of the other; or the flattery only, caring not that bullfinch's feather on the carpet for him? There's not much in her face to guide me; I can only see, for certain, that she is pleased.

"I—I shall never forget those airs; they—you know, you sang them the first time I heard you sing; and I'am afraid I have been awfully unreasonable about them, asking you to sing them for me every time nearly I had an opportunity; and I—I assure you, I don't know what I shall do without my poor bird; and——"

Exactly at this point Aunt Dinah returned, and Mr. Vane Trevor, with admirable presence of mind, said:

"I was just saying to Miss Darkwell, I am sure I have heard her sing those little songs the bird whistles."

"So she does," interrupted Miss Perfect. "I could not think where I heard them. You know those airs, Vi?"

"Yes—I think they *are* among my songs," answered Violet, carelessly.

"It would be very good of you, Miss Perfect—now that I've parted with my—my—musician, you know—if you would allow me—just perhaps once before I leave Revington—I shall be away probably some months—to look in some evening, when Miss Darkwell is at her music—it is very impertinent I'm afraid to ask—but knowing those airs so well, I should like so much to hear them sung, if you happened to—to be able to find them." The concluding words were to Violet.

"Oh, dear yes—won't you, Vi—certainly, any evening, we shall be very happy; but you know we are very early people, and our tea hour seven o'clock."

"Oh, quite deligthful," exclaimed the accomodating Vane Trevor, "I have no hours at all at Revington; when I'm alone there, I just eat when I'm hungry and sleep when I'm sleepy."

"The certain way to loose your health!" exclaimed Miss Perfect.

"Very much obliged—I'll certainly turn up, you know, seven o'clock, some evening.

And so he took his leave, and was haunted day and night by Violet Darkwell's beautiful down-cast face, as he had seen it that morning.

"I knew I'd make her like me—by Jove, I knew I should—she does, I'm quite sure of it, she's beginning to like me, and if I choose I'll make her like me awfully.

Now, all the rest of that day, Trevor thought a great deal less than he had ever done before, of the pomps and vanities of Revington, and the vain glories of the Trevors of that Ilk. Wrestling with love is sometimes like wrestling with an angel, and when the struggle seems well nigh over, and the athlete sure of his victory, one unexpected touch of the angelic hand sets him limping again for many a day. Little did he fancy that the chance meeting in the shadowy porch of Saxton church would rivet again the sightless chains which it had taken some time and trouble to unclasp, and send him maundering and spiritless in his fetters among the woods and lonely paths of Revington; not yet, indeed, bewailing in vain his captivity, but still conscious of the invisible influence in which he was again intangled, and with no very clear analysis of the present, or thoughts for the future.

Time had brought no tidings of William Maubray, and except on occasions, Aunt Dinah's fits of silence were growing longer, and her old face more wan and sad.

"Ungrateful creature!" said she, unconsciously aloud.

"Who, ma'am?" asked old Winnie, mildly. Her mistress was disrobing for bed.

"Eh, who? repeated Miss Perfect. "My nephew, William Maubray, to think of his never once sending me a line, or a message! we might all be dead here and he never know. Not that I care for his indifference and heartless ingratitude, for as I told you before, I shall never see his face again. You need not stare, you need not say a word, Winnie; it is quite fixed. You may go to see him at Cambridge, if he's there, or wherever he is, but the door of Gilroyd he shall never enter more while I live, and he and his concerns shall trouble me just as little as I and mine do him."

It was about this time that William Maubray, who was permitted regularly to look into the *Times*, saw the following notification among its advertisements:—

"If the young gentleman who abruptly left his old relative's house, under displeasure, on the night of——, is willing to enter the Church, a path to reconciliation may be opened; but none otherwise. If he needs pecuniary assistance it will be supplied to the extent of £50, on his applying through his tutor, Doctor S——, but not directly."

"How insulting—how severe and unforgiving," murmured William. "How could she fancy it possible that I could accept the insult of her gift?"

With a swelling heart he turned to another part of the paper, and tried to read. But the odious serpent coiled and hissing at him from its little tabulated compartment, was too near, and he could think of nothing else.

CHAPTER XXX.

THE LORD OF BURLEIGH.

One morning at breakfast, the Kincton letters having arrived, Miss Clara, who had only one, tossed it carelessly to her mamma, who, having just closed one of her own, asked—

"Who is it?"

"Vane; he's coming here he says on Thursday, instead of Wednesday," answered the young lady.

"Cool young gentleman!" observed Mrs. Kincton Knox. "He ought to know that people don't invite themselves to Kincton—any news?"

"Yes; there has been an awful battle, and young Maubray has gone off, no one knows where, and everyone curious to find out—quite irreconcileable, they say."

"Does he say what about?" inquired the old lady, taking up the letter.

"No, nothing; only that," answered Clara.

"Mamma, Mr. Herbert's blushing all over, like fun," cried Master Howard from the other side of the table, with a great grin on his jam-bedaubed mouth, and his spoon pointed at poor William's countenance.

The ladies involuntarily glanced at William, who blushed more fiercely than ever, and began to fiddle with his knife and fork. Miss Clara's glance only, as it were, touched him, and was instantly fixed on the view through the window, in apparent abstraction. Mrs. Kincton Knox's prominent dark eyes rested gravely a little longer on poor William's face, and the boy, waving his spoon, and kicking his chair, cried, "Ha, ha!"

"Don't, sir, that's extremely rude — lay down spoon; you're never to point at any one, sir. Mr. Herbert's quite ashamed of you, and so am I."

"Come here," said William. "May he come to me?" asked William.

"Oh, no! you all want me to hold my tongue. It's always so, and that great beast of a Clara," bawled "the hope of the house," as his mamma was wont to call him.

"Come to me," said poor William, mildly.

"Or, if you permit *me*, Mr. Hebert," said Mrs. Kincton Knox. "*Howard!* I can't tolerate this. You are to sit quiet, and eat your breakfast—do you hear—and do you like sardines? — Mr. Hebert, may I trouble you — thanks; and no personalities, mind — never! Mr. Hebert, a little more tea?"

The ladies fell into earnest conference that morning after breakfast, so soon as William and his pupil had withdrawn.

"W. M.! Everything marked with W. M. —Wynston Maubray. Don't you see?" said the old lady, with a nod, and her dark and prominent eyes fixed suddenly on her daughter.

"Yes, of course; and did you look at his face when I mentioned the quarrel with Sir Richard?" said the young lady.

"Did you ever see anything like it?" exclaimed her mother.

Miss Clara smiled mysteriously, and nodded her acquiescence.

"Why, my dear, it was the colour of that," continued Mrs. Kincton Knox, pointing her finger fiercely at the red leather back of the chair that stood by them. "I don't think there can be a doubt. I know there's none in *my* mind."

"It is very curious—very romantic. I only hope that we have not been using him very ill," said Miss Clara, and she laughed more heartily than was her wont.

"Ill! I don't know what you mean. I trust, Clara, no one is ever ill-used at Kincton. It certainly would rather surprise me to hear anything of the kind," retorted the lady of Kincton, loftily.

"Well, I did not mean ill, exactly. I ought to have said rudely. I hope we have not been treating him like a—a—*what* shall I say?—all this time," and the young lady laughed again.

"We have shown him, Clara, all the kindness and consideration which a person entering this house in the capacity he chose to assume could possibly have expected. I don't suppose he expected us to divine by witchcraft who and what he was; and I am very certain that he would not have thought as—as highly of us, if we had acted in the slightest degree differently."

But though she spoke so confidently, Mrs. Kincton Knox, that perfect woman, was secretly troubled with misgivings of the same uncomfortable kind, and would have given a good deal to be able to modify the past, or even distinctly to call its incidents to mind.

"Of course, Clara, I shan't observe upon those odd coincidences to Mr.—Mr. *Herbert* himself. It is his wish to be private for the present. We have no right to pry. But there is certainly justifiable—I may say, even *called* for—some little modification of our own demeanour toward him, in short; and knowing now—as I feel confident we do—who he is, there is no need of the same degree of reserve and—and distance; and I am very glad, if for this reason only, that you may more frequently, my dear Clara, look in and see your little brother, who is so much shut up; it would be only kind."

In fact this old warrior, with the Roman nose and eagle eye, surveying the position, felt, in Cromwell's phrase, that the "Lord had delivered him into her hand." There he was domesticated, in what she might regard as a romantic incognito, without parental authority to impede or suspicion to alarm him! Could a more favourable conjuncture be fancied? How a little real kindness would tell just now upon his young heart; and he would have such an opportunity in his disguise of estimating and being touched by the real amiability of the Kincton Knoxes; and the Maubray estates and an old baronetage would close Miss Clara's campaigning with *eclat*.

The young lady did look into the school-room.

"I'm afraid, Mr. Herbert. you'll think me very tiresome," she said.

William had risen as she entered, with a bow.

"But mamma is thinking of taking Howard a drive, if you approve, and Howard, we are going to Bolton Priory. Mamma wishes so much to know whether you will allow him to come."

"I—I can have no objection. He's not now at his lessons. I'm sure it will do him a great deal of good."

Miss Clara, in a pretty attitude, leaning with one hand on the table, was smiling down on Master Howard, and caressingly running her taper fingers through his curls.

"Let my head be—will you," he bawled, disengaging himself, with a bounce and a thump at her hand.

The young lady smiled and shrugged plaintively at William, who said, "Howard, I shall tell your mamma, if you are rude to Miss Knox, and I'll ask her not to take you out to-day."

"That's just it," retorted Master Howard. "That's the way you men always take her part against me, because you think she's young and pretty. Ah-ha! I wish you'd ask her maid—Winter."

"Be quiet, sir," said William, in so stern a tone, and with so angry a flash of his blue eyes, that the young gentleman was actually overawed, and returned lowering and muttering to the ship he had been rigging, only making an ugly grimace over his shoulder, and uttering the word "crocodile!"

Though Miss Clara smiled plaintively down upon the copy of Tennyson which lay open on the table, and turned over a page or two with her finger-tip, serenely, she inwardly quaked while Howard declaimed, and in her soul wished him the fate of Cicero; and when she got to her room planted her chair before the cheval glass with a crash, and exclaimed, "I do believe that the fiendish imp is raised up expressly to torture me! Other parents would beat such a brat into mummy, and knock his head off rather than their daughter should be degraded by him; but mine seem to like it positively. I wish—oh! don't I, just." And the aposiopesis and the look were eloquent.

But she had not yet left the school-room, and as she looked down on the open pages, she murmured, sadly, "The Lord of Burleigh!" And looking up she said to William, "I see you read my poet and my favourite poem, too, only I think it too heart-rending. I can't read it. I lose my spirits for the whole day after, and I wonder whether the story is really true." She paused with a look of sad inquiry, and William answered that he had read it was so.

And she said, with a little sigh, "That only makes it sadder," and she seemed to have something more to say, but did not; and after a moment, with a little smile and a nod, she went from the room. And William thought he had never seen her look so handsome, and had not before suspected her of so much mind and so much feeling, and he took the book up and read the poem through, and dreamed over it till the servant came with a knock at the door, and his mistress' compliments, to know if Master Howard might go now.

CHAPTER XXXI.

A FRIEND APPEARS.

William Maubray's harmless self love was flattered by the growing consideration with which he was treated. The more they saw of him plainly the better they liked him, and William began, too, dimly to fancy that there must be something very engaging about him.

A night or two later, his pupil having just gone to bed, a footman came with a little scrap of pink paper, pencilled over, in Mrs. Kincton Knox's hand, on a salver, for William. who found these words:

"It has just struck me that I might possibly prevail upon your good-nature, to look in upon our solitude for half an hour; though we don't like abridging your hours of liberty, it would really be quite a kindness to indulge me; and if you can lay your hand upon your volume of Tennyson, pray bring it with you."

Up got William, and with his book in his hand followed the servant, who announced Mr. Herbert at the drawing-room door, and William found himself in that vast apartment, the lights of which were crowded about the fire, and the rest comparatively dim.

"So good of you, Mr. Herbert," said Mrs. Kincton Knox, with a superb smile, and even extending her fingers in the solemn exuberance of her welcome. "It is so very kind of you to come; so unreasonable, I fear; we had a debate, I assure you," and she smiled with awful archness toward Miss Clara, "but my audacity carried it—you've brought the book too—he has brought the book, Clara: how very kind, is not it?"

Miss Clara answered by a glance at their visitor, almost grateful, and a smile at her mother, who continued—

"You have no idea, Mr. Herbert—pray sit where we can both hear and see you—how very lonely we are in these great rooms, when we are *tête-à-tête*, as you see."

William's remarks in reply were not very original or very many, but such as they were nothing could be more successful, and the ladies exchanged smiles of approbation over the timid little joke, which had all but broken down.

So William read aloud, and the ladies each in her way, were charmed, and next night he was invited again, and there was more conversation and rather less reading, and so he grew much more easy and intimate, and began to look forward to these little reunions with a very pleasant interest; and Miss Clara's brilliant beauty and some little indications of a penchant very flattering began to visit his fancy oftener than I should have supposed likely; although it is hard to say when the way-side flowers on the longest journey quite lose their interest; or how much care and fatigue are needed to make a man cease to smile now and then, or whistle a stave on his way.

William and his pupil were walking down the thick fir wood that lies on the slope between Kincton and the Old London road, when just at a curve in the path, within twenty yards, whom should he come upon suddenly in this darksome by-way but Mr. Vane Trevor.

They both stopped short.

"By Jove! Maubray?" exclaimed Trevor, after a pause, and he cackled one of his agreeable laughs.

"Did not expect to see you here, Trevor," replied William, looking on the whole rather dismally surprised.

"Why, what are you afraid of, old Maubray? I'm not going to do you any harm, upon my honour," and he laughed again, approaching his friend, who likewise advanced to meet him, smiling, with rather an effort. "Very glad to see you, and—and I've a lot to tell you," said he, "I don't mean any nonsense, but—but really serious things."

"All well at home?" asked William eagerly.

"Oh, dear, yes, quite well—all flourishing. It is not—it's nothing unpleasant, you know, only I mean something, I—I, it's of importance to me, by Jove! and to—to, I fancy, other people also; and I—I see you're puzzled. Can we get rid of that little wretch for a minute or two?" and he glanced at Howard Seymour Knox, to whom, he just remembered, he had not yet spoken.

"And how do you do, Howard, my boy? Flourishing, I see. Would you like to have a shot with my revolver? I left it at the game-keeper's down there. Well, give them this card, and they'll give it to you—and we'll try and shoot a rabbit—eh?"

Away went Master Howard, and Trevor said—

"And do tell me, what are you doing here, of all places in the world?"

"I'm a resident tutor—neither more nor less," said William Maubray, with a bitter gaiety.

"You mean you've come here to Kincton to teach that little cur—I hope you lick him a trifle?" inquired Trevor.

"Yes; but I don't lick him, and in fact the situation—that's the right word, isn't it?—is very, what's the word? We get on quietly, and they're all very civil to me, and it's very good of a swell like you to talk so to a poor devil of a pedagogue."

"Come, Maubray, none of your chaff. I knew by your aunt's manner there was a screw loose somewhere—something about a living, was'nt there?"

It was plain, however, that Trevor was thinking of something that concerned him more nearly than William Maubray's squabble with his aunt.

"It's a long story," said William; "she wants me to go into the Church, and I won't, and so there's a quarrel, and that's all."

"And the supplies stopped?" exclaimed Trevor.

"Well, I think she would not stop them; she is very generous—but I could not, you know, it's time I should do something; and I'm here—Dr. Sprague thought it right—under the name of Herbert. They know it's an assumed name—we took care to tell them that—so there's no trick, you know, and please don't say my name's Maubray, it would half break my aunt's heart."

"Secret as the tomb, *Herbert*, I'll remember, and—and I hope that nasty little dog won't be coming back in a minute—it's a good way though—and, by Jove! it's very comical, though, and almost providential this, meeting you here, for I did want a friend to talk a bit to, awfully, and, you know, Maubray, I really *have* always looked on you in the light of a friend.

There was a consciousness of the honour which such a distinction conferred in the tone in which this was spoken, and William, in the cynical irony which, in this interview, he had used with Trevor, interposed with—

"A humble friend and very much flattered."

"You're no such thing, upon my honour, and I think you're joking. But I really do regard you as a friend, and I want to tell you no end of things, that I really think will surprise you."

William Maubray looked in Trevor's face, gravely and dubiously, and said he, with the air of a man of the world, "Well, I should like to hear—and any advice I can offer, it is not of any great value I fear, is quite at your service."

"Let's sit down here," said Trevor, and side by side they seated themselves on a rustic seat, and in the golden shade of the firs and pines, Vane Trevor began to open his case to William.

CHAPTER XXXII.

A CONFIDENCE.

"I DON'T know what you'll think of it after all I've said, but I'm going to marry your cousin, Violet Darkwell," said Vane Trevor, after a little pause, and with a kind of effort, and a rather deprecatory smile.

"Oh?" exclaimed William Maubray, cheerily, and with a smile. But the smile was wan, and the voice sounded ever so far away.

"There's no use, Maubray, in a fellow resisting his destiny; and there's an old saying, you know, about marriages being made in heaven. By Jove! when it comes to a certain point with a fellow, it's all over; no good struggling, and he may as well accomplish his —his destiny—by Jove, with a good grace. And—and I know, Maubray, you'll be glad to hear, and—and I really believe it's the best, and wisest thing I could have done—don't you think so?"

"I'm sure of that," said William, in the same tone, with the same smile. "You're—everyone says it's better to marry, when a fellow can afford it; but—but, I did not think you had a notion; that is, for ever so long; and then, some—some great lady."

"No more I had," answered Trevor. "By Jove! a month ago, *you* weren't a more unlikely man; but how can *I* help it? You never were spoony on a girl in all your life, and of course you can't tell; but you've no idea how impossible it is for a fellow, when once he comes to be really in—in love—to—to make himself happy, and be content to lose her. *I* can't I know."

"No, of course," answered William, with the same smile and an involuntary sigh.

"And then, you know, money and that sort of thing, it's all very fine, all very good in a wife; but by Jove! there's more than you think in—in fascination and beauty, and manner, and that sort of thing. There's Sir John Sludgeleigh—old family, capital fellow —he chose to marry a woman from some of those cotton mill places, with no end of money, and by Jove, I think he has been ashamed to show ever since; you never saw such a brute. He's ashamed of her, and they say he'd give his right hand he had never set eyes on her. I can quite understand, of course, a fellow that has not a guinea left; but, by Jove, if you saw her, you could conceive such a thing. And there's old Lord Ricketts, he married quite a nobody. Sweetly pretty, to be sure, but out of a boarding school, and so clever, you know, but no money, and no family, and he so awfully dipt; and she set herself to work and looked after everything, awfully clever, and at this moment the estate does not owe a guinea, and she found it with a hundred and twenty thousand pounds mortgage over it; and when he married her every one said it was all up, and his ruin certain, and by Jove it was that marriage that saved him."

"Very curious!" said William, dismally.

"To be sure it is; there's no subject, I tell you, there's so much nonsense talked about as marriage; if a woman brings you a fortune or connexion, by Jove, she'll make you pay for it. I could tell you half a dozen who have been simply ruined by making what all the world thought wonderfully good marriages."

"I dare say," said William, in a dream.

"And then about family and connexion, really the thing, when you examine it, there's wonderfully little in it; the good blood of England isn't in the peerage at all, it is really, as a rule, all in the landed gentry. Now, look at us, for example, I give you leave to search the peerage through, and you'll not find *four* houses—I don't speak of titles, but families—older than we. Except four, there is not one as old. And really, if people are nice, and quite well bred, what more do you want?"

"Oh, nothing," sighed William.

"And do you know, I've rather a prejudice against barristers, I mean as being generally an awfully low, vulgar set; and I assure you, I—I know I may say whatever I think to you; but I, when I was thinking about all this thing, you know, I could not get the idea out of my head. I knew her father was a barrister, and he was always turning up in my mind; you know the sort of thing, as—as a sort of fellow one could not like."

"But he's a particularly gentlemanlike man," broke in William, to whom Sergeant Darkwell had always been very kind.

"Oh! you need not tell *me*, for I walked with him home to Gilroyd, last Sunday, from church. I did not know who he was—stupid of me not to guess—and you can't think what an agreeable—really nice fellow."

"I know him; he has been always very kind to me, and very encouraging about the bar," said Maubray.

"Yes," interrupted Trevor, "and they say, certain to rise, and very high, too. Chancery, you know, and that—and—and such a really gentleman-like fellow, might be anything, and so—and so clever, I'm sure."

"Come down to draw the settlements,"

thought William, with a pang. But he could not somehow *say* it. There are events to which you can submit, but the details of which you shrink from. Here was for William, in some sort, a *death*. A familiar face gone. The rest was the undertaker's business. The stretching and shrouding, and screwing down, he had rather not hear of.

"You are going to tell the people here?" said William Maubray, not knowing well what to say.

"Tell them here, at Kincton! Not if I knows it. Why, I know pretty well, for fifty reasons, how *they'll* receive it. Oh! no, I'll just send them the prettiest little bit of a note in a week or two, when everything is quite settled, and I'll not mind seeing them again for some time, I can tell you, Here's this little wretch coming again. Well, Howard, have you got the revolver?"

Master Howard's face was swollen with tears and fury?

"No, they wouldn't give it me. You knew right well they would not, without mamma told 'em. I wished mamma was hanged; I do; she's always a plaguing every one; her and that great brute, Clara."

This explosion seemed to divert Mr. Trevor extremely; but William was, of course, obliged to rebuke his pupil.

"If you say that again, Master Howard, I'll tell your mamma."

"I don't care."

"Very well, sir."

"I say, come with me," said Trevor. "We'll ask mamma about the pistol. May he come? and I shall be here again in half an hour."

"Very well, do so, and just remember, though I don't much care," said Maubray, in an under tone, "they don't know my name here."

"All right," said Trevor; "I shan't forget," and he and his interesting companion took their departure, leaving William to his meditations.

"So! going to be married—little Vi—pretty little Vi—little Vi, that used to climb up at the back of my chair. I'll try and remember her always the same little wayward, beautiful darling. I've seen my last of her, at least for a long time, a very long time. I wonder—I wonder—Gilroyd—I'll never see it again."

And thoughts, vague and sad, came swelling up the stormy channels of his heart, breaking wildly and mournfully one over the other, and poor William Maubray, in his solitude, wept some bitter tears.

——o——

CHAPTER XXXIII.

THE LADIES MAKE INQUISITION.

On the steps Vane Trevor was encountered by Mr. Kincton Knox, in his drab gaiters and portly white waistcoat, and white hat, and smiling in guileless hospitality, with both hands extended. "Very glad, Vane, my dear boy—very happy—now we've got you, we'll keep you three weeks at least. You must not be running away as usual. We"ll not let you off this time, mind."

Vane knew that the hospitable exuberances of the worthy gentleman were liable to be overruled by another power, and did not combat the hospitable seizure, as vigorously as if there had been no appeal. But he chatted a while with the old gentleman, and promised to walk down and see the plantations, and the new road with him. By a sort of silent compromise, this out-door department was abandoned to Mr. Kincton Knox, who seldom invaded the interior administration of the empire, and in justice, it must be alleged that the empress seldom interfered directly with the 'woods and forests,' and contented herself with now and then lifting up her fine eyes, and mittened hands, as she surveyed his operations from the window in a resigned horror, and wondered how Mr. Kincton Knox could satisfy his conscience in wasting money the way he did!

She had learned, however, that his walks, trees, and roads, were points on which he might be raised to battle; and as she knew there was little harm in the pursuit, and really little, if anything done, more than was needed, and as some one *must* look after it, she conceded the point without any systematic resistance, and confined herself to the sort of silent protest I have mentioned.

While Vane Trevor lingered for a few minutes with the old gentleman, Master Howard Seymour Knox, who was as little accustomed to wait as Louis XIV., stumped into the drawing-room, to demand an order upon the gamekeeper's wife for Vane Trevor's revolver.

"Vane Trevor come?" exclaimed Clara.

"I want a note," cried Howard.

"We shall hear all about the quarrel," observed the old lady emphatically, and with a mysterious nod, to her daughter.

"I won't be kept here all day," cried Master Howard, with a stamp.

"Well, wait a moment," cried Clara, "and you shall have the other box of bon-bons. I'll ring and send Brooks; but you've to tell me where Vane Trevor is."

"No I won't till I get the bon-bons."

Miss Clara was on the point of bursting forth into invective, but being curious, she did not choose a rupture, and only said

"And why not, pray?"

"Because you cheated me of the shilling you promised me the same way, and I told all the servants, and they all said you were a beast."

"I don't know what you mean, sir."

"You *do*, right well," he replied, "you asked me to tell you all about the tutor, and when I did you said it was not worth a farthing, and you would not give the shilling you promised, that was cheating; you cheat?"

"Do you hear him, mamma?"

"Howard, my dear! what's all this? Tut, tut!" exclaimed Mrs. Kincton Knox.

The arrival of the bon-bons, however, did more to re-establish peaceful relations; and the boy, who was anxious to get away, delivered his news as rapidly as he could.

"Yes, Vane Trevor's come. When I and Herbert were in the long larch walk he met us, and they seemed very glad to meet."

"Ah! Like people who knew one another before?" asked Miss Clara, eagerly, in tones little above a whisper.

"Yes, and Vane called Herbert, *Maubray*—yes he did."

"*Maubray?* Are you *quite* sure of that?" demanded the elder lady, peering into his face and forgetting her dignity in the intensity of her curiosity.

"Yes, that I am, quite sure," replied the boy wagging his head, and then spinning himself round on his heel.

"Be *quiet*, sir," hissed Miss Clara, clutching him by the arm; "answer me,—now do be a good boy and we'll let you away in a minute. How do you remember the name was Maubray, and not some other name *like* Maubray?"

"Because I remember Sir Richard Maubray that you and mamma's always talking about."

"We're *not* always talking about him," said Clara.

"No, sir, we're *not*," repeated the matron, severely.

"I'll tell you no more, if your both so cross. I *won't*," retorted Master Howard, as distinctly as the bonbons would allow him.

"Well, *well*, *will* you have done, and answer my question? Did he call him Maubray often?" repeated Clara.

"Yes—*no*. He *did*, though—he called him Maubray twice. I'm sure of that."

Mother and daughter exchanged glances at this point, and Mrs. Kincton made a very slow little bow with compressed lips, and her dark eyes steadily fixed on her daughter, and then there was a little "h'm!"

"And they seemed to know one another before?" said Mrs. Kincton Knox.

"Yes, I told you that before."

"And glad to meet?" she continued.

"Yes, that is, *Vane*. I *don't* think *Herbert* was."

Again the ladies interchanged a meaning glance.

"Where is Vane Trevor now?" inquired the elder lady, gathering up her majestic manner again.

"He was talking to the governor at the hall-door."

"Oh! then we shall see him in a moment," said Mrs. Kincton Knox.

"Mind now, Howard, you're not to say one word to Mr. Herbert or to Vane Trevor about your telling us anything," added Miss Clara.

"Ain't I though? I just will, both of them, my man, unless you pay me my shilling," replied Master Howard.

"Mam*ma* do you *hear* him!" exclaimed Miss Clara in a piteous fury.

"What do you *mean*, sir?" interposed his mamma vigorously, for she was nearly as much frightened as the young lady.

"I mean I'll *tell* them; yes I *will*, I'm going," and he skipped with a horrid grimace, and his thumb to his nose, toward the door.

Come *back*, sir; how dare you?" almost screamed Miss Clara.

"Here, sir, *take* your shilling," cried Mrs. Kincton Knox, with a stamp on the floor and flashing eye, fumbling hurriedly at her purse to produce the coin in question. "There it is, sir, and *remember*."

Whether the oracular "remember" was a menace or an entreaty I know not; but the young gentleman fixed the coin in his eye after the manner of an eyeglass, and with some horrid skips and a grin of triumph at Miss Clara, he made his exit.

"Where *can* he learn those vile, low tricks?" exclaimed Miss Clara. "I don't believe there is another such boy in England. He'll *disgrace* us, you'll find, and he'll kill *me*, I know."

"He has been extremely troublesome; and I'll speak to him by-and-bye," said the matron.

"*Speak*, indeed; much he cares!"

"I'll make him care, though."

There was a little silence, and the ladies mentally returned to the more momentous topic from which the extortion of Howard Seymour had for a moment diverted them.

"What do you think of it?" murmured Mrs. Kincton Knox.

"Oh! I think there's but *one* thing to think," answered Miss Clara.

"I look upon it as *perfectly conclusive*; and, in fact, his appearance tallies so exactly with the descriptions we have heard that we hardly needed all this corroboration. As it is, I am satisfied."

At this moment the door opened, and Vane Trevor was announced.

———o———

CHAPTER XXXIV.

TREVOR AND MAUBRAY IN THE DRAWING-ROOM.

Vane Trevor was a remote cousin, and so received as a kinsmen; he entered and was greeted smilingly.

"We have secured *such* a treasure since we saw you, a tutor for my precious Howard; and such a young man—I can't tell you *half* what I think of him." (That, perhaps, was true.) "He's so accomplished."

"Accomplished—is he?" said Trevor.

"Well, not perhaps in the common acceptation of the term, that I know of, but I referred particularly to that charming accomplishment of reading aloud with feeling and point, you know, so sadly neglected, and yet so conducive to real enjoyment and one's appreciation of good authors, when cultivated. You would hardly believe what a resource it is to us poor solitaries. I am quite in love with Mr. Herbert; and I will answer for Clara there; she is as nearly so as a young lady ought to be."

Playfulness was not Mrs. Kincton Knox's happiest vein. She was tall, tragic, and ungainly; and her conscious graciousness made one uncomfortable, and her smile was intimidating. "He certainly does read charmingly," threw in Miss Clara.

"We have grown, I fear," continued Mrs. Kincton Knox, "almost too dependent on him for the enjoyment of our evenings; and I sometimes say, quite seriously to my girl there, Clara, I do trust we are not spoiling Mr. Herbert."

"He does not look like a spoiled child—rather sad and seedy, doesn't he?" replied Vane Trevor.

"Tut—does he?" said Miss Clara.

"You've seen him, then?" supplemented her mother.

"Yes; had that honour as I mounted the steep walk—how charming that walk is—among the fir-trees. But I did not see anything very unusual about him."

"I can only say I like him *extremely*," observed Mrs. Kincton Knox, in a tone which concluded debate.

"And what do you say, Miss Knox?" inquired Vane Trevor, with one of his arch cackles.

"No; young ladies are not to say all they think, like us old people," interposed Mrs. Knox; "but he's a very agreeable young man."

"Is he?" said Vane Trevor, with irrepressible amazement. "That's the first time by Jove! I ever heard poor Maubray"—and hereupon he stopped, remembering that Maubray's identity was a secret, and he looked, perhaps, a little foolish.

Mrs. Kincton Knox coughed a little, though she was glad to be quite sure that Mr. Wynston Maubray was safe under her roof, and did not want him or Vane Trevor to know that she knew it. She therefore coughed a little grandly, and also looked a little put out. But Miss Clara, with admirable coolness, said quite innocently—

"What of Mr. Maubray? What have you heard of him? *do* tell us. How is poor Sir Richard? We never saw his son, you know, here; and is the quarrel made up?"

"That's just what I was going to tell you about," said Vane Trevor, scrambling rather clumsily on his legs again after his tumble. "Not the least chance—none in the world—of a reconciliation. And the poor old fellow, in one of his fits of passion, got a fit, by Jove, and old Sprague at Cambridge told me one half his body is perfectly dead, paralytic, you know, and he can't last; so Wynston, you see, is more eligible than ever."

"Poor old man! you ought not to speak with so much levity," said Mrs. Kincton Knox. "I did not hear a word of it—how horrible! And when had poor Sir Richard his paralytic stroke?"

"About a week ago. He knew some people yesterday; but they say he's awfully shaken, and his face all—you know—pulled up on one side, and hanging down at the other; old Sprague says, a horrible object; by Jove, you can't help pitying him, though he was a fearful old screw."

"Melancholy!—and he *was* such a handsome man! Dear me! Is his son like him?" said Mrs Kincton Knox ruefully.

"Why, not particularly just now. They say the two sides of his face are pretty much alike; and his right limbs are about as lively as his left;" and Vane Trevor cackled very agreeably over this sally.

"So I should hope, Mr. Trevor," said the matron of the high nose and dark brows with a gloomy superiority, "and if there is any objection to answering my question, I should rather not hear it jested upon, especially with so shocking a reference to Sir Richard's calamity—whom I knew, poor man! when he was as strong and as good-looking as you are."

"But seriously," said Miss Clara, who saw that her mother had not left herself room to repeat her question, "What is he like?" is he light or dark, or tall or short—or what?"

"Well, he's dark at night, you know, when he's put out his candle, and light enough in the daytime, when the sun's shining, and he's decidedly *short* sometimes—in his temper, I mean—he, he, he!—and tall in his talk always," replied Vane Trevor, and he enjoyed a very exhilarating laugh at his witty conceits.

"You used to be capable of a little conversation," said the matron grandly. "You seem to have abandoned yourself to—to——"

"To *chaff* you were going to say," suggested Vane, waggishly.

"No, certainly not, that's a slang phrase such as is not usual among ladies; nor ever spoken at Kincton," retorted the old lady.

"Well, it is though, whenever I'm here," he replied agreeably. "But I'll really tell you all I can: there's nothing very remarkable in his appearance; he's rather tall, very light; he has light hair, blue eyes, pretty good bat."

"What's that?" demanded the elder lady.

"He handles the willow pretty well, and would treat you to a tolerably straight, well pitched slow underhand."

"I think you intimated that you were about making yourself intelligible?" interposed Mrs. Kincton Knox.

"And don't you understand me?" inquired Vane Trevor of Miss Clara.

"Yes, I think its cricket, ain't it?" she replied.

"Well, you see I was intelligible; yes, cricket, of course," replied Vane.

"I can't say, I'm sure, where Miss Kincton Knox learned those phrases; it certainly was not in this drawing-room," observed her mamma, with a gloomy severity.

"Well, I mean he's a tolerable good cricketer, and he reads poetry, and quarrels with his father, and he's just going to step into the poor old fellow's shoes, for, jesting apart, he really is in an awful state from all I can hear."

"Is it thought he may linger long?" inquired Mrs. Kincton Knox; "though, indeed, poor man, it is hardly desirable he should, from all you say."

"Anything but desirable. I fancy he's very shaky indeed, not safe for a week—may go any day—that's what Sprague says, and he's awfully anxious his son should come and see him; don't you think he ought?" said Mr. Vane Trevor.

"That depends," said the old lady thoughtfully, for the idea of her bird in the hand flitting suddenly away at Old Sprague's whistle, to the bush of uncertainty, was uncomfortable and alarming. "I have always understood that in a case like poor Sir Richard's nothing can be more unwise, and, humanely speaking, more certain to precipitate a fatal catastrophe than a—a—adopting any step likely to be attended with agitation. Nothing of the kind, at least, ought to be hazarded for at least six weeks or so, *I* should say, and not even then unless the patient has rallied very decidedly, and in such a state as the miserable man now is, a reconciliation would be a mere delusion. I should certainly say *no* to any such proposition, and I can't think how Dr. Sprague could contemplate such an experiment in any other light than as a possible *murder*."

At this moment the drawing-room door opened, and William Maubray's pale and sad face appeared at it.

"Howard says you wished to see me?" said he.

"We are very happy, indeed, to see you," replied the old lady, graciously. "Pray come in and join us, Mr. Herbert. Mr. Herbert, allow me to introduce my cousin, Mr. Trevor. You have heard us speak of Mr. Vane Trevor, of Revington?"

"I had the pleasure—I met him on his way here, and we talked—and—and—I know him quite well," said William, blushing, but coming out with his concluding sentence quite stoutly, for before Vane Trevor's sly gaze he would have felt like a trickster if he had not.

But the ladies were determined to supect nothing, and Mrs. Knox observed—

"We make acquaintance very quickly in the country—a ten minutes' walk together. Mr. Herbert, would you object to poor Howard's having a holiday?—and, pray, join us at lunch, and you really must not leave us now."

"I—oh! very happy—yes—a holiday—cersainly," replied he, like a man whose thoughts were a little scattered, and he stood leaning on the back of a chair, and showing, as both ladies agreed, by his absent manner and pale and saddened countenance, that Vane Trevor had been delivering Doctor Sprague's message, desiring his presence at the death-bed of the departing baronet.

———o———

CHAPTER XXXV.

THEY CONVERSE.

"We were discussing a knotty point, Mr. Herbert, when you arrived," said Mrs. Kincton Knox. "I say that nothing can warrant an agitating intrusion upon a sick bed. Mr. Trevor here was mentioning a case—a patient in a most critical state—who had an unhappy quarrel with his son. The old gentleman, a baronet, is now in a most precarious state." Miss Clara stole a glance at William, who was bearing it like a brick. "A paralytic stroke; and they talked of sending for his son! Was ever such madness heard of? If they want to kill the old man outright, they could not go more direct to their object. I happen to know something of that awful complaint. My darling Clara's grandfather, my beloved father, was taken in that way—a severe paralytic attack, from which he was slowly recovering, and a servant stupidly dropped a china cup containing my dear father's gruel, and broke it—a kind of thing which always a little excited him—and not being able to articulate distinctly, or in any way adequately to express his irritation, he had, in about twenty minutes after the occurrence, a second seizure, which quite prostrated him, and in fact he never spoke intelligibly after, nor were we certain that he recognised one of his immediate family. So trifling are the ways, so mysterious—h—hem!—and apparently inadequate the causes, which of course, under Divine regulation, in paralytic affections, invariably overpower the patient. Now, what I say is this, don't you think a son, in such a case, instead of obtruding himself at the sick man's bedside, ought to wait quietly for a month or two—quietly, I would say, in France or wherever he is, and to allow his father just to rally?"

William had been looking rather drearily on the carpet during this long statement, and I am afraid he had hardly listened to it as closely as he ought, and on being appealed to on the subject he did the best he could, and answered—

"It's an awful pity these quarrels."

"He knows something of the case, too," interposed Vane Trevor.

The ladies looked, one upon the flowers in the vase, and the other out of the window, in painful expectation of an immediate *eclaircissement*. But William only nodded a little frown at Trevor, to warn him off the dangerous ground he was treading, and he went on.

"The blame is always thrown on the young fellows; it isn't fair." William spoke a little warmly. "It's the fault of the old ones a great deal oftener, they are so dictatorial and unreasonable, and expect you to have no will or conscience, or body or soul, except as they please. They forgot that they were young themselves once, and would not have submitted to it; and then they talk of you as a rebel, by Jove! and a—a *parricide* almost, for presuming to have either a thought or a scruple, or——" On a sudden William perceived that, fired with his subject, he was declaiming a little more vehemently than was usual in drawing-rooms, and his inspiration failed him.

"Hear, hear, hear!" cried Trevor, with a tiny clapping of his hands, and a laugh.

Miss Clara looked all aglow with his eloquence, and her mama said grandly—

"There's truth, I'm *sorry* to say, in your remarks. Heaven knows *I've* suffered from unreasonableness, if ever mortal has. Here we sit in shadow of that great ugly, positively *ugly* tree there, and *there* it seems it must stand! *I* daren't remove it;" and Mrs. Kincton Knox lifted her head and her chin, and looked round like a queen shorn of her regalities, and inviting the indignant sympathy of the well affected. "There *is*, no question of it, a vast deal of unreasonableness and selfishness among the old. We all feel it," and she happened to glance upon Miss Clara, who was smiling a little cynically on the snowy ringlets of her little white dog, Bijou. She continued fiercely, "And to return to the subject. *I* should think no son, who did not wish to kill his father, and to have the world believe so, would *think* of such a thing."

"Killing's a serious business," observed Trevor.

"A man killed," observed Mrs. Kincton Knox, "is a man lost to society. His place knows him no more. All his thoughts perish."

"And they're not often any great loss," moralized Trevor.

"Very true!" acquiesced Mrs. Kincton Knox, with alacrity, recollecting how little rational matter her spouse ever contributed to the council board of Kincton. "Still, I maintain, a son would not like to be supposed to have caused the death of his father. That is, unless my views of human nature are much too favourable. What do *you* think, Mr. Herbert?" and the lady turned her prominent dark eyes, with their whites so curiously veined, encouragingly upon the young man.

"I think if *I* were that fellow," he replied, and Mrs. Kincton Knox admired his diplomacy, "I should not run the risk."

"Quite right!" approved the lady radiantly.

Trevor looked at his watch and stood up.

"Your trunk and things, gone up to your room, Vane?" inquired Mrs. Kincton Knox.

"I've no trunk; ha, ha! and no things—he, he, he! no, upon my honour. I can't stay, really; I'm awfully sorry; but my plans were all upset, and I'm going back to the station, and must walk at an awful pace too; only half an hour—a very short visit; well, yes, but I could not deny myself—short as it is—and I hope to look in upon you again soon."

"It's very ill-natured, I think," said Miss Clara.

"Very," said Mrs. Kincton Knox, yet both ladies were very well pleased to be relieved of Vane Trevor's agreeable society. He would have been in the way—unutterably *de trop*. His eye upon their operations would have been disconcerting; he would have been taking the—the tutor long walks, or trying, perhaps, to flirt with Clara, as he did two years ago, and never leaving her to herself. So the regrets and upbraidings with which they followed Vane Trevor, who had unconsciously been helping to mystify them, were mild and a little hypocritical.

CHAPTER XXXVI.

THE EVENING.

William Maubray was bidden to luncheon, and was sad and abstemious at that pleasant refection, and when it was over Mrs. Kincton Knox said—

"My dear Clara, it's quite out of the question my going with you to-day, I'm suffering so—that horrid neuralgia."

"Oh! darling! how sorry I am!" exclaimed Miss Clara, with a look of such beautiful pity and affection as must have moved William Maubray if he had the slightest liking for ministering angels. "What *can* I do for you? You must, you know, try something."

"No, love, no; nature—nature and rest. I shall lie down for a little; but you must have your ride all the same to Coverdale, and I am certain Mr. Herbert will be so kind as to accompany you.

William Maubray would have given a great deal for a solitary ramble; but, of course, he was only too happy, and the happy pair scampered off on their ponies side by side, and two hours after Miss Clara walked into her mamma's room, looking cross and tired, and sat down silently in a chair, before the cheval glass.

"Well, dear?" inquired her mother, inquisitively.

"Nothing, mamma. I hope your head's better!'

"My head? Oh! yes, better, thanks. But—a—how did you like your ride?"

"Very stupid," answered the young lady.

"I suppose you've been in one of your tempers, and never spoke a word—and you know he's so shy? Will you ever learn, Miss Kincton Knox, to command your miserable temper?" exclaimed her mother very grimly, but the young lady only flapped the folds of her skirt lazily with her whip.

"You quite mistake, mamma, I'm not cross; I'm only tired. I'm sorry you did not let him go off to the sick old man. He's plainly pining to go and give him his gruel and his medicine."

"Did he speak of him?" asked the old lady.

"No, nor of anything else; but he's plainly thinking of him and thinks he has murdered him—at least he looks as if he was going to be hanged, and I don't care if he was," answered Miss Clara.

"You must make allowances, my dear Clara, said she. "You forget that the circumstances are very distressing.

"Very cheerful I should say. Why, he

hates his father, I dare say. Did not you hear the picture he drew of him, and it's all hypocrisy, and I don't believe his father has really anything to do with his moping."

"And what do you suppose *is* the cause of it?" inquired Mrs. Kincton Knox.

"I really can't tell; perhaps he's privately married, or in love with a milliner, perhaps, and *that* has been the cause of this quarrel," she said with an indolent mockery that might be serious, and, at all events, puzzled the elder lady.

"Ho! stuff, my dear child!" exclaimed her mother with an uneasy scorn. "You had better call Brookes and get your habit off. And where did you leave him?

"At the hall door," replied Miss Clara, as she walked out of the room.

"H'm, stuff!" repeated Mrs. Kincton Knox, still more uneasily, for she knew that Clara had her wits about her. "Married, indeed! It's probable just this—Vane Trevor has come here with a foolish long exhortation from Doctor—what's his name?—*Sprague*—and upset the young man a little, and perhaps agitated him. He'll be quite a different person to-morrow."

And so indeed it proved. Whatever his secret feelings, William Maubray was externally a great deal more like himself. In the state which follows such a shock as William had experienced before the monotony of sadness sets in, there is sometimes an oscillation of spirits from extreme depression to an equally morbid hilarity, the symbol of excitement only. So in a long ride, which William took with the youn lady to-day, accompanied by his pupil, who, on his pony, entertained himself by pursuing the sheep on the hill side, Miss Clara found him very agreeable, and also ready at times to philosophize, eloquently and sadly, in the sort of Byronic vein into which bitter young lovers will break. So the sky was brightening, and William who suspected nothing of the peculiar interest with which his varying moods were observed, was yet flattered by the gradual but striking improvement of his relations, accepted the interest displayed by the ladies as a feminine indication of compassion and appreciation, and expressed a growing confidence and gratitude, the indirect expressions of which they, perhaps, a little misapprehended.

In the evening Mrs. Kincton Knox called again for the "Lord of Burleigh," not being fertile in resource—Miss Clara turned her chair toward the fire, and with her feet on a boss, near the fender, leaned back, with a handscreen in her fingers, and listened.

"That *is* what I call poetry!" exclaimed the matron with the decision of a brigadier, and a nod of intimidating approbation, toward William, "and so *charmingly* read!"

"I'm afraid Miss Kincton Knox must have grown a little tired of it," suggested William.

"One can never tire of poetry so true to nature," answered Miss Clara.

"She's all romance, that creature," confidentially murmured her mamma, with a compassionating smile.

"What is it?" inquired Miss Clara.

"You're not to hear, but we were saying, weren't we, Mr. Herbert? that she has not a particle of romance in her nature," replied her mamma with her gloomy pleasantry.

"No romance certainly, and I'm afraid no common sense either," replied the young lady naively.

"Do you write poetry?" asked the old lady of William.

"You need not ask him, he could not read as he did, if he did not write," said Miss Clara turning round in an eager glow, which momentary enthusiasm some other feeling overpowered, and she turned away again a little bashfully.

"You *do* write, I see it confessed in your eyes," exclaimed Mrs. Kincton Knox. "He does, Clara, you're right. I really think sometimes she's a—a—fairy."

"Ask him, mamma, to read us some of his verses," pleaded Clara, just a little timidly.

"You really *must*, Mr. Herbert—no, no, I'll hear of no excuses; our sex has its privileges, you know, and where we say must, opposition vanishes."

"Really," urged William, "any little attempts of mine are so unworthy"—

"We must, and will have them to-morrow evening; *dear* me, how the hours *do* fly. You have no idea, Clara dear, how late it is, quite dreadful. I'm really angry with you, Mr. Herbert, for beguiling us into such late hours."

So the party broke up, and when Mrs. Kincton Knox entered her daughter's room where she was in a dishevelled stage of preparation for bed; she said, her maid being just despatched on a message—

"I really wish, mamma, you'd stop about that Lord of Burleigh; I saw him look quite oddly when you asked for it again to-night, and he must know, unless he's a fool, that you don't care two pence about poetry, and you'll just make him think we know who he is."

"Pooh! nonsense, Clara! don't be ridiculous," said her mother, a little awkwardly, for she had a secret sense of Clara's superiority. "I don't want *you* to teach me what I'm to do, I hope, and who *brought* him here, pray, and investigated, and, in fact—here's Brookes back again—and you know we are to have his own verses to-morrow night, so we don't want that, nor any more, if you'd rather not, and you can't possibly be more sick of it than I am."

So, on the whole well pleased, the ladies betook themselves to their beds, and Mrs. Kincton Knox lay long awake, constructing her clumsy castles in the air.

———o———

CHAPTER XXXVII.

VANE TREVOR AT THE GATE OF GILROYD.

NEXT morning, at breakfast, as usual, the post-bag brought its store of letters and news, and

Mrs. Kincton Knox dispensed its contents in her usual magisterial manner. There were two addressed in Vane Trevor's handwriting; one to the tutor, which the matron recognized, as she sent it round to him in Howard's hand, the other to herself.

"Pray, no ceremony with us," said the lady of the house, with a gorgeous complacency; "read your letter here, Mr. Herbert: we are all opening ours, you see."

"So William Maubray, with an odd little flutter at his heart, opened the letter, which he knew would speak of those of whom it agitated him to think.

It was dated from Revington, whither, with a sort of home sickness new to him, Trevor had returned almost directly after his visit to Kincton.

Vane Trevor had, without intending it, left, perhaps, on Maubray's mind an impression, that a little more had occurred than the progress of the drama could actually show. He had not yet committed himself irrevocably; but he had quite made up his mind to take the decisive step, and only awaited the opportunity.

The day after his arrival he joined the Gilroyd ladies as they left the Rectory, where—for the great law of change and succession is at work continually and everywhere—the Mainwarings were no more, and good old Doctor Wagget was now installed, and beginning to unpack and get his books into their shelves, and he and old Miss Wagget were still nodding, and kissing their hands, and smiling genially on the door-steps on their departing visitors..

Just here Vane Trevor lighted upon them. How lovely Miss Violet Darkwell looked! Was not that a blush, or only the rosy shadow under her bonnet?

"A blush, by Jove!" thought Vane Trevor, and he felt as elated as, a few weeks before, he would have been had he got a peerage.

So they stopped in a little group on the road under the parsonage trees; and, the usual greeting accomplished, the young man accompanied them on their way toward Gilroyd, and said he—

"I looked in the other day, on my way back from Lowton, on my cousins, the Kincton Knoxes, at Kincton, you know, and, by Jove! I met—*who* do you think?"

"I haven't an idea," replied Miss Darkwell, to whom he had chiefly addressed himself.

"Anne Dowlass, I dare say, my roguish, runaway little girl," suggested Miss Perfect inquisitively.

"Oh. no! not a girl," answered Trevor.

"Well, it was the Bishop of Shovel-on-Headly," said she firmly.

"No; by Jove! I don't think you'd guess in half an hour. Upon my honour! He! he! he! Well, what do you think of Maubray?"

"William?" repeated Miss Perfect, faintly, and in a tone such as would indicate sudden pain.

"Yes, by Jove! the very man, upon my honour—as large as life. He's——"

Suddenly, Vane Trevor recollected that he was not to divulge the secret of his being there in the office of tutor.

"Well, he's—*what* is he doing?" urged Aunt Dinah.

"He's—he's staying there; and, upon my honour—you won t tell, I know, but, upon my honour—the old lady, and—he! he! he!—the young one are both—I give you my honour—in *love* with him!"

And Trevor laughed shrilly.

"But, I really ain't joking—I'm quite serious, I do assure you. The old woman told me, in so many words almost, that Clara's in love with him—awfully in love, by Jove!"

Trevor's narrative was told in screams of laughter.

"And you know, she's really, awfully pretty: a stunning girl she was a year or two ago; and—and—you know that kind of thing could not be—both in the same house—and the girl in love with him—and nothing come of it. It's a case, I assure you; and it will be a match, as sure as I'm walking beside you."

"H'm!" ejaculated Aunt Dinah, with a quick little nod and closed lips, looking straight before her.

"How pretty that light is, breaking on the woods; how splendid the colours;" said Miss Darkwell.

"Yes—well. It really *is* now, *jolly!*" responded Vane Trevor; and he would have made a pretty little speech on that text; but the presence of Miss Perfect, of course, put that out of the question.

Miss Perfect was silent duringnearly all the rest of the walk; and the conversation remained to the young people, and Vane Trevor was as tenderly outspoken as a lunatic in his case dare be under restraint and observation.

They had reached the poplars, only a stone's throw from the gate of Gilroyd, when Miss Perfect asked abruptly, "How was the young man looking?"

Vane Trevor had just ended a description of old Puttles, the keeper of the "Garter," whom he had seen removed in a *drunken* appoplexy to the hospital yesterday; and Aunt Dinah's question for a moment puzzled him, but he quickly recovered the thread of the by-gone allusion.

"Oh! Maubray? I beg pardon. Maubray was looking very well, I think; a little like a hero in love, of course, you know, but very well. He was just going to lunch with the ladies when I left, and looked precious hungry, I can tell you. I don't think you need trouble yourself about Maubray, Miss Perfect, I assure you you needn't, for he's taking very good care of himself, *every* way, by Jove."

"I *don't* trouble myself," said Aunt Dinah, rather sternly, interrupting Trevor's agreeable cackle. "He has quite broken with me, as I already informed you—*quite*, and I don't care who knows it. I shall never interfere with him or his concerns more. He shall never enter that gate, or see my face more; that's no great privation, of course; but I don't wish his death or destruction, little as he deserves of me, and that's the reason I asked how he looked; and, having heard, I don't desire to hear more about him or to mention his name again."

And Miss Perfect stared on Vane Trevor with a grim decision, which the young man was a little puzzled how to receive, and, with the gold head of his cane to his lip, looked up at a cloud, with a rueful and rather vacant countenance, intended to express something of a tragic sympathy.

He walked with them to the pretty porch; but Aunt Dinah was still absent and grim; and bid him good-bye, and shook hands at the door, without asking him in; and though he seemed to linger a little, there was nothing for it, but to take his departure, rather vexed.

That evening was silent and listless at Gilroyd, and though Miss Perfect left the parlour early, I think there was a *séance*, for, as she lay in her bed, Violet heard signs of life in the study beneath her, and Miss Perfect was very thoughtful, and old Winnie Dobbs very sleepy, all next day.

It was odd, now that Vane Trevor had come to set his heart upon marrying Violet Darkwell, that his confidence in his claims, which he would have thought it simple lunacy to question a few weeks ago, began to waver. He began to think how that gentlemanlike Mr. Sergeant Darkwell, with the bright and thoughtful face, who was, no doubt, ambitious, would regard the rental and estate of Revington with those onerous charges upon it; how Miss Perfect, with her whims and fancios, and positive temper, might view the whole thing; and, lastly, whether he was he was quite so certain of the young lady's "inclinations," as the old novels have it, as he felt a little time before: and so he lay awake in an agitation of modesty, quite new to him.

—o—

CHAPTER XXXVIII.

VANE TREVOR WALKS DOWN TO SEE MISS VIOLET.

Looking at himself in his glass next morning, Vane Trevor pronounced the *coup d'œil* "awfully seedy. This sort of thing, by Jove, it will never do, it would wear out any fellow; where's the good in putting off? there's no screw loose, there's nothing against me; I hope I stand pretty well here—hang it—I'll walk down to-day," and he looked over the slopes to sunny Gilroyd, "and if a good opportunity turns up, I'll speak to Miss Darkwell."

And though he had taken care, in secret mercy to his nerves, to state his resolve hypothetically, his heart made two or three strange throbs, and experienced a kind of sinking like that said to attend, on the eve of battle, an order to prepare for action.

Accordingly, before twelve o'clock, Vane Trevor walked into the porch of Gilroyd, and rang the bell beside the open door, and stood with the gold head of his cane to his chin, looking on the woodlands toward Revington, and feeling as he might have felt in an ominous dream.

"Miss Perfect at home?" he inquired of the maid, with a haggard simper.

"She was in the drawing-room," into which room, forgetting the preliminary of announcement, he pushed his way. She was not there, but he heard her talking to Winnie Dobbs in the gallery.

"Just passing by; afraid I'm very troublesome, but I could not resist," pleaded Vane Trevor, as he glanced over Miss Perfect's gray silk shoulder, and somewhat old-fashioned collar, toward the door, expecting, perhaps, another apparition.

"I'm very glad you've come, Mr. Trevor.—Shall we sit down, for I—I want to ask you to satisfy me upon a point."

This was a day of agitations for Trevor, and his heart made an odd little dance, and a sudden drop, and though he smiled, he felt his cheek grow a little pale.

"By Jove!" thought Trevor as he placed himself near Aunt Dinah, "she'll save me a lot of trouble and open the subject all in a sentence."

He was leaning against the window case, and the damask curtains, though somewhat the worse of the sun, made a gorgeous drapery about him, as with folded arms, and trying to look perfectly serene, he looked down on Miss Perfect's face. The lady seemed to have some little difficulty about speaking, and cleared her voice, and looked out of the window for help, and all the time the young man felt very oddly. At last she said—

"I had made up my mind not to allude to the subject, but I—I—last night, in fact, something occurred which has induced me just to ask a question or two." Aunt Dinah paused; and with rather pale lips, Vane Trevor smiled an assurance that he would be too happy to answer any question which Miss Perfect might please to ask.

Again a little silence—again the odd sensation in Vane's heart, and the same sickening sense of suspense, and he felt he could not stand it much longer.

"I—I said I would not allude again to William Maubray, but I—I have altered that resolution. I mean, however, to ask but a question or two."

"Oh?" was all that Trevor uttered, but he felt that he could have wished the old woman and William Maubray in a sack at the bottom of his best pond at Revington.

"I—I wish to know, the Kincton Knoxes, aren't they a leading people rather, in their part of the world?"

"Oh, dear, yes. Kincton is one of the best places in the county," ejaculated Trevor, who being a kinsman, bore a handsome testimony.

"And—and—the young lady, Miss Clara Knox, she, I suppose, is—is admired?"

"So she is, by Jove—I know, *I* admired her awfully—so admired that the fellows won't let one another marry her, by Jove!—he, he, he! Very fine girl, though, and I believe her father, or rather her mother, will give her a lot of money."

Miss Perfect looked on the table, not pleased, very thoughtfully, and Vane Trevor looked down at her fore-shortened countenance listlessly.

"And—and you spoke, you remember, of an idea that—that in fact it would end in a *marriage*," resumed Miss Perfect

"Did I really say? well, but you won't mention what I say, I, upon my honour, and quite seriously, I should not wonder a bit. It is not altogether what she said, you know, Mrs. Kincton Knox, I mean, though that was as strong as you could well imagine—but her manner; I know her perfectly, and when she wishes you to understand a thing; and I assure you that's what she wished me to suppose—and I really, I can't understand it; it seems to me perfectly incomprehensible, like a sort of infatuation, for she's one of the sharpest women alive, Mrs. Kincton Knox; but, by Jove, both she and Clara, they seem to have quite lost their heads about Maubray. I never heard anything like it, upon my honour."

And Trevor, who had by this time quite shaken off the chill of his suspense, laughed very hilariously, till Aunt Dinah said, with some displeasure—

"For the life of me, I can't see anything ridiculous in it. William Maubray is better connected than they, and he's the handsomest young man I ever beheld in my life; and if she has money enough of her own, for *both*, I can't see what objection or difficulty there can be."

"Oh! certainly—certainly not on those grounds; only what amused me was, there's a disparity; you know—she's, by Jove! She *is*—she's five years elder, and that's something."

"And—and if it *is* to be, how *soon* do you suppose it likely?" asked Miss Perfect, fixing her eyes anxiously on him.

"Well, you know I know no more than the man in the moon; but if they really mean it, I don't see what's to delay it," answered Trevor.

"Because—because"—hesitated Aunt Dinah, "I have reason to know that if that unfortunate young man—not that I have any reason to care more than any one else, should marry before the lapse of five years, he will be utterly ruined, and undone by so doing."

Vane Trevor stood expecting an astounding revelation, but Aunt Dinah proceeded—

"And therefore as *you* are his friend—of course it's nothing to me—I thought you might as well hear it, and if you chose to take that trouble, let him know," said Miss Perfect.

He looked a little hard at Miss Perfect, and she as steadily on him.

"I will, certainly—that is, if *you* think I *ought*. But—but I hope it won't get me into a scrape with the people there."

"I *do* think you ought," said Miss Perfect.

"I—I suppose *he'll* understand the reasons?" suggested Vane Trevor, half interrogatively.

"If you say—I *think*, if you say—that I said I had *reason* to *know*"—and Aunt Dinah paused.

Vane Trevor, looking a little amazed, repeated—

"I'm to say you said you had reason to know?"

"*Yes*, and—and—I *think* he'll understand—and if he should not, you may say—a—*yes*, you *may*, it has reached me through Henbane."

"I beg pardon—through *what?* said Vane Trevor, inclining his ear.

"Henbane," said Miss Perfect very sharply.

"Henbane?"

"*Yes.*"

"By Jove!" exclaimed Trevor.

A considerable silence ensued, during which a variety of uncomfortable misgivings respecting the state of Miss Perfect's mind, floated through his own. He concluded, however, that there was some language of symbols established between Miss Perfect and her nephew, in which Henbane stood for some refractory trustee, or rich old uncle.

So he said, more like himself—

"Well, I shan't forget. I'll take care to let him know, and you may depend upon me."

—o—

CHAPTER XXXIX.

VANE TREVOR OPENS HIS MIND.

After a silence, Mr. Vane Trevor, whose thoughts were not *quite* abandoned to Henbane and his friend William Maubray, but had begun to flow in a more selfish channel, said—

"Miss Darkwell, I suppose, in the garden?"

"Violet's gone for a few days to our friends, the Mainwarings, at their new Rectory; they seem to like it extremely."

"Oh, *do* they? That's delightful," said Trevor, who looked very dismal. "And so Miss Darkwell is there?"

Miss Perfect nodded.

"I'm—I'm very unlucky. I—I thought such a fine day, I—I might have induced you both to—to—there's such a pretty drive to Wilton."

"Yes—I know—I'm sure she'd have liked it of all things."

"Do you *really* think so?" exclaimed the young man, inquiringly. "I wish—I wish very much I could—I could flatter myself."

Aunt Dinah looked up, and at him earnestly but kindly, and said nothing, and so looked down again. There was encouragement in that look, and Trevor waxed eloquent.

"I—I wish I could—I wish I dare—I—I think her so beautiful. I—I can't express all I think, and I—there's nothing I would not do to make her friends approve—a—a—in fact I should be so much obliged if I thought you would wish me well, and be my friend—and—and——"

And Vane Trevor for want of anything distinct to add to all this, came to a pause.

And Miss Perfect, with a very honest surprise in her face, said:

"Am I to understand, Mr. Vane Trevor?" and she too came to a stop.

But with those magical words the floodgates of his eloquence were opened once more.

"Yes, I do. I do indeed. I mean to—to propose for Miss Darkwell, if—if I were sure that her friends liked the idea, and that I could think really she liked me. I—I came to-day with the intention of speaking to her."

He was now standing erect, no longer leaning against the window shutter, and holding his walking-cane very hard in both hands, and impressing Miss Perfect with a conviction of his being thoroughly in earnest.

"I—I tell you frankly, Mr. Trevor," said Aunt Dinah, a little flushed with a sympathetic excitement, and evidently much pleased, "I did not expect this. I—I had fancied that you were not a likely person to marry, and to say truth, I sometimes doubted whether I ought to have allowed your visits here so frequently, at least as you have made them for the last few weeks. Of course I can see nothing that is not desirable, in fact highly advantageous in the proposal you make. Am I at liberty to write to Sergeant Darkwell on the subject?"

"Oh! certainly, exactly what I should wish."

"I'm very sure he will see it in the same light that I do. We all know the Trevors of Revington, the position they have always held; and though I detest the line they took in the great civil war, and think your poor father had no business helping to introduce machinery into this part of the world as he did, and I always said so, I yet can see the many amiable qualities of his son, and I have no doubt that you will make a kind and affectionate husband. I must, however, tell you candidly, that I have never spoken of you to Violet Darkwell as a—in fact, in any other light than that of an acquaintance, and I cannot throw any light upon her feelings. You can ascertain them best for yourself. My belief is, that a girl should be left quite free to accept or decline in such a case, and I know that her father thinks exactly as I do."

"I—I may write to Miss Darkwell, do you think? I suppose I had better?"

"*No*, said Miss Perfect, with decision; "were I you I should much prefer speaking. Depend upon it, there's more to be *done* by speaking. But as you are acquainted with her father, don't you think you might write to him. Violet may return in three days, but will not, I think, quite so soon; and meanwhile you will have heard from him."

"I think so. I'll do it, certainly; and I—I feel that you're my friend, Miss Perfect;" and he took her hand, and she took his very kindly.

"I've said my say, I *highly* approve, and I'm quite certain her father will also; he agrees with me on most points; he's a very superior man."

Vane Trevor, there and then, with Aunt Dinah's concurrence, wrote his letter to Mr. Sergeant Darkwell; and then he walked with Aunt Dinah in the garden, talking incessantly of Violet, and it must be added, very much pleased with Miss Perfect's evident satisfaction and elation; and he remained to dinner, a situation which two months ago would have appeared the most ludicrous and dismal in nature, and he gabbled of his lady love, asking questions and starting plans of all sorts.

And time flew so in this *tête-à-tête*, that they were surprised by the entrance of the household with the Bible and Prayer-book; and Mr. Vane Trevor, though not a particularly sober minded youth, could not avoid accepting the role of the absent William Maubray, and officiated, much to the edification of the maids, in whose eyes the owner of Revington was a very high personage indeed; and, "the chapter" for that evening delighted and overawed them, and they could hardly believe their eyes that the great squire of Revington was pent up with them in that small drawing-room, and kneeling and saying "amen," and repeating the Lord's Prayer after Miss Perfect, "as mild and humble" as one of themselves.

When he got home to Revington, not being able to tranquilize his mind, he vented his excitement upon the two letters which I have mentioned as having reached the family of Kincton, at the breakfast-table.

"Read that, Clara, my dear," said Mrs. Kincton Knox, with a funereal nod and in a cautious under-tone.

Miss Clara read the letter, and when she came to the passage which related that poor old Sir Richard Maubray had had a second and much severer paralytic stroke, and was now *in articulo*, she raised her eyes for a moment to her mother's, and both for a moment looked with a solemn shrewdness into the other's, Miss Clara dropped hers again to the letter, and then stole a momentary glance at William, who looked as if he were very ill.

As a man who receives a letter announcing that judgment is marked, and bailiffs on his track, will hide away the awful crumpled note in his pocket, and try to beguile his friends by a pallid smile, and a vague and incoherent attempt to join in the conversation, so William strove to seem quite unconcerned, and the more he tried the more conscious was he of his failure.

CHAPTER XL.

MRS. KINCTON KNOX PROPOSES A WALK WITH WILLIAM.

In fact William Maubray had received a conceited and exulting letter from Trevor, written in the expansion of his triumph once more as the Lord of Revington, the representative of the historic Trevors, the man of traditions and *prestige*, before whom the world bowed down and displayed its treasures, and who, being restored to reason and self-estimation by his conversation with Miss Perfect, knew well what a prize he was—what a sacrifice he was making, and yet bore and gave away all with a splendid magnanimity.

So as he says, "it is all virtually settled. I have talked fully with Miss Perfect, a very intelligent and superior woman, who looks upon the situation just as I could wish; and I have written announcing my intentions to her father, and under such auspices, and with the evidence I hope I have, of not being quite indifferent where I most wished to please, I almost venture to ask for your congratulations," &c.

"He is quite right, it *is* all over, she likes him, I saw that long ago, I fancied she would have been a little harder to please; they fall in love with any fellow that's tall, and pink, and white, and dresses absurdly, and talks like a fool, provided he has money—money—d—— money!"

Such were the mutterings of William Maubray, as he leaned dismally on the window of the school-room, and looked out upon the sear and thinning foliage of the late autumn.

"This is very important—this about unfortunate Sir Richard; his son will succeed immediately; but he seems a good deal, indeed very much agitated, however, it's a—a great point in his favor *other*wise." So said Mrs. Kincton Knox to her daughter, so soon as being alone together they could safely talk over the missives of the breakfast table.

"I rather think he has been summoned to —to the dying man, and he'll go—he *must*— and we shall never see more of him," said Miss Clara, with superb indifference.

"Yes, of course it *may* have been, I was going to say so," said her mother, who, however, had not seen that view. "I'll make him come out and walk up and down the terrace with me a little, poor young man."

"You'll do him no good by that," said the young lady, with a sneer.

"We'll see that, Miss Kincton Knox; at all events, it will do no good sitting here, and sneering into the fire; please sit a little away and raise the hand-screen, unless you really *wish* to ruin your complexion."

"It can't be of the least importance to any one whether I do or not, certainly not to *me*," said the young lady, who, however, took her advice peevishly.

"You are one of those conceited young persons; pray allow me to speak, I'm your mother, and have a right I hope to speak in *this house*—who fancy that no one can speak anything but *they*—I'm not disposed to flatter you—I never *did* flatter you, but I think the young man (her voice was lowered here) *likes* you—I *do*. I'm *sure* he does. It can't possibly be for *my* sake that he likes coming every evening to read all that stuff for us. You make no allowance for the position he is in, his father dying, in the very crisis of a painful domestic quarrel, it must be most uncomfortable; and then he's here in a position which precludes his uttering any sentiments except such as should be found on the lips of a resident teacher. I've frequently observed him on the point of speaking in his real character, and chilled in a moment by the recollection of the apparent distance between us; but I think I know something of countenance, and tones, and those indications of feeling, which are more and more significant than words."

Miss Clara made no sign by look, word, or motion; and after a little pause her mamma went on sturdily.

"Yes, I ought, at my time of life, and having been, I may say, a good deal admired in my day, and *married*, not quite as I *might* have been perhaps, but—but still pretty *well*. I ought to know something more of such matters than my *daughter*, I think, and I can't be mistaken. I don't say *passion*, I say a *liking*—a *fancy*, and that there *is* I'll stake my life. If you only take the trouble to think you'll see, I hold it quite impossible that a young man should be as he is, alone for several weeks in a country-house with a person. I will say, of your advantages and—and attractions without some such feeling, *im—possible*."

Miss Kincton Knox looked indolently on her fair image in the mirror at the further end of the room.

"In those rides he and Howard have taken with you, I venture to say he has said things which *I* should have understood had I been by."

"I told you he never said anything—anything particular—anything he might not have said to any one else," said the young lady, wearily. "He is evidently very shy, I allow."

"*Very! extremely* shy," acquieced her mamma, eagerly; "and when all these things are considered, I don't think in the time you could possibly have expected more."

"I never expected anything," said Miss Clara, with another weary sneer.

"Didn't you? then I did," answered the matron.

Miss Clara simply yawned.

"You are in one of your unfortunate tempers. Don't you think, Miss Kincton Knox, even on the supposition that he *is* about leaving our house, that you may as well command your—your spirit of opposition and—and ill temper, which has uniformly defeated every endeavour of mine to—to be of use to you, and here you are at eight-and-twenty." The young lady looked round alarmed, but there was no listner, "and you seem to have *learned nothing*."

"I'll write all round the country, and tell the people I'm eight-and-twenty or thirty, for anything I know, if you have no objection. I don't see any harm it can do, telling truth perhaps mayn't do one much good; but if I've learned nothing else, I've learned this at all events, that there's absolutely no good in the other course."

"I don't know what you mean by *courses.* No one I hope has been committing any fraud in this house. If you please to tell people you are thirty, which is perfectly contrary to fact, you must only take the consequences. Your miserable temper, Clara, has been the ruin of you, and when I'm in my grave you'll repent it."

So saying she left the room, and coming down in a few minutes in a black velvet garment, trimmed with ermine, and with a muff of the same judicial fur, she repaired to the schoolroom, where, much to William's relief, she graciously begged a holiday for Howard, and then asked William with, at the end of her invitation, a great smile which plainly said, "I know you can hardly believe your ears, but it's true notwithstanding," to lend an old woman his arm in a walk up and down the terrace.

William was of course at her service, though the honour was one which at that moment was almost oppressive.

CHAPTER XLI.

HOW THEY TALKED.

After a few turns, and some little talk, Mrs. Kincton Knox said:

"I'm afraid, Mr. Herbert, like most of us, young as you are, you have your troubles. You will excuse an old woman, old enough to be your mother, and who likes you, who really feels a very deep interest in you, for saying so. I wish—I wish, in fact, there was a little more confidence, but all in good time. I said you were—you were—it's perhaps impertinent of me to say I observed it, but my motive is not curiosity, nor, you will believe, unkind. I did see you were distressed this morning by the letter that reached you. I trust there was no illness, nor——"

"No, nothing—that is which I had not—which was not," he replied. "Nothing very unexpected."

"For if there was any necessity, any *wish* to leave Kincton for a little, I should offer my poor services as a substitute with your pupil, if you would trust him to me."

Although her graciousness was oppressive, and her playfulness awful, there were welcome signs of sympathy in this speech, and William Maubray greeted them with something like confidence, and, said he:—

"It's awfully kind of you, Mrs. Kincton Knox, to think about me. I—I don't know exactly what to say, except that I am very grateful, and—and it's quite true I've had a great deal of vexation and suffering—a kind of quarrel—a very bad quarrel, indeed, at home, as I call it, and—and some other things."

"Other things!—no doubt. There is one trouble to which the young are exposed, and from which old people are quite exempt. The course of true love, you know, as our great moralist says, never did run smooth."

Her prominent eyes were fixed with an awful archness upon Maubray, and, conscious as he was, he blushed and paled under her gaze, and was dumb.

"My maxim in all such cases is, *never despair.* When a young man is endowed, like you, with good looks, and a—a refinement. You see I am talking to you almost as I would to a son, that darling boy of mine is such a link, and one grows so soon to know a *guest*, and those delightful evenings, and I think—I *think*, Mr. Herbert, I can see a little with my old eyes, and I've divined your secret."

"I may—that is, I think it may have been —a *fancy*, just. I don't know," said William, very much put out.

"But *I* know. You may be perfectly certain you *are* in love, if you ain't quite certain that you are *not.* Trust an old woman who has seen something of life—that is, of human nature," insisted Mrs. Kincton Knox.

"I—I don't know, I did not know it myself until, I think, within the last few days. I dare say I'm a great fool. I'm sure I am, in fact, and I ought not to have allowed—but I really did not know."

He suspected that Trevor had told all he knew of his story, and that the women, with the sagacity of their sex, had divined the rest.

"You see, Mr. Herbert, I have not guessed amiss. When I see a young person very much dejected and *distrait*, I at once suspect a *romance;* and now let me say a word of a—*comfort*, derived from observation. As I said before—I've known such things happen—*never despair.* There is a spark of romance in our sex as well as in yours. I think I *may* be of use to you. I dare say things are not quite so desperate as they appear. But do trust me —do be frank."

"I will. I'll tell you everything. I—I don't know where to begin. But I'm so much obliged. I've no one to speak to, and——"

At this moment the "darling boy" Howard bounced from behind a thick shrub, with a shriek which was echoed by his fond mother, who, if anything so dignified could jump, *did* jump, and even William's manly heart made an uncomfortable bounce in his breast. At the same time Master Howard Seymour turned his ankle, and tumbled with a second horrid roar on the walk, from which his mother and his instructor lifted him, not much hurt, but bellowing in a fury, and requiring to be conducted for comfort to the house.

"I shall call upon you again, Mr. Herbert, when my poor darling is better, and we can—there, there! my rosebud," began Mrs. Kincton Knox, distracted between her curiosity and her compassion.

"Shall I take him on my back? Get up. May he?" And so, with the lady's approval, he took the urchin, who was hopping round them in circles with hideous uproar, in his arms, and bore him away beside his anxious parent towards the house, where, having ministered to the sufferer, Mrs. Kincton Knox looked into the drawing-room, and found Miss Clara seated by the fire, with her slender feet as usual, on a boss, reading her novel.

Mrs. Kincton Knox, stooping over her, kissed her, and Miss Clara, knowing that the unusual caress indicated something extraordinary, looked up with a dreary curiosity into her mother's face. When they were *tête-à-tête*, these ladies did not trouble one another much with smiles or caresses. Still her mother was smiling with a mysterious triumph, and nodded encouragingly upon her.

"Well?" asked Miss Clara.

"I think you'll find that I was right, and that somebody will ask you a question before long," answered her mother, with an oracular smile.

Miss Clara certainly did look a little interested at this intimation, and sat up with comparative energy, looking rather earnestly into her mother's prominent, hard brown eyes.

"He's been talking very, I may say, frankly to me, and although we were interrupted by a —an accident, yet there was no mistaking him. At least that's *my* opinion."

And Mrs. Kincton Knox sat down, and with her imposing coiffure, nodding over her daughter's ear, recounted, with perhaps some little colouring, her interesting conversation with William Maubray. While this conference was proceeding, the door opened, and Mr. Kincton Knox, his gloves, white hat, and stick in his hand, walked in.

It was one of Mrs. Kincton Knox's unpublished theories that her husband's presence in the drawing-room was a trespass, as that of a cow among the flower-beds under the windows.

As that portly figure in the gray woollen suit and white waistcoat entered mildly, the matron sat erect, and eyed him with a gaze of astonishment, which, however, was quite lost upon him, as he had not his spectacles on.

"I hope, Mr. Kincton Knox, your shoes are not covered with mud?—unless you are prepared to buy another carpet," she said, glancing at the clumsy articles in question.

"Oh, dear! no—I haven't been out—just going, but I want you and Clara to look over there," and he pointed with his stick, at which Mrs. Kincton Knox winced with the ejaculation, "the China!"

"You see those three trees," he continued, approaching the window with his stick extended.

"Yes, you *need*n't go on, *perfectly*," she answered.

"Well, the one to the right is, in fact, I think it's an ugly tree; I've been for a long time considering it. You see it there, Clara, on the rising ground, near the paling?"

She did.

"Well, I'm thinking of taking him down; what do you say?"

"*Do* lower your stick, Mr. Kincton Knox, *pray*, we can see perfectly without *breaking* anything," expostulated his wife.

"Well, what do you say?" he repeated, pointing with his hand instead.

"Do you want my opinion as to what trees should come down?" said Mrs. Knox, with admirable perseverance, "I shall be happy to give it with respect to *all*—as to that particular tree it is so far away, I really don't think the question worth debating."

"Take it down, papa," said Miss Clara, who rather liked her father, and encouraged him when too much put down. "I really think you're always right about trees. I think you've such wonderful taste, I do indeed, and judgment about all those things."

The old man gave her a hearty kiss on the cheek, and smiling ruddily, said—

"Well, I think I ought; I've read something, and *thought* something on the subject, and as *you* don't dissent, my dear, and Clara says it's to come down—down it comes. She's looking very pretty; egad she is—wonderfully pretty she is to-day."

"Folly!" exclaimed Miss Clara, pleased notwithstanding.

"Other people think her good-looking too, I can tell you," exclaimed her mother, whose thoughts were all in that channel, and who could not forbear saying something on the subject; "I think, even you, Mr. Kincton Knox, will see that I have done my duty by our child, and have been the means under Providence of promoting her happiness."

"And what is it?" said Mr. Kincton Knox, looking solemnly on his daughter.

"I don't know that there is anything at all," replied she quietly.

Mrs. Kincton Knox beckoned him imperiously, and they drew near the window, while the young lady resumed her novel.

"He's in love with her," she murmured.

"Who, my dear?"

"Mr. Maubray."

"Oh! is he?—*what*, Mr. Maubray," inquired the old gentleman.

"Wynston Maubray—probably *Sir* Wynston Maubray, at this moment, his father, you know, is dying; if not dead."

"Sir Richard, you mean?"

"Of course, I mean Sir Richard.

"Yes, he is; he wasn't a bad fellow, poor Maubray. But it's a long time—thirty—thirty-*eight* years—yes—since we were at Oxford."

"And his son's in the house."

"Here?"

"Yes, this house, *here*."

"Very happy to see him, I'm sure, very happy—we'll do all in our power," said Mr. Kincton Knox, very much at sea as to the cause of his arrival.

"You know Mr. Herbert?"

"Yes."

"Well, that's he—Mr. Herbert is Mr. Wynston Maubray. If you were to stare till

Doomsday it won't change the fact; here he is, and *has* been—and has confessed to me that he likes Clara. He's very modest, almost shy, and without any kind of management on my part; had I stooped to that as other mothers do, she'd have been married, no doubt, long ago—simply placing them under the same roof, perceiving that he was a gentleman; ascertaining *who* he *was*, I left the rest to—to—you see, and the consequence is—as I've told you, and—and *humanly* speaking—she'll be Lady Maubray."

"Oh!" said Mr. Kincton Knox.

"Perhaps you don't like it?"

"Oh! like it?—very well; but—but she's very young—there's no great hurry; I—I would not *hurry* her.'

"Pooh!" exclaimed Mrs. Kincton Knox, turning abruptly away from her husband, one of whose teazing hallucinations was that Clara had hardly emerged from the nursery.

CHAPTER XLII.

CONFIDENCES.

Mrs. Kincton Knox, still in walking costume, entered the school-room, intending to invite the pseudo-tutor to continue his walk with her; and with one of her awful smiles she began:

"I've come to claim your promise, Mr. Maubray." The name had escaped her. It reverberated in her ear like a cannon-shot. Hardly less astounded stood our friend William before her. For a full minute she could not think of a presentable fib, and stared at him a good deal flushed; and dropped her huge, goggle eyes upon a "copy-book" of Master Howard's, which she raised and inspected with a sudden interest, and having read—

"Necessity is the mo"
"Necessity is the moth"
"Necessity is the moth'r"
"Necessity is the mo"

upon its successive lines, she replaced it firmly, raised her head and said—

"I have addressed you by the name of Maubray, which I've learned, just five minutes since, is your real name; but, should you prefer my employing that of Herbert—my using the other, indeed, was simply an accident; and, perhaps, it *is* better—I shall certainly do so. Your little confidence has interested me unaffectedly—very much, indeed—deeply interested me; the more particularly as Mr. Kincton Knox was once acquainted with a family of your name. Sir Richard Maubray, possibly a relation."

William, who was still a little confused, assented, and the lady, with growing confidence, proceeded:

"You mentioned some unhappy family discord; and it struck me—Mr. Kincton Knox, you know, and I—in fact, we have a good many friends, that possibly some—a—intervention—"

"Oh! thanks; *very* kind of you; but I don't know any one likely to have much influence—except, perhaps, Mr. Wagget; and I was thinking of writing to him, although I hardly know him sufficiently."

"And may I ask who Mr. Wagget is?" inquired the lady, who had intentions of taking the carriage of the affair.

"The—a clergyman—a very good man, I believe."

Oh! in attendance at the sick bed?" inquired the matron, with proper awe.

"No—no; not that I know of; but a very old friend of my aunt's."

"I see—I understand—and he and your aunt would unite their influence to reconcile you."

"Oh, my quarrel, as we've been calling it, is with my aunt."

"Oh! oh!—I see, and your father has taken it up?" suggested Mrs. Kincton Knox, promptly.

"My father's dead," said William, with the gravity becoming such an announcement.

"Oh! dear me!—I'm shocked to think I should—I beg your pardon. I ought to have anticipated. You have, I assure you, my deep sympathy—all our sympathies. I do recollect *now* having heard something of his illness; but, dear! oh, dear! *What* a world it is."

William could only bow with his former seriousness. It was more than twenty years since his excellent father had deceased; and though *he* could not remember, Mrs. Kincton Knox very well might, an event of that date. Still the fervour of her surprise and her sympathy were, considering all things, a little uncalled for.

"The rupture, then, is with your aunt—dear me! you must have wonderful self-command, admirable—admirable, in so young a person." A brief pause followed this oracular speech.

"And your aunt is married?" inquired Mrs. Kincton Knox.

"No, unmarried—in fact, an old maid," he replied.

"Oh! yes, quite so. Then she's Miss Maubray?" said the lady.

"No, Miss *Perfect*," said he.

"Miss Perfect, *maternal* aunt, it must be;" and Mrs. Kincton Knox paused, a little perplexed, for she did not recollect that name in that interesting page in the Peerage, which she had looked into more than once. She concluded, however, it must be so, and said, slowly, "I see—I *see*."

"And what—you'll do me the justice to believe, it ain't curiosity but a higher motive that actuates me—what is the *ground* of this unhappy dispute?"

"She has set her heart on my going into the Church," said William sadly, "and I'm not fit for it."

"*Certainly*;" exclaimed Mrs. Kincton Knox,

"nothing, begging the old lady's pardon, *could* be more absurd—you're *not* fit of course, nor is *it* fit for *you*—there is *no* fitness *whatever*. There's the Very Rev. the Earl of Epsom, and the Rev. Sir James St. Leger, and many others I could name. Can anything be more ridiculous? They both have their estates, and—and position to look after; and their ordination vow pledges them to give their entire thoughts to their holy calling. I and Mr. Kincton Knox have had many arguments upon the subject; as you see, I'm quite with you. Mr.—Mr. *Herbert*, you must allow me still to call you by that name—that dear old name. I was going to say"——

William could only acquiesce—a little puzzled at her general exuberance; she seemed, in fact, quite tipsy with good nature. How little one can judge of character at first sight!

"And, of course, it is not for *me* to say—but your reserve about your name—I suppose *that* is at an end. Since the—the melancholy termination of your hopes and fears—I mean there can hardly be—now that you apprize me of your domestic loss"——

"It was entirely in deference to my *aunt's* prejudices, that I—Doctor Sprague, in fact," began William.

"I know, an old friend of poor Sir Richard's; but whatever else you do, I suppose we must make up our minds to lose you for a week or so; your absence would be of course remarked upon, in fact, those feelings never survive the grave, and there are sacrifices to decorum. Your friends, and you know there are those here who feel an interest; *no* one could advise your staying away."

"My aunt is not ill?" said William with a sudden and horrible misgiving, for the lady's manner was unmistakably funeral.

"Ill?—I haven't heard. I have not the honour of knowing Miss Purity," said Mrs. Kincton Knox.

"*Perfect*," interrupted William—"thank God! I mean that she's not ill."

"I was thinking *not* of your aunt, but of your poor father; there are things to be looked after; you are of age."

"Yes, three-and-twenty," said William, with a coolness that under so sudden a bereavement, was admirable.

"Not quite that, *two*-and-twenty last May," said the Student of the Peerage.

William knew *he* was right, but the point, an odd one for Mrs. Kincton Knox to raise—was not worth disputing.

"And, considering the circumstances under which, although you will not admit the—the estrangement, poor Sir Richard Maubray has been taken"——

"Sir Richard! Is Sir Richard dead?" exclaimed William.

"Dead! of course he is dead. Why you told me so yourself, this moment."

"I—I *couldn't*; I—I didn't know—I—if I said anything like that, it was the merest slip."

"He's either dead or alive, sir, I *suppose*; and, whether intentionally or by *slip*, it is for you to determine; but I'm positive you did tell me that he's *dead*; and if he be so, pray, as between friends, let there be an end of concealments, which can have no object or effect but a few hours' delay in making known a fact which must immediately appear in all the newspapers," expostulated Mrs. Kincton Knox as nearly offended as it was possible to be with so very eligible a young man, so opportunely placed, and in so docile a mood.

"He's *dying*, at all events," she added.

"*That* I know," said William, with that coolness which had before struck Mrs. Kincton Knox, during this interview, as a new filial phenomenon.

"And although we shall miss you, *some* of us *very* much, yet, of couse, knowing *all*, we have no claim—no right—only you must pledge me your honour—you really must." She was holding his hand and pressed it impressively between both hers, "that you won't forget your Kincton friends—that so soon as you can, you will return, and give us at least those weeks on which we reckon."

"It is very kind—it's very good of you. It is very odd, but I had such a wish to go, just for a day or two—only to see Dr. Sprague—and—and to consult him about writing to Gilroyd before finally determining on a course of life. I was thinking of—in fact going away and leaving England altogether."

Mrs. Kincton Knox stared, and at last asked: "Who *is* Gilroyd?"

"My aunt's house, a small place, Gilroyd Hall."

"I was merely thinking of your attending poor Sir Richard's obsequies."

"The funeral? I—I should not like to attend it uninvited," answered William. "I don't know that I should be a welcome guest; in fact, I know I should not—young Maubray——"

"Your brother?" inquired the lady, who did not remember any such incumbrance in the record she had consulted.

"No, my cousin."

"*Cousin?* And what right *could* a cousin pretend to exclude *you* from your father's funeral?" exclaimed Mrs. Kincton Knox, unfeignedly amazed.

"I'm speaking of Sir Richard Maubray, my uncle. My father has been a long time dead—when I was a mere child."

"Oh, yes, of course—dead a long time," repeated Mrs. Kincton Knox, slowly, as the horrible bewilderment in which she had been lost began to clear away. "Oh, yes, your *uncle*, Sir Richard Maubray; of course—of course that would alter—I—*I* was speaking of your father—I did not know you had lost him so long ago—it, of course, it's quite another thing, and—a—and—you wish to go to Mrs. Purity?"

"No—a—*Perfect*—not to go there—not to Gilroyd, only to Cambridge, to see Doctor Sprague."

"Very well—a—very well—I don't see, I shall mention it to Mr. Kincton Knox; have you anything more to say to me. Mr. — Mr. —pray what am I to call you? Herbert, I suppose?"

"Nothing, but to thank you—you've been so good, so very kind to me."

"I—I make it a rule to be kind to—a—to *every* body. I *endeavour* to be so—I believe I *have*," said the majestic lady with a dignity indescribably dry. "I shall mention your wish to Mr. Kincton Knox. Good evening, Mr.—Mr. Herbert."

It seemed to our friend William, that the lady was very much offended with him; but what he had done to provoke her resentment he could not divine. He reproached himself after the door had closed, for not having asked her; but perhaps an opportunity would offer, or he might make one, he could not bear the idea of having wounded a heart which had shown such friendly leanings towards him.

——o——

CHAPTER XLIII

MR. KINCTON KNOX RECEIVES A SUMMONS.

Mr. Kincton Knox, with a couple of dogs at his heels, was tranquilly consulting his chief commissioner of woods and forests, when he was summoned from his sylvan discourses by a loud tapping on his study window, within whose frame he he saw, like a full-length portrait of Mrs. Siddons, on a sign-board, if such a thing exists, the commanding figure of his wife, who was beckoning him imperiously.

The window at which she stood was in fact a glass door opening upon two steps, to which the peaceable old gentleman of sixty-two wonderingly drew near.

"Come in," she exclaimed, beckoning again grimly, and superadding a fierce nod.

So up went the sash, and the little hatch which simulated a window-sill was pulled open by the old gentleman, who was vexed somewhat at the interruption.

She read this in his honest countenance, and said, as he entered—

"I don't mean to detain you, Mr. Kincton Knox, I shan't keep you more than five minutes away from your timber; but I think, for once, you may give that time to your *family*. It's becoming a little too much for me perfectly unaided as I've always been."

"Well, I'm sorry you're annoyed. Something will happen, I suppose. What do you wish me to do?" said that accommodating gentleman in the grey tweed and copious white waistcoat.

"I told you, Mr. Kincton Knox, if you remember, when your friend, Dr. Sprague, of whose character, recollect, *I* know nothing, except from your representations—I *told you distinctly* my impression when that gentleman was persuading you to accept the—the—a person who's here in the capacity of tutor, under a feigned name. I then stated my conviction that there was danger in disguise. I declared myself unable to assign any creditable reason for such a step. Wiser people, however, thought differently—my scruples were overruled by you and your friend Doctor—Doctor —*what's* his name?"

"Sprague—eh?" said her husband.

"Yes—Sprague. It is not the first time that my warning voice has been disregarded. It does not in this case signify much—fortunately very little; but it is not pleasant to have one's house made a scene of duplicity to please Dr. Sprague, or to convenience some low young puppy."

"I thought you said he was the son of my friend Maubray—Sir Richard, you know?"

"It signifies very little whose son he is; but he's not—I simply conjectured he might, and certainly everything was artfully, or not I can't say, laid in train to induce that belief on my part; but he's not—I thought it best to clear it up. He says he's some relation—goodness knows; but in point of everything else he's a mere pretender—the—the merest adventurer, and the sooner we part with him the better."

"And what do you wish me to do?" said Mr. Kincton Knox, with some little vehemence.

"I've given you my views," replied the lady.

"Yes, but you like to do everything yourself, and you always say I'm wrong whatever I say or *do*," said the old gentleman, sonorously, flushing a little, and prodding the point of his stick on the floor.

"See the young man and dismiss him," said his wife peremptorily.

"Well, that's easily done, of course. But what has he *done?* I—I—there ought to be a *rea*-son."

"The reason is that I'm tired of disguises. We can't go on in that absurd manner. It never was known at Kincton, and I—I——"

Suddenly Mrs. Kincton Knox paused in her sentence, and with a great rustling hurried to the study window, where she began to knock with a vehemence which alarmed her husband for the safety of his panes.

The object of the summons was Miss Clara in that exquisitely becoming black velvet cloak and little bonnet which was so nearly irresistible, all grace and radiance, and smiling—upon whom? Why, upon that odious tutor to whom she was pointing out some of those flowers which she claimed to have planted and tended with her own fingers.

Her mother beckoned fiercely.

"Assist me, if you please, Mr. Kincton Knox; open this horrid window, no one else can."

So it was opened, and she called rather huskily to Clara to come in.

"I want to say a word to you, please."

And without condescending to perceive William Maubray, who had raised his hat, she said with an appearance of excitement not of a pleasant kind, and in presence of which somehow the young lady's heart sunk with a sudden misgiving—

"We'll go up, my dear, to my room, I've a word to say,—and—and I think Mr. Kincton

Knox, as you asked me what you shall do, you may as well, in this instance, as usual, do *nothing*. I'll write. I'll do it myself. Come, Clara."

So suspending questions until the apartment up stairs was reached, the young lady, in silence and with a very grave face, accompanied her mother.

"Charming day—sweet day—we shall soon have the storms, though—they must come; we had them ten days earlier last year. Will you come with me to the Farm-road plantation, and give me your ideas about what I'm going to do?"

And the old gentleman came down the two steps from the glass door upon the closely-shorn grass, looking a little red, but smiling kindly, for he saw no reason for what his wife intended, and thought the young man was about to be treated unfairly, and felt a liking for him.

"No; she can't come down again; I know her mother wants her, so you may as well come with me."

So off they set together, and I dare say William liked that ramble better than he would have done the other. The old man was sociable, genial, and modest, and had taken rather late in life, tempted thereto, no doubt, by solitude, to his books, some of which, such as "Captain Lemuel Gulliver's Travels," were enigmatical, and William was able to throw some lights which were new to the elderly student, who conceived a large and honest admiration for his young friend, and would have liked to see a great deal more of him than he was quite sure Mrs. Kincton Knox would allow.

In the course of their walk, William Maubray observed that he seemed even more than usually kindly, and once or twice talked a little mysteriously of women's caprices, and told him not to mind them; and told him also when he was at Oxford he had got once or twice a little dipped—young fellows always do—and he wanted to know—he was not, of course, to say a word about it—if fifty pounds would be of any use to him—he'd be so happy, and he could pay him any time, in ten years or twenty for that matter, for the old gentleman dimly intended to live on indefinitely.

But William did not need this kindly help, and when his pleasant ramble with the old man and his dogs was over, and he returned to the "school-room," William found a note awaiting him on the table, in the large-hand of Mrs. Kincton Knox.

—o—

CHAPTER XLIV.

BACK TO CAMBRIDGE.

The letter upon the table was thus:—

"—— October, —— 1860.

"Mrs. Kincton Knox understanding from Mr. *Herbert* that he wishes to visit Cambridge upon business, begs to say that she will oppose no difficulty to his departing on to-morrow morning with that view; she begs also to mention that Mr. Kincton Knox will write by an early post to the Rev. Dr. Sprague upon the subject of Mr. Herbert's engagement. A carriage will be at the door at eight o'clock, A.M., to convey Mr. Herbert to the railway station."

"What *have* I done. I've *certainly* offended her—she who wrote all those friendly little notes; I can't think of anything, unless that boy Howard has been telling lies. She'll give me an opportunity of explaining, I *suppose*, and it will all be right; it can't be much."

Glad he was to get away even for two or three days to his old haunts, and to something like his old life. He made his preparations early for his next morning's journey, and late in the evening with his ingenious pupil, wondering whether a change of mood might not bring him a relenting note on the usual pink paper, inviting him to visit them in the drawing-room, and debating whether it might not be a wholesome lesson to the capricious old lady to excuse himself, and so impose on her the onus of explanation.

"I say, old chap, listen. What do you think?" said Master Howard, who had been whistling, and on a sudden, being prompted to speak, poked the point of his pen uncomfortably into the back of William's hand.

"Stop that, young un. I told you before you're not to do that. What have you got to say? Come."

"I say, I heard mamma say to Clara this afternoon, that you ain't to to be trusted; and I told Clara I'd tell you, because she teazed me; and mamma said you deceived papa. I heard every word."

"She could not have said that, because I never did anything of the kind," said William, flushing a little.

"Yes, but she did. I heard her, I'd swear; and Clara said, he's a low person. I told her I'd tell you. She did, upon my word—a low person and I said I'd tell you; and I'll tell you ever so much more."

"Not now, please, nor ever. I don't want to hear that sort of thing, even if it *was* said. I'd rather not, I think, unless it was said to myself."

"And I heard Clara say, let him go about his business. I did, upon my honour."

"I say, young un, this is one of your fibs to vex Miss Knox.'"

Master Howard began to vociferate.

"Quiet, sir! If your mamma had any complaint to make, she'd make it to me, I suppose; and if you say a word more on the subject, I'll go in and mention the matter to your mamma," said William, growing angry.

"Catch me telling you anything ever again, as long as I live, that's all," said Master Howard, and broke into mutterings; and then whistled a tune as loud as he could, with his hands in his pockets, and his heels on the table. But he did not succeed in disturbing William. Thoughts that are thoroughly unpleasant hold fast like bull-dogs. It is only the pleasant ones that take wing at noise, like a flight of birds.

Away in due time went Master Howard—no sign appeared from the drawing-room—and William Maubray, who in his elevation and his fall had experienced for the second time something of the uncertainty of human affairs, went to his bed mortified and dismal, and feeling that, go where he would, repulse and insult awaited him.

His early breakfast despatched—William mounted the dog cart, which, in her official letter, Mrs. Kincton Knox had dignified with the title of carriage, and drove at a rapid pace away from Kincton, with a sense of relief and hope as the distance increased, and a rising confidence that somehow he was to see that abode of formality and caprice no more.

Doctor Sprague was now at Cambridge, and greeted him very kindly. He had not much news to tell. It was true Sir Richard Maubray was actually dead at Gilston, whence the body was to be removed that day to Wyndelston, where in about a week would be the funeral.

"No, William would not go—he was not recognised, it would not do—Sir Wynston, as he now was, would take care to let him know he was not wanted."

So said William in reply to the Doctor's question, and having related his experience of Kincton, Doctor Sprague told him frankly, that although Kincton Knox was a very good fellow, and very kind, though a little weak, you know, that he had always heard his wife was a *particularly* odious woman.

"Well, and what of Miss Perfect; any conciliatory symptoms in that quarter?" asked Doctor Sprague.

"Oh, none; she is very inflexible, sir; her dislikes never change."

While they were talking some letters arrived, one of which was actually from Kincton, and in the hand of its mistress.

"Hey? Haw! ha—ha! I protest, Maubray, the lady has cut you—*read*," and he threw the letter across the table to William.

———o———

CHAPTER XLV.

VIOLET DARKWELL AT GILROYD AGAIN.

"Mrs. Kincton Knox" it said, "presents her compliments to the Rev. W. H. Sprague, and as Mr. Kincton Knox is suffering from gout in his hand, which though slight, prevents his writing, she is deputed to apprise him that the gentleman calling himself Mr. Herbert, who has been acting as tutor at Kincton, need not return to complete his engagement. Mr. Kincton Knox desires to remit to him, through your hands, the enclosed cheque, payable to you, and for the full amount of the term he was to have completed. Should the young man feel that under the circumstances, he can have no right to retain the entire amount, he will be so good as to return that portion of the sum to which he feels himself unentitled. We wish to mention that we part with him not in consequence of any specific fault, so much as from a feeling, upon consideration, that we could no longer tolerate the practice of a concealment at Kincton, the character and nature of which—although we impute nothing—might not consist with our own ideas upon the subject."

"She begins in the third person and ends in the first," said Doctor Sprague, "otherwise it is a very fine performance. What am I to do about the cheque?"

"I will not touch a farthing," said William.

"Tut, tut; I think you've a right to it all, but if you object, we'll send them back all that represents the unexpired part of your engagement, but I'll have no Quixotism. I'm half sorry, Maubray, we ever thought of tuitions; we must think of some other way. You're quite right in resolving not to vex Miss Perfect more than you can help, I'm clear upon that; but I've been thinking of quite another thing—I have not time now to tell you all." He glanced at his watch. "But you can speak French, and you would have to reside in Paris. I think it would answer you very nicely, and I think you ought to let Miss Perfect know something of your plans, considering all she has done. I'll see you here again in an hour."

And William took his leave.

That evening Miss Violet Darkwell arrived at Gilroyd. She did not think old "grannie" looking well—was it a sadness or a feebleness—there was something unusual in her look that troubled her. *She* thought her Violet looking quite beautiful—*more* so than ever—so perhaps she was. And she asked her all sorts of questions about all sorts of things, and how the Mainwarings had arranged the rooms, for Aunt Dinah had known the house long ago, and whether the paint had ever been taken off that covered the old oak wainscot in the parlour, and ever so many other particulars besides.

And at last she said—

"Great news Mr. Trevor tells me of William." She had already resolved against opening the Trevor budget to its more interesting recesses. "William Maubray—he's going to marry—to make a great match in some respects—money, beauty—"

"Oh!" said Violet with a smile.

"Yes; a Miss Kincton Knox. He has been residing in the house; an only daughter. *Kincton* is the place."

Something of this Violet had heard before

she left Gilroyd, but not all; and Aunt Dinah went on—

"They are connected somehow with Mr. Trevor, whom I've grown to like extremely, and he saw William there; and from what he told me *I* look upon it as settled, and so in fact does he."

"It's very cold, isn't it, to-night?" said Miss Violet. "That's all very nice—very well for William Maubray."

"Very well; better, perhaps, than he deserves. Had I been, however, as we used to be, I should have endeavoured to postpone it, to induce the parties to defer it for a little—in fact for five years. I may say, indeed, I should have made a point of it; because I—I happen to *know* that his marrying within that time will be attended with the worst consequences."

There was a silence.

"*Very* cold," repeated Miss Violet, drawing a little nearer to the fire.

"It seems odd, as a mere matter of *respect*—that's all, of course, he should not have written me a single line upon the subject," said Miss Perfect, grimly.

"Well, perhaps, not *very* odd," answered Miss Darkwell carelessly, yet somehow, ever so little, sadly. "I'm beginning to think it a worse world than I used to think it, and—and so hard to know any one in it, except dear old grannie."

And up got the girl, and threw her pretty arms round old Aunt Dinah's neck, and kissed her.

"Little Vi, little Vi!" said Aunt Dinah, with a tender tremour in her voice, and she laughed a little.

"I think you are tired, darling. Your long drive," she added.

"I believe I *am*, grannie. Shall I run away to my bed?"

"God bless you, darling!" said grannie, and rang the bell for old Winnie Dobbs, who appeared; and away, with a second good night, they went.

"Well, old Winnie Dobbs, great doings, I hear. Grannie says Mr. William's to be married—a great lady, Miss Kincton Knox, she says—and very pretty—quite a beauty, quite a belle."

She was looking with a faint little smile down upon the trinkets she was laying upon the dressing table, and she spoke in the tones in which people recall a very far off remembrance.

"Well, she did tell me so, Miss Vi; and very glad I was, poor fellow; but very young. I that knows him when he was only the length o' my arm—to think of him now. But very sensible—always was; a good head—wiser than many an older body."

"You've never seen the lady?" said Vi.

"No; but Mr. Trevor's groom was stopping there last summer for a week with Mr. Trevor, you know, and he did not much like the family—that's the old lady—no one has a good word of her; and the young one, Miss Clara—do you like the name Clara, miss?"

"Yes; a pretty name I think."

"Well, they don't say much about her; only she's very distant like?"

"And *she's* the lady?" asked Violet.

"Ah, *that* she is, miss—the only daughter."

"She's tall?"

"Well, yes; he says she is."

"Taller than I, I dare say?"

"Well, he did not say that; you're a good height you know yourself, miss—a nice figure, yes, indeed."

"And what colour is her hair?" asked Vi.

"Light—light hair," he said.

"Yes; he always liked light hair, I think," she said, still with the same faint smile and in the same soft and saddened tones. Vi was arranging her own rich dark brown tresses at the glass.

"And blue eyes—large—something the colour o' yours, he said, miss; he used to take great notice to her, the groom—everything. She used to go out a ridin'. A hair pin, miss?"

"No, Winnie, thanks."

"He says she's a fine rider; showy, handsome, that sort you know."

"And when is it all to be?"

"Well, they don't know; but once it's settled, I do suppose it won't be long delayed. Why should it?"

"*No* why, once it's settled, as you say."

"And is it not well for him, poor fellow, he should have some one to love him, and look after him? What's the good o' life without kindness, both o' them handsome, and young, and loving. What more need they ask?" said old Winnie. "And if they aren't happy, who will?"

"Yes, old Winnie, they will, very happy, I'm sure; and now I'll bid you good night, I'm so *tired*, very tired; it's a long tedious way, and I'm always wishing to come back to you, and dear old grannie, and poor old Gilroyd, where we were all so happy, where I always feel so safe—but I believe we always fancy the old times the pleasantest—when I was a child, I think—Good night, old Winnie."

———o———

CHAPTER XLVI.

VANE TREVOR AT THE WINDOW.

WILLIAM MAUBRAY liked the appointment which his kind friend, Doctor Sprague, had virtually secured for him. It was not a great deal in salary, but opening abundant opportunities for that kind of employment which he most coveted, and for which, in fact, a very little training would now suffice to accomplish him. Literary work, the ambition of so many, not a wise one perhaps for those who have any other path before them, but to which men will devote themselves, as to a perverse marriage, contrary to other men's warnings, and even to their own legible experiences of life—in a dream.

For three years he would sojourn in Paris. He preferred that distant exile to one at the gates of the early paradise from which he had been excluded. From thence he would send to his good friend, Doctor Sprague, those little intimations of his doings and his prosperings, which he, according to his wisdom, might trasmit for inspection to the old lady at Gilroyd, who might, if she pleased, re-open a distant correspondence with the outcast.

Doctor Sprague, at William's desire, had written to accept and arrange, and would hear by the return of post, or nearly, and then William might have to leave at a day's notice. Three years! It was a long time, and Aunt Dinah old! He might never see her or Gilroyd more, and a kind of home-sickness fell upon him.

At Gilroyd that morning, Aunt Dinah and Vi sat at breakfast *téte-à-tête.* The spirits of the old lady were not altogether so bright, the alacrity was gone, and though she smiled there was a sadness and a subsidence. William was banished. The pang of that sharp decision was over. Some little help he should have circuitously through Doctor Sprague; but meet again on earth they never should. So that care was over; and now her other tie, pretty Violet Darkwell, she, too, was going; and although she sat beside her at the little breakfast-table, prattling pleasantly, and telling her all the news of her friends, the Mainwarings and their new neighbours, yet her voice sounded already faint in distance, and the old lady's cares were pretty well over. Our business here is work of some sort, and not for ourselves; and when that is ended it is time, as Fuller says, to put out the candle and go to bed.

"I'm going to see old Mrs. Wagget to-day. I promised her the day before I went to the Mainwarings," said Vi, recalling this engagement.

"But, my dear, some one may call here. Your friends and mine will be looking in," said Aunt Dinah, who knew that Trevor would arrive at about twelve o'clock.

"Well, I can return their visits all the same, and see them in their own houses," said Vi, "just as well."

"And what need to go to Mrs. Wagget to-day—to-morrow I fancy would answer," said Miss Perfect.

"But I *promised,* you know, and she wrote to remind me."

"*Promised* to *leave* your old Granny alone again the day after your return!" she exclaimed, a little huffed.

"Why, darling, it was you who made me promise, don't you recollect?" pleaded Miss Violet, "the day we paid them our last visit."

"H'm—did I? Well, if there really was a promise, and I suppose you remember, we must keep it I suppose." Aunt Dinah had made that kind of scrupulousness an emphatic point in Violet's simple education, and of course it could not now be trifled with. And now she did recollect the appointment, and something about walking to the school-house together at twelve o'clock—could anything be more unlucky? Aunt Dinah looked up at the sky; but no, it was *not* threatening—clear blue, with a pleasant white cloud or two, and a sea of sunshine.

"I'm so sorry, Granny, we settled, it would have been so much pleasanter to have staid with you to-day, and I'm afraid it's very wicked; but that school, except to *very* good people, it is really insupportable," said Miss Vi, whose inflexible estimate of such appointments rather vexed Aunt Dinah, and not the less that she could not deny that it was her own work.

"It's right in the main," thought she. "But there are distinctions—there's danger, however, in casuistry, and so let it be," There was an odd little sense of relief too in the postponement of the crisis.

At about half-past eleven Vane Trevor arrived. He came by the path, and from the drawing-room window Miss Perfect, sitting there at her work, saw him, and knocked and beckoned with her slender mittened hand.

"He looks pale, poor young man," he was smiling as he approached, "and haggard too," she pronounced, notwithstanding. "He's anxious I dare say," and she pushed up the window as he approached. "What a sweet morning," she said, taking off her gold spectacles, and smiling with that soft look of sympathy which in such cases makes even old women's faces so pretty again.

"Charming morning—quite—really—quite charming."

She saw him peeping into the shadow of the room for a second figure. Aunt Dinah's hand was now within reach, and they exchanged a friendly greeting.

"My little Violet has returned," she said, still holding Trevor's hand kindly, "quite well—looking so well—and most unluckily I quite forgot; but I had made an appointment for her this morning with Mrs. Wagget, and—and in fact I have always made the keeping of appointments so much a moral duty with her, that unless I had opened the subject on which you talked with me, and told her plainly that I expected your call, and that she must wait—which would have been a—a—not a favourable way of proceeding; and in fact I should have been obliged to say very badly what you would say, probably, very well; and indeed it is a thing that makes me nervous—always did. When my dear sister was proposed for, I refused to take the message, in fact—I could not—and—he spoke for himself—poor Charles Maubray—like a man and —and a very happy"——Suddenly she stopped, and Trevor saw that tears were trickling slowly down her cheeks; and her lips were resolutely closed; and she fumbled for a minute or two among her silks and worsteds; and the young man felt that he liked her better than ever he did before; and he sat on the window-stone outside, and they chatted kindly for a long time. Then they took a little walk together among the flowers, and under the chesnuts till it grew to be near two o'clock, and Aunt Dinah began to look for Violet's return; and if the great Duke of Wellington on the field of Waterloo consulted his watch half so often as Mr. Vane Trevor did his on the green sward of Gilroyd that afternoon, I'm not surprised at it having excited all the observation it did, and being noted in the history of that great day of thunder and suspense.

Not the Iron Duke, however, but his Imperial rival on the field, when lowering his glass, he muttered, "c'est les Prussien," is the fitter representative of our friend Vane Trevor when, not Miss Violet Darkwell, but old Mrs. Wagget's page, a thick and stunted "buttons," in rifle green regimental, moved down upon his flank, with a note in his hand for Miss Perfect, who was entreated by the writer to allow Miss Violet to stay dinner, with a promise that she should arrive safe at Gilroyd in the brougham that evening at nine!

There was nothing for it but submission. It would not do, in presence of that dwarfish page, who was eyeing Vane with the curiosity of a youthful gossip, to order the young lady home, detain the young gentleman where he stood, and thus by a feat of discipline compel a meeting.

So Miss Perfect despatched her reply, thanking—I hope it was sincerely—Felicia Honoria Wagget, and accepting the arrangement with the best grace she might.

"You must come in and take some luncheon," said Aunt Dinah.

Gilroyd was somehow so charming a spot, its resources had grown so inexhaustible, and old Miss Perfect so sensible and altogether interesting that Trevor was glad to linger a little, and postpone the evil hour of departure. It came at last, however, and Aunt Dinah called old Winnie Dobbs, and went listlessly to her room to make her toilet for her solitary dinner.

—o—

CHAPTER XLVII.

MISS PERFECT'S TOILET.

"Short the evenings growing," said Aunt Dinah, looking out upon the slanting amber sun-light, that made the landscape all so golden. "Long shadows already!" and she glanced at her broad old gold watch. "How the years go over us; Winnie, you've been a long time with me now—ha, ha, a long time. When first you came to me, you thought me such a shrew, and I thought you such a fool, that we both thought a parting must very soon come of it—an old termagant and an old goose, continued Miss Perfect, nodding her head at her image in the glass. "We were not altogether wrong in that, perhaps, old Dobbs—don't interrupt me—but, though we were neither lambs nor Solomons, we answered one another. We never parted, and we'll live on so, don't you think, to the end of the chapter, and a pretty long chapter it has been, and pretty near the end, Winnie Dobbs, it must be for both of us. 'Here endeth the first lesson,' and then comes the judgment, Winnie—'here endeth the second lesson,'—our two great lessons, death and judgment: think of that, my good old Winnie, when you hear Doctor Mainwaring, or Doctor Wagget, it is now, saying, 'here endeth the first lesson,' and 'here endeth the second lesson,' and much good may it do you."

Aunt Dinah's lectures on such themes were generally very odd, and her manner sometimes a little flighty—people who did not know her would have almost said waggish. But her handmaiden received them always with a reverent acquiescence, having as full a faith in her mistress as honest Sancho, in his most trusting moods, ever reposed in the wisdom of the Knight of La Mancha.

"Death and judgment, sure enough. Death, at any rate, that's certain," maundered old Dobbs.

"And judgment, too, I hope," said Aunt Dinah, sharply.

"And judgment, too," supplemented Winnie.

"What do you mean, old Dobbs, as if one was more certain than the other?"

"Ay, indeed. What is there certain?—nothing—nothing," she continued, not exactly apprehending her mistress.

"Tut, tut! Dobbs. Give me a pin—you don't intend—but you sometimes say things that make my flesh creep—*yes*—you don't know it—but you do."

"*Dear* me! ma'am," ejaculated old Winnie, who was never very much startled by Aunt Dinah's violent remarks.

"So, I think, old Dobbs, we shall soon have a wedding here," said Miss Perfect, after a silence, changing the subject.

"Well, well, I should not wonder, ma'am," answered she.

"But you're not to say one word about it to Miss Violet until she speaks to you—do you mind—not a word—and that will be, I think, to-morrow."

"To-morrow!" exclaimed Winnie.

"Not the wedding, old goose, but the talk of it. I think it will be all settled to-morrow, and I'm glad, and I'm sorry. Give me my snuff-box—thanks. She has never spoken to you on the subject?" said Aunt Dinah.

"No, no, ma'am; never," answered Winnie.

"Nor to me. But I know all about it from another quarter, and I hope she'll not be a fool. She'll never have so good an offer again. I like him extremely. I have the best opinion of him, and the Sergeant is very much pleased; indeed, it's quite unexceptionable, and I do expect, Winnie Dobbs, if she *should* talk to you, you'll not try to frighten her. You and I are old maids, and I believe we chose wisely; but we are not to frighten nervous girls by drawing terrific pictures of matrimony, and maundering about bad husbands and unprovided children; young girls are so easily frightened away from anything that's prudent: and, though we are old maids, there's a good deal to be said on the other side of the question—so, do you mind?

"Dear me, ma'am, I'd be sorry she wasn't to get a good husband, I would."

"And you remember the last evening, Friday last, when we were in the study, at the table, you know, where the word 'eminently' came. Do you remember?"

"Well, I ought to, I'm sure; but my old head is not as good at bringing a thing to mind as it used to be," hesitated Winnie.

"No more it is; but the word eminently was all we got that night, and you didn't know what the question was. Well, I'll tell you. I asked simply, will Violet Darkwell's marriage—hook my body, please—will Violet Darkwell's marriage prove happy? and the answer was *eminently*."

"Ay, so it was, I'll be bound, though I can't bring it to mind; but it's a hard word for the like o' me to come round."

"You *are* provoking, Winnie Dobbs," exclaimed her mistress, looking at herself defiantly in the glass.

"Well, dear me! I often think I am," acquiesced Winnie.

"Well, Winnie, we are too old to change much now—the leopard his spots, and the Ethiopian his skin. There's no good in trying to teach an old dog tricks. They must make the best of us now, Winnie, such as we are; and if this wedding does happen, I'll trick you out in a new dress, silk every inch, for the occasion, and the handsomest cap I can find in Saxton. I'll make you such a dandy, you'll not know yourself in the looking-glass. You'll come to the church as her own maid, you know; but you're not to go away with her. You'll stay with me, Winnie. I don't think you'd like to leave Gilroyd."

Old Winnie hereupon witnessed a good and kindly confession.

———o———

CHAPTER XLVIII.

THE PRODIGAL.

Then came one of those little silences, during which thoughts glide on with the stroke, as it were, of the last sentence or two; and old Winnie Dobbs said at last:

"But I don't think it would be like a wedding if Master Willie wasn't here."

"Stop that," said Miss Perfect, grimly, and placing the end of the comb, with which she had been adjusting her grey locks, that lay smoothly over her resolute forehead, on a sudden upon old Winnie's wrist. "I never change my mind when once I've made it up. You don't know, and you *can't* know, for your wits are always wool-gathering, all I've done for that boy—young *man*, indeed, I ought to call him—nor the measure of his perversity and ingratitude. I've supported him—I've educated him—I've been everything to him—and, at the first opportunity, he has turned on me. If I were a total stranger, a Cambridge doctor, or—or anything else that had never cared or thought about him, he'd have listened to what I had to say, and been influenced by it. He has refused me for his friend—renounced me—chosen other advisers—he'll soon be married."

"Dearie me!" interpolated old Winnie, in honest sympathy.

"And although Mr. Trevor wrote to him yesterday to mention my view and conviction, that his marriage ought to be postponed for some little time, I know perfectly it won't have the slightest effect, no more than those birds twittering."

The sparrows in the glittering ivy were gossipping merrily in the beams of the setting sun.

"I simply told his friend, Mr. Trevor, and left it to him to acquaint him, not as having any claim whatever on my particular regard any longer, but as a—a human being—just that; and *you* know, Winnie Dobbs, when I make a resolution I can keep it; you remember——"

Miss Perfect had reached this point in her oration when old Winnie, who had been looking out of the window with unusual scrutiny, on a sudden exclaimed—

"I'm blest if here baint Master William a comin'!"

Aunt Dinah uttered a little exclamation, with her shut hand pressing on her breast, as she looked over her old servant's shoulder.

I don't know how it was, but as William Maubray entered the old iron gate, he heard the swift tread of a light foot, and Aunt Dinah, hurrying from the red brick porch, ran towards him with a little cry, and "my darling!" and threw her thin arms round his neck, and they both stood still.

"Oh! Willie, you've come back."

William did not answer, he was looking down in her face, pale, with his hands very gently on her shoulders

"Come in, darling," she said at last.

"*Am* I to come in?" said William, wistfully and softly.

And she looked at him, pleadingly with tears in her eyes, and said—

"Poor old Aunt Dinah."

And he leant down and kissed her.

"Come in?" my boy—my Willie man—my only precious boy that I was so proud of."

And William kissed her again, and cried over her thin shoulder, and she, close laid to his breast, sobbed also; each felt the tremble in the other's kindly arms. Thank God, it was made up now—the two loving hearts so near again—sweet and bitter the angelic love and mortal sadness—the sense of uncertainty and parting mingling with the great affection that welled up from the eternal fountain of love. Improve the hours of light. The time is near when the poor heart will tremble no more, and all the world of loving thoughts lie in dust and silence.

"I am going to give you the silver tobacco-box that was on Marston Moor—it is the most valuable thing I have—it has the inscription on the inside of the cover. It was in my foolish old head to send it to Doctor Sprague for you. It was your ancestor's. The 'Warwickshire Knight,' we called him—Sir Edwin. He joined the Parliament, you know, and took the name of Perfect. I always intended the tobacco-box for you, Willie, even when I was offended—come in—come, my darling."

And she drew in the prodigal with her arm in his, and her hand on his fingers, liking to feel as well as to see and to hear him—to be *quite* sure of him!

"Dinner, Tom, this minute," said she to old Tom, who grinning spoke his hearty word of welcome in the hall, "Master William is very hungry—he has come ever so far—tell Mrs. Podgers—come Willie—are you cold?"

So before the bright fire, which was pleasant that clear red, frosty evening, they sat—and looking fondly on him—her hand on his, she said—

"A little thin—certainly, a little thin—have you been quite well, Willie—quite well?"

"Yes, quite well—all right—and how have you been?" he answered and asked.

"Very well—that is, pretty well—indeed I can't say I *have*—I've *not* been well—but time enough about that. And tell me—and tell me about this news—about Miss Kincton Knox—is it true—is there really an engagement?"

"I've left them—I came from Cambridge. Engagement! by Jove! I—I don't know exactly what you mean."

So said William, who was struck by something more in Aunt Dinah's look and tone than could possibly arise from the contemplation merely of that engagement he had been fulfilling at Kincton.

"I—I heard—I thought—was not there—isn't there"—Aunt Dinah paused, gazing dubiously on William—"I mean—something of—of—she's very handsome—I'm told."

"Going to be married to Miss Kincton Knox!—I assure you, if you knew her, such an idea would strike you as the most absurdly incredible thing the people who invented it could possibly have told you"—and William actually laughed.

"Ha!" exclaimed she, rather dismally—"that's very odd—that is really very odd—it must have been a mistake—people do make such mistakes—it must—and you have heard of—Vi—it seems so odd—little Vi! There's no mistake *there*, for Mr. Trevor has had a long conversation with me, and has written to her father, and we both approve highly. But—but about Miss Kincton Knox—it was an odd mistake, though I can't say I'm sorry, because—but it does not signify now; you would never have waited, and so sure as you sit there, if you had not, you'd have regretted your precipitation all the days of your life."

And thrice she nodded darkly on William, in such a way as to assure him that Henbane had been looking after his interests.

After dinner she ordered Tom to call Winnie Dobbs, who had already had *her* chat with William.

"Winnie," said she, producing a large key from her bag, "you must go to the store room and fetch one of the three bottles on the shelf."

"We dust them every week, old Winnie and I," said she as soon as Dobbs had gone. "They have been there fifteen years—Frontignac—the doctor ordered it—sillabubs in the morning, when I was recovering, and I don't think they did me a bit of good; and we must open one of them now."

William protested in vain.

"Yes, it's the kind of wine young people like—they like it—sweet wine—you *must*. I hear her coming. What are you dawdling there for, Winnie? Come in—bring it in—why *don't* you?"

So, sitting side by side, her hand on his, and looking often in his face as they talked, they sipped their wine; and old Winnie, standing by, had her glass, and drank their healths, and declared it was "a beautiful sight to see them." And Aunt Dinah sent Tom to Saxton for some muffins for tea. Mr. William liked muffins—"be quiet—you know you do."

"I'm so sorry Violet should have been out, drinking tea at the Rectory; but you're to stay to-night; you say you'll be in time at Mr. Clever's chambers at five to morrow evening; and you have a London up train at half-past eleven at our station: and you must sleep at Gilroyd; it would not be like the old times if you didn't."

CHAPTER XLIX.

"AFTER DEATH MY GHOST SHALL HAUNT YOU."

It was a clear, frosty moonlight night, and the stars blinking and staring fiercely in the dark sky, as William Maubray peeped between the drawing-room shutters, and listened in vain for the ring of the wheels of the promised brougham; and Aunt Dinah returned just as he let the curtains fall together, having in her hand a little card-board box tied round with a little blue ribbon.

"Blue, you see, for loyality—not to princes, but to right—I tied it with blue ribbon," said Aunt Dinah, sitting down beside him, and untying the knot, and taking out the silver box, with embossed windmills, trees, dogs, and Dutchmen upon it. "Here it is—the tobacco-box; it is yours, mind and your eldest boy's to have it—an heirloom," said she, with a gentle smile, looking into that dim but sunny vista, and among the golden haired and blue-eyed group, painted in fancy, where she would have no place; "and it's never to go out of the family, and who knows what it may inspire. It was a brave man's tobacco-box—*my* hero. The courtiers, I believe did not smoke, and he did not like tobacco, indeed I can't abide the smell, except in snuff—the kind you know you bring me sometimes; but he would not be different from the other officers about him, and so he did smoke; though, my dear father told me, always sparingly; and so, dear William here it is, and I have had your name placed underneath, and you can take it with you."

Hereupon the tea and muffins entered, and after a time the conversation took another turn.

"And I'm not sorry, William, about that Kincton Knox business; indeed I'm very glad; I never knew before—I never knew intimations—and you know I implicitly believe in them—so peremptory upon any point as on that; and you're not to marry—mind, you shall promise me you will not—till after the expiration of five years.'

"I think I might promise you safely enough, I'll never marry," said William, with a little laugh.

"Don't be rash—no—don't promise more than I ask; but *that* you *must*," replied the old lady.

"You'll not ask me to make promises, I'm sure?" said William; "I hate them so."

"For five years," said Miss Perfect, holding up her head a little sternly.

"For five years, dear aunt?" replied William, with a smile, and shaking his head.

"It is not much," said Aunt Dinah, looking sadly down on her muffin, and chopping it lightly with the edge of her knife, as if she cut off the head of a miniature argument at every stroke. "I don't think it's *very* much for a person, that is, who says he'll *never* marry."

"I'll never marry—I'm sure I shall never marry—and yet I can't promise *any*thing. I hate vows; they are sure to make you do the very thing you promise not to do," said William, half provoked, half laughing, "and if I *were* to promise, I really can't tell *what* the consequence might be."

"Ha!" said Miss Perfect. "Well! It *is* odd!" and up she got and stood very erect and grim on the hearth-rug.

"Now don't, dear aunt, don't be vexed with me; but I assure you I *could* not. I *can't* make vows about the future; but I really and honestly think I shall *never* be a married man; it's all—all—*odious*."

"Well," said she with an effort, "I *won't* quarrel. It was not much—five years." A little pause here she allowed William to reflect upon its reasonableness, but he made no sign. "Not a great deal; but I won't quarrel—*there*—I won't," and she extended her hand to him in amity, and he clasped it very affectionately.

"But I'll speak to you seriously. I'm not fanciful, I think, I don't believe things without *evidence*, and I don't much care what very young, or very prejudiced people may think about me, that which I know I declare, and I don't shrink an atom—no, not at the stake."

William looked at her with respectful amazement.

"No—truth first—truth *always*—in the face of ridicule and bigotry never abandon the truth. I say I know perfectly well we are surrounded by spirits—disprove it if you can—and unequivocally have they declared themselves to me, and from that one among them, who is always near me, who is present at this moment, a friendly spirit—Henbane! Why should I hesitate to name him?—I have learned the *condition*, I may say of your *fate* and *I* won't hide it, nor suffer you, if I can help it, to disregard it. Marry for five years you shan't. If I be alive I'll leave no stone unturned to prevent it; and if I'm dead, there's nothing that spirit can do, if you so much as harbour the thought, I'll not do to prevent it. I'll be about you, be I good or evil, or mocking, I'll trouble you, I'll torment you, I'll pick her eyes out, but I won't suffer you to ruin yourself.

Preposterous as was this harangue, Aunt Dinah delivered it like a Pythoness, with a vehemence that half awed her nephew.

"I'll speak of this no more," she said, more like herself, after two or three minutes silence. "I'll not mention it—I'll let it rest in your mind—it's nothing to me, but for your sake, my mind's made up though, and if I have power in this world or the next, you'll hear of me, remember that, William Maubray."

William was bound to listen to this flighty rigmarole, with respect as coming from his aunt, but her spiritual thunders rather amused than alarmed him, and of Henbane he entertained, I must confess, the meanest possible opinion. Connected with all this diablerie, indeed there was but one phenomenon which had unpleasantly fastened upon his imagination, and that was the mysterious adventure which had befallen him in this old house of Gilroyd when in his bed, his wrist was seized and held fast in the grasp of an unseen hand, and the intensely disagreeable sensations of that night recurred to his memory oftener than he would care to admit.

"I wonder you have so little curiosity, sometimes," said Aunt Dinah, speaking now, though gravely, much more in her usual way, "you young people think, you are so far away from the world of spirits, material and sceptical. You've never once cared to ask me for Elihu Bung. I'll lend it to you with pleasure, while you are here. But that portion of the Almighty's empire has no interest—is dead—for you."

There was abundant truth in this reproach, for William indeed could not without great offence, have told his aunt what rubbish he thought it all. But said he:

"I dare say it is very curious."

"Not a bit curious; that's not the word; it is serious and it's certain; bread and butter is not very curious, your foot is not very curious, nor your hat; but there they are, facts! that's all. I'm glad you say you have no present intention of marrying, in fact, dear William, the idea has caused me the most extreme anxiety, having the warning I *have;* as for me, however, my course is taken. I expect to be what we call a mocking spirit—yes a mocking spirit—and I'll play you such tricks as will make you think twice, if such an idea should be in your head. Mind I told you, though I be dead you shan't escape me," and she smiled oddly, and nodded her head, and then frowned a little bit.

"But I dare say it won't happen. Now that this Kincton Knox business has turned out a mistake—thank God—a *canard.* There's no hurry; you are too young. Remember it was on the 28th of September the warning came, five years, and you count from that; but goodness knows you have time enough. I think I hear the brougham."

William was already at the window and the gate-bell ringing.

"And William, remember, not a word to Violet about Mr. Trevor—not a hint."

"Oh! certainly," cried he, and he was at the hall door in time to open the carriage door, and take little Violet's hand.

"Oh! *you* come?" said she, smiling, and descending lightly with a bouquet of old Miss Wagget's best flowers in her fingers. "I had not an idea—only just come, I suppose?"

"Yes, this evening; and you quite well, Violet?"

"Quite well, flourishing, Grannie in the drawing-room? And I'm glad you've come to Gilroyd, poor old Grannie, I think she has been in very low spirits; let us go to her."

CHAPTER L.

VIOLET AND WILLIAM IN THE DRAWING-ROOM.

Violet seemed merry and good-natured, William thought, but somewhat cold. No one else would have perceived it; but this little chill, hardly measurable by the moral thermometer, was for him an Icelandic frost, in which his very heart ached.

This pretty girl kissed Aunt Dinah, and put off her bonnet, and out gushed her beautiful dark brown hair, but kept her other mufflers on, and said smilingly towards William,

"I was so surprised to see him at the door, I could scarcely believe my eyes."

"And looking very well—a little thin perhaps, but very well," added Aunt Dinah.

"And how is Mr. Wagget?" asked William, who did not care to come formally under critical discussion.

"Oh, very well, and Miss Wagget too; but I don't know that you've made her acquaintance. She's quite charming, and I doubt very much whether so susceptible a person as you would do wisely in putting himself in her way."

She has been hearing that nonsense about Miss Kincton Knox, thought William, and he said rather drily,

"I'm not a bit susceptible. How did I ever show it? I'd like to know who I ever was in love with in my life. Susceptible, by Jove! but I see you're laughing.

Miss Vi looked curiously at him for a moment, and then she said,

"We heard quite another account of him, didn't we, Grannie?"

"It was all a mistake though, it seems," said Aunt Dinah.

"I should like to know who the kind person is who cares enough about me to invent all these lies."

"The ladies there liked you extremely, we have the best authority for believing that," said Miss Perfect.

"I don't know; I'm sure they detest me now, and I really don't know any reason they have ever had for doing either."

"Detest you, my dear!" exclaimed Aunt Dinah.

"Mrs. Kincton Knox is awfully offended with me, I don't know for what. I've nothing on earth to charge myself with, and I really don't care two pence, and I hate to think about them," said William testily; "and I'd rather talk about anything else."

Miss Vi looked at William, and glanced at Aunt Dinah, and then laughed, with a pleasant little silvery cadence.

"Dear me! Grannie, what a disappointment. We simple people in this part of the world have been lost for weeks in wonder and respect—we heard such stories of your prowess, and here comes the lady-killer home, harmless William Maubray, as he went."

"Just so," said he. "Not William the Conqueror—nothing of the kind; and I don't think it likely I shall ever try to kill a lady, nor a lady ever kill me. Weapons of iron won't do now-a-days, and a knight-errant of that sort must arm himself with the precious metals, and know how to talk the modern euphuism, and be a much finer man than ever I can hope to be; and even so, when all's done, it's a poor profession enough. By Jove! I don't envy them their adventures, and their exploits, and their drubbings and their Dulcineas—the best among them is often laid on his back; and I'm not ashamed to say I have more of Sancho Panza than of the Don in my nature."

"He rails like a wounded knight—doesn't he, Grannie?" laughed Violet.

"I'd like to know who wounded me," said he.

"We'll take your own account, William," said Aunt Dinah, who saw that he was vexed and sore, "and whoever is to blame, I'm very glad—Oh! prayers," and the little household of Gilroyd trooped solemnly into the room, and the family devotions were performed, William officiating in his old capacity.

"William leaves us early to-morrow," said Aunt Dinah, glancing regretfully at him.

"Oh?" said Miss Violet.

"Yes, to London! and from London perhaps to Paris, there to remain for some time," said William, spiritedly.

"Charming excursion," exclaimed the young lady.

"Why London is not particularly lively at this moment, and I hope to be pretty hard worked in Paris. There's nothing very charming about it, but I'm glad to go;" and thinking this a little strong he added, "because it is time I should begin, if ever I am to do any good for myself or any one else."

"He's like the good boy in a story-book, he makes such wise reflections; and I'm certain he'll grow rich and prosper," said Miss Vi to Aunt Dinah. "My only wise saw is, 'Early to bed and early to rise, makes a man healthy, wealthy, and wise.' I learned it from good old Winnie, and I'm going to act on it now. Good night, dear old Grannie," and she kissed her in a fond little embrace. "All this wise talk makes one sleepy, I think; and I've been walking about with Miss Wagget all day. Good night." This was to William with a smile.

"Good night, he answered quietly, and a little bitterly, as without smiling he took her hand. Then he lighted her candle and gave it to her with a little nod, and a smile, and stood at the door while she ran up the broad stair, humming an air.

He came back, looking sulky, and sat down with his hands in his pocket, looking at the fire-irons that rested on the fender.

"How do you think she's looking?" asked Aunt Dinah.

"Very well; much as usual," said William, with a dreary carelessness.

"I think she's looking particularly beautiful," said Miss Perfect.

"Perhaps so—very likely; but I've plenty of work before me, thank God, the sort of work I like; and I'm in no admiring mood, like Trevor and other fellows who have nothing better to do. I like work. 'Man delights not me, nor woman neither.' And, dear Aunt, I'm a little bit sleepy, too; but I'll see you early, shan't I?"

And William yawned dismally.

"Good night, dear, it *is* better," said Aunt Dinah; "but I don't know, it strikes me that you and Vi are not as friendly together as you used to be, and I think it is a pity."

"Not so friendly," exclaimed William. "Ha, ha! That did not strike me; but I assure you there's no change, at least that I know of—none on my part, I'm sure. I suppose it's just that our heads are full of other things; we have each got our business to think of—don't you see?—and her's you know, is very serious," and William Maubray laughed again a little bitterly.

"Well, she is a dear little creature, an affectionate little soul. I've always found her quite the same," said Aunt Dinah.

"I'm *sure* she is—I dare say—I don't see why she shouldn't, that is, as affectionate as other young ladies. You know it isn't I who say she's changed."

"I did not say *she's* changed more than *you*. I think you don't seem so kindly as used, and more disposed to be agreeable; and I think, considering you have been so long together, and are so soon to part, and life is so uncertain, I think it a pity; and *you* can't see even how pretty she is looking."

"I must have been thinking of something else, for she is in particularly good looks;" and he added, quite like himself, "Yes, indeed, I think she improves every time I see her, but that may be the old partiality, you know. Good night, Aunt Dinah."

Aunt Dinah took both his hands to hers, and kissed him.

"Good night, my dear William—my dear boy. You will never know, dear William, all the pain you have cost me. Pray, my dear child, for a reasonable spirit, and that you may have power to conquer the demon of pride—the besetting sin of youth, and, my dear William, you *must* reconsider the question of ordination, and pray for light. God bless you, and don't forget to put out your candle. *There*"—another kiss—"Good night."

CHAPTER LI

A DREAM.

"AFFECTIONATE indeed!" said William. "I do believe they have no other idea but to mortify and wound every one that seems to like them—cats and monkeys."

William had closed the door; he poked his fire, and sat before it eyeing it scornfully.

"I can't think why anyone likes them,—why we go on liking them—they are so odious. I suppose they used not to be so. There's Aunt Dinah—kind, true old Aunt Dinah—she never could have been a heartless, insolent creature like that—never. We are all growing worse; the world will soon be ripe for judgment."

And William pulled off his coat as savagely as if he was going to fight "Old Crump" again, behind the Chapel at Rugby.

"I hate myself for liking her. No, I don't like her—for *admiring* her; but she *is* pretty. She is—there's no good in denying it—she's *awfully* pretty—*lovely!* and till that great goose, Trevor, came and turned her head with his boots, and his gloves, and his house, and his trumpery, she was the nicest little creature in the world. Yes, there was no one like her; not one on earth, I'll maintain."

And he knocked his hand so hard on the back of the chair beside him, that he thought his knuckles were bleeding.

"I wish they *were*, by Jove!" he said. "I don't care what happens, I don't care if I was knocked to smash, to think of that great, gawky, goose. What on earth *can* she *see* in him? Such rot?"

"Yes, she *is*—there's no use in *disputing* it—she's the prettiest girl I ever *saw*, in all my *life*," he went on, putting himself down and overbearing his affected indifference with honest vehemence. "Aunt Dinah has promised me her *carte de visite*. I'll have it copied in large the first money I have, in Paris, at that great fellow's there—and tinted; and I'll make old Winnie get me a lock of her hair; I have the one safe when she was nine years old—so bright—who would have thought it would ever have grown so dark? Old Winnie will get it for me. If I asked *her* she'd only refuse, or put me off some way. I'll hang up her picture and the little drawing of Gilroyd in my garret in Paris, and I'll be a jolly old bachelor. Marry in five years, indeed? My poor aunt might easily find something more likely to fret about. Yes, I'll be the most tremendous, dry old quiz of a bachelor; and when she and her precious husband come to Paris, as they will some day, I'll get a peep at her, perhaps, in the theatres and places, from some dark corner, and I wonder what she will be like then—always handsome, those eyes, and her lips so scarlet, and her beautiful hair; and I'll compare her with little Vi of Gilroyd. She may be handsomer and more showy, but the little Vi of Gilroyd will always be the brightest and best."

In this mood William rambled over many old recollections of the place and people he was leaving, and he laid his waistcoat on the chair much more gently than his coat; and he thought how Aunt Dinah had taught him to say his prayers long ago, under that friendly roof, and so down he kneeled and said them with a sadder heart, and rose up with a great sigh, and a sense of leave-taking that made his heart ache.

And now his candle was out, and he soon fast asleep; and again he had a dream so strange that I must relate it.

The scenery of his dream, as before, presented simply the room in which he lay, with the flickering firelight in which he had gone to sleep. He lay, in his vision, in his bed, just as he really did, with his back to the fire and looking toward the curtains, which were closed on the side between him and the door, when he heard a sound of naked feet running up to his chamber door, which was flung open with a precipitation which made the windows rattle, and his bed curtain was drawn aside, and Miss Perfect, with only a sheet, as it seemed, wrapt over her night dress, and with a face white, and fixed with horror, said, "Oh, my God! William, I'm dead—don't let me go!" and under the clothes she clasped his wrist with a hand that felt like cold metal. The figure crouched, with its features advanced towards his, and William Maubray could neither speak nor move, and lay so for some time, till with a "Ho!" he suddenly recovered the power of motion, and sprang out of bed at the side farthest from the visionary Aunt Dinah; and as he did so, he distinctly felt the grasp of a cold hand upon his wrist, which just as before, vanished as he recovered the full possession of his waking faculties, leaving, however, its impression there.

William lighted his candle at the fire, and listened for a long time before he could find courage to look to the other side of the bed. When he did, however, no sign of Aunt Dinah, sane or mad, was there. The door was shut, and the old fashioned furniture stood there prim and faded as usual, and everything maintained its old serenity. On his wrist, however, were the marks of a recent violent pressure, and William was seized with an uncontrollable anxiety about aunt Dinah which quite overcame his panic; and getting on his clothes, and making a preliminary survey of the gallery, which was still and empty, he hurried to Aunt Dinah door, and knocked.

"It's I—William. How are you, aunt? are you quite well?" asked he, in reply to her.

"Who's there? what's all that?"

"I, William."

"Come in, child; you may. I'm in my bed; what takes you out of yours?"

"I had a dream, and fancied you were in my room, and—and ill."

"Pooh, pooh, my dear William, get back to your room. It is all a fancy. I've been here in bed for an hour or more, reading my dear fathers's sermon on the Woman of Endor."

There she was, sitting up in a flannel dressing gown, with the sometime dean's large and legible manuscript before her, and no doubt investigating, with the lights thrown by Elihu Bung, the phenomena in which the witch of those remote times dealt.

"I heard you talk a little time ago," said Aunt Dinah, after a short and curious stare at William's pallid countenance.

"No," said William, "I didn't; I heard it too. It was that in fact that partly alarmed me. It is very odd."

"Were there knockings? inquired she.

"No, no knocking," said William; "it opened with a push."

"*What*, my dear?" demanded Aunt Dinah, sitting very erect as she gazed with a dark curiosity in William's face, and abandoned the dean's manuscript on the coverlet.

"The door," he answered. "It *is* very odd. It's the most horrid thing I ever heard of. I'm sorry I slept in that room."

———o———

CHAPTER LII.

NEXT MORNING.

Aunt Dinah leaned on her thin hand, looking with something like fear at William fixed and silently.

"What o'clock is it, aunt?" asked he.

"Three minutes to four," she replied, consulting her broad old gold watch, and then holding it to her ear. "Yes; three minutes to four. I thought it was later. You *saw* something, William Maubray—you *did*. You *have* seen something; haven't you?"

So William, bit by bit, scared and very uncomfortable, recounted his adventure, to which Miss Perfect listened attentively, and she said—

"Yes—it *is* remarkable—*very* wonderful—if anything can be said to be particularly so, where all is marvellous. I understand it, quite."

"And what is it? asked he.

"The spirit key again—my name and image—don't you see; and 'don't let me go,' and the other intimation—take it all together, it's quite plain."

"Do tell me, dear aunt, what you mean?"

"It all connects, dear William, with what I told you; the grasp of that hand links you with the spirit world; the image was mine—my *double*, I do suppose. Hand me that snuff-box. It spoke as if after my death; it urged upon you to maintain your correspondence with me—'don't let me go'—and it plainly intimates that I shall have the power of doing as I promised and certainly shall, in case you should meditate disregarding my solemn warning about your marriage, and think of uniting yourself, William dear, to any one, before the expiration of five years—there's the whole thing in a nutshell."

"May I sit here for a little?" asked William, who from childish years had been accustomed to visit his aunt's room often, and when she was ill used to sit there and read for her.

"Certainly, my dear; but don't go to sleep and fall into the fire."

Aunt Dinah resumed her sermon, with now and then a furtive reference to Elihu Bung, concealed under her pillow, and William Maubray sat near the bed with his feet on the fender; and thus for nearly five minutes—he looking on the bars, and she on her sermon and her volume of reference—at the end of that time she laid it again on the coverlet, and looked for some time thoughtfully on the back of William's head; and she said so suddenly as to make him start—

"Five years is nothing; it's quite ridiculous making a fuss about it. I've known girls engaged that time, and longer, too; for ten and even *twelve* years."

"Pretty girls they must have been by that time," thought William, who was recovering from the panic of his *vision*.

"And I think they made fonder couples than people that are married three weeks after their engagement," added Aunt Dinah. "Therefore *do* have a little patience."

"But I'm in no hurry about anything," said William; "least of all about marriage. I have not an idea; and if I had I *couldn't;* and my honest belief is I shall die an old bachelor."

"H'm! I never mind what people say on that subject," said Miss Perfect; "but I hope what you've experienced to-night will be a warning. Yes, dear William, I'm very glad it has happened; it is always well to know the *truth*—it may affright, but when it comes in the shape of warning it is always welcome—that is it ought to be. I needed nothing more to convince me, but you did, and you've got it. Depend upon it, if you disobey you are a ruined man all your days; and if I die before the time, I'll watch you as an old grey cat watches a mouse—ha, ha, ha! and if you so much as think of it, I'll plague you—I will. Yes, William, I'll save you in spite of yourself, and mortal was never haunted and tormented as you'll be, till you give it up."

William could not have forborne a joke, though a kindly one, upon such a speech at another time; but somehow now he could not. The spectre of Aunt Dinah cowering at his bedside was present with him; and when she bid him good-night, although he was ashamed to confess his trepidation, he hated a return to that old-fashioned room where he had twice experienced the same kind of visitation.

When he returned he made up his fire, drew his window curtains wide open to admit the earliest streak of sunrise, pulled his bed-curtains back to the posts, and placed his candle on the table in the centre of the room, resolved that Aunt Dinah's double should not at all events steal on him unawares.

At last the pleasant October morning came. The wind that had blown wildly in the night was quiet now, having left its spoil of yellow leaves strewn upon the lawn or rustling over the gravel walks.

The cheerful yellow light cleared the room of all unearthly shadows, and the song of birds refreshed his ears, as he made his early tiolet

The joyous bark of little Pysche scampering before the windows, the call of the driver to his team, the whistling of birds, the voices of the inmates of the house, and at last the laugh of Violet Darkwell from the porch.

Beautiful music! like merry spirits in the air, departing soon to be heard no more. He stood with his hand on his half open door—smiling—scarcely breathing—listening, as never did *Fanatico per la musica*, to the favourite roulade of Prima Donna. It ceased—he listened still, and then sighed in the silence, and seemed to himself to waken.

In his ear that music sounded sadly, and his heart was full as he ran down the stairs smiling. And pretty Violet's slender figure was leaning at the side of the porch; and she looked up, knowing his step, with a smile. The old kindly smile, for a moment, and then its character a little changed, something of the inscrutable but beautiful reverses of girlhood, which baffled, and interested, and pained William so. He would have liked to have called her Vi. The name was at his lips; but there was something of pride, which even thus, while his boat is on the shore and his bark is on the sea, restrained him.

"Miss—mind I'm calling you rightly—*Miss* Violet Darkwell, I'm so glad I've found you so early," he said, smiling, "my hours—I ought to say *minutes*—are so precious. I go at half-past ten, and I hardly saw or heard you last night, you were so anxious to be off."

"You forget how wise we all were, and wisdom, though it's a very good thing, is not lively; and its chief use, I suppose, is *that*—a sort of lullaby, for I'm sure nobody ever minds it. *You* don't, nor *I*, nor darling Grannie; and I think if you wanted to be put to sleep there would be nothing like having a tranquil old sage, like Winnie Dobbs, at your bedside to repeat a string of her sayings, like 'early to bed and early to rise make a man healthy, wealthy, and wise;' and besides being very wise, I think you were just, if it is not very disrespectful to say so, ever so little cross, so that altogether I thought it best to go to bed and to sleep as fast as I could."

"I quite forget. Was I cross? I dare say I was. I think ill-temper is one expression of suffering; and I have not been very happy lately," said William.

"You have been strangely misrepresented, then," said the young lady, slily.

"So I have; and I do so wish you'd stop about that nonsense. You can't conceive unless you knew the people——"

"I thought she was very pretty," interrupted Miss Darkwell, innocently.

"So she *is*—perhaps—I dare say; but pretty or plain, as I said before, I'm not in love with her. *I'm* not in love, thank heaven, with any one, and I——"

"Come in to prayers, William dear," Aunt Dinah called aloud from the parlour door. "I've had breakfast early, expressly for you, and you must not delay it."

———o———

CHAPTER LIII.

THE FLOWER.

At breakfast the little party had a great deal to talk about, topics of hope, and topics of regret, glanced at in all sorts of spirits, sad and cheerful, black spirits and white, blue spirits and grey but on the whole one would have said, looking on and a stranger to all that was possibly passing within, that it was a cheerful meal.

"Five miles and a half to the Station, and the up train at 'eleven forty-five.' The cab, or whatever it is, will be here at half-past ten, and then good-by. Farewell, perhaps, for three years to Gilroyd," so said William, as he and Violet Darkwell stood side by side, looking out from the window, upon the glowing autumnal landscape.

"Three years! you don't mean to say you'd stay away all that time, without ever coming to see Grannie"

"Of course if she wants me I'll come; but should she *not*, and should she at the same time continue, as I hope she will, quite well, and should *I* be kept close to my work, as I expect, it's sure to turn out as I say. Three years—yes, it *is* a long time—room for plenty of changes, and changes enough, great ones, there *will* be, no doubt."

The uplands of Revington formed the background of the pretty prospect before him, and it needed the remembrance of the promise he had made to Aunt Dinah to prevent his speaking with less disguise, for he always felt of late an impetuous longing, almost fierce, to break through conventional hypocrisies, and lay bare his wounded heart, and upbraid, and implore, in the wildest passion before Violet Darkwell. To be alone with her, and yet say nothing of all that was swelling and rolling at his heart—was pain. And yet to be alone with her, even in this longing and vain anguish, and near her was a strange despairing delight.

"Oh, yes, everyone changes every day almost, except dear Grannie and old Winnie Dobbs. I'm sure *I* change, and so do you, and what won't three years do? You've changed very much, and not for the better," and saying this Miss Violet laughed.

"My changes, be they what they may, don't seem to trouble you much," replied William.

"Trouble?—not at all. I dare say they are improvements, though I don't like them," laughed she.

"I don't think I'm a *bit* changed. I *know* I'm not, in fact. Tell me any one thing in which I am changed."

"Well, it is *generally*; you have grown so disagreeable, that's all—it is not much to me, but I dare say it will be to other people," said she.

"I'm disagreeable—yes, of course—because I have my opinion about men and things, and fools and nonsense. I don't know anything I've said to you, at least since I came yesterday, that could annoy you. I have not mentioned a single subject that could possibly even interest you. I dare say it is tiresome my talking so much as Aunt Dinah makes me, about myself. But I couldn't help it."

"It won't do, William; you know very well how cross you always are now, at least with me, not that I mind it much, but there's no denying."

"You accused me of that before, and I said I was sorry. I—perhaps I am. I'm going away, and everything breaking up, you know, and you must make allowances. I used not to be cross long ago, and I'm *not* changed. No—I'm the same—I never said an unkind word to you, Vi, all the time when you were a little thing, and if I ever speak differently now, it is not from unkindness, only that things have gone wrong with me, and I've seen something of the world; and things happen to sour one, and—I don't know—but I'm *not* changed. You mustn't think it now that I'm going away. I'm such a fool, I'm such a beast, I can't help talking bitterly sometimes, and sometimes I think I am a—a *fiend* almost, but I hope I am not as bad as I seem."

So spoke this Penruddock, who fancied himself soured for life, and soliloquized at times in the vein of Elshender of Muckle-stane Muir, but still cherished at the age of three-and-twenty some sparks of his original humanity.

"There goes Tom with my things to the gate. Yes, it ought to be here now," said William, looking at his watch. "I'll send you something pretty from Paris if you let me; nothing very splendid, you know, only a little reminder such as a poor beggar like me can offer," and he laughed, not very merrily. "And I shall hear all the news from Aunt Dinah, and send her all mine; and I like flowers. I always remember the Gilroyd flowers along with you. You were always among them, you know, and will you give me that little violet—a namesake. No one ever refuses a flower, it is the keepsake every one gets for the asking."

"Here it is," said Violet, with a little laugh, but looking not mockingly, but a little downward and oddly, and William placed it very carefully in a recess of his complicated purse, that was a cardcase also, and I know not what else beside. He was on the point of saying something very romantic and foolish, but suddenly recollected himself, and pulled up at the verge just before he went over.

"This is a souvenir of very old days, you know," said William, remembering Trevor, how humiliating because vain any love-making of his own must prove, "of a very early friend—one of your earliest. Wasn't I?"

"Yes, so you were, a very good-natured friend, and very useful. Sometimes a little bit prosy, you know, always giving me excellent advice; and I think I always, *often*, at least, listened to your lectures with respect. But why is it, will *you* tell me who know everything, that gentlemen always ask for a rose or a violet, or a flower of some sort, as a keepsake? Nothing so perishable. Would not a thimble or even a slipper be better? I suppose you have us all in what you used to call a *hortus siccus*, brown roses, and yellow violets, and venerable polyanthuses, thoroughly dried up and stiff as chips, and now and then with a sort of triumph review your prisoners, and please yourselves with these awful images of old maidhood. How can we tell what witchcrafts go on over our withering types and emblems. Give me back my violet and you shall have a hair-pin instead."

"Many thanks; I'll keep my violet, however. It may grow dry and brown to other eyes to mine it will never change. Just because it is an enchanted violet, and there is a spell upon my eyes as often as I look on it, and the glow and fragrance will never pass away."

"Very good song, and very well sung! only *I* suspect that's the usual speech, and you asked for the violet for an opportunity of making it."

At this moment Aunt Dinah entered the room, accompanied by old Winnie Dobbs, supporting a small hamper, tray fashion. William recognised the old commissariat of Gilroyd in this nutritious incumbrance, against which he had often and vainly protested, as he now did more faintly by a smile and lifting his hands.

"Now there's really very little in this; just a fowl cut up, half a ham, one of the Saxton plumcakes, and a pint bottle with a little sherry. You'll find bread by itself, and some salt in white paper, and a few Ripston pippins, and it is really no weight at all; is it, Winnie?"

"No, nothing to them porter fellows. What else be they paid for, if it baint to carry loads; what's a hamper like this here to one of them? and he'll want something on the way. You'll be hungry, you will, Master William."

"And whatever's left will be of use to you when you reach your destination," said Aunt Dinah, repeating her ancient formula on similar occasions. "Now, William, you promise me you'll not leave this behind. Surely you can't be such a fool as to be ashamed to take a little refreshment before the passengers. Well-bred people won't stare at you, and I know you won't vex me by refusing the little provision."

So William laughed and promised, and Miss Vi looked as if she could have quizzed him, but at this moment the Saxton vehicle from the Golden Posts pulled up at the iron gate of Gilroyd, and William glanced at his watch, and though he smiled, it was with the pale smile of a man going to execution, and trying to cheer his friends rather than being of good comfort himself.

———o———

CHAPTER LIV.

DOCTOR DRAKE GOES TO GILROYD.

"And now I must say farewell, and if I *can*, or if you want me, I'll come soon and see you again; and God bless you, Violet; and goodbye, my darling Aunt. I'll write from London this evening, and let you know what my Paris address will be."

"God Almighty bless you, my precious man, Willie; and I'm very glad—" and here Aunt Dinah's sentence broke short, and tears were in her eyes, and she bit her lips. "I *am*, my darling, Willie, that we met; and you'll really come soon, if I write for you; and you won't forget your Bible and your prayers; and, oh! goodness gracious! have you forgot the tobacco-box?"

It was safe in his dressing-case. So another hurried farewell, and a smiling and kissing of hands. "Good-by, good-by!" from the cab window; and away it rattled, and William was gone; and the two ladies, and old Winnie in the rear, stood silently looking for a minute or so where the carriage had been, and then they turned, with the faded smile of farewell still on their faces, and slowly re-entered old Gilroyd Hall, which all in a moment had grown so lonely.

In the drawing-room they were silent. Violet was looking through the window, but not, I think, taking much note of the view, pretty as it is.

"I'm going away, and everything breaking up, and you must make allowances"—William's words were in her lonely ears now. A break-up had partly come, and a greater was coming. William's words sounded like a prophecy. "Breaking-up." Poor Gilroyd! Many a pleasant summer day and winter evening had she known in that serene old place.

Pleasant times, no doubt, were before her—a more splendid home, perhaps. Still memory would always look back regretfully on those early times, and the familiar view of Gilroyd; its mellow pink-tinted brick, and window-panes, flashing in the setting sun, half seen through the stooping branches of the old chestnuts, would rise kindly and quaint before her, better beloved than the new and colder glories that might await her. Had the break-up indeed come? There was a foreboding of change, a presage as of death at her heart. When she looked at Miss Perfect she saw that she had been crying, and it made her heart heavier.

"Remember, he said he'd come to you whenever you write. You can bring him back whenever you please; and really Paris is no distance at all."

"I don't know, little Violet, I'm very low, It's all very true, what you say, but I've a misgiving. I've looked my last on my fine fellow—my boy. If I did as I am prompted, I think I should follow him to London, just to have one look more."

"You're tired, Grannie, darling, and you look pale; you must have a little wine."

"Pooh, child—no—nothing," said Aunt Dinah, with a flicker of her usual manner; but there was a fatigue and feebleness in her look which Violet did not like.

"Give me my desk, like a darling," said Miss Perfect; and she wrote a note, pondering a good while over it; and she leaned back, tired, when she had completed it. "I did my duty by him, I hope. I think he does me credit—a handsome fellow! I don't see anywhere——"

There was a pause here, and a kind of groan, and, coming near, Violet Darkwell saw that she had fainted.

Great commotion was there in Gilroyd Hall. Miss Perfect's seizure did not pass away like a common swoon. Away went Tom for Doctor Drake, and Vi and the servants got poor Aunt Dinah, cold, and breathing heavily, and still insensible, to her bed.

Dr. Drake arrived quickly, and came up to her room, with his great coat buttoned up to his chin, looking rather stern, in a reserved but friendly sort of fuss.

"Hey—yes, yes—*there* it *is*. How long ago did this happen, my dear?"

"Not quite half an hour—in the drawing-room. Oh, Doctor Drake, is it anything very bad?" answered Violet.

"Well, my dear, it's—it's serious—but I hope it will be all right; it's a smart, little attack of apoplexy—upon my word it is. There was no convulsion—that's right. It was very well he came when he did—just caught me at the door. Open the window and door. Mrs. Dobbs, give me cold water. Have *you* a scissors? We'll cut the strings of her dress and stay-lace. One of you run down and bring up a kettleful of hot water. Her feet are a little cold. Get her head up a little more. We'll get her sitting up, if you please, in this armchair here. We'll bathe her feet, and you'll see she'll do very well, presently. It's not a case for bleeding; and bring up mustard. I think you'll see she'll come round in a little time."

And so on the doctor talked; and directed, and actively treated his patient; and in a little time consciousness returned, and there was time at last, to think of William Maubray.

"Shall we telegraph a message to London?" asked Violet.

"Not a bit; she's going on as nicely as possible. He'd only be in the way here, and it would frighten her. She's doing capitally; and she may never have a return, if she just takes care. She *must* take *care*, you know, and I'll give you full directions how to treat her."

And so he did; Miss Vi being accurate and intelligent, and rising with the occasion, so that Doctor Drake that evening celebrated Miss Darkwell to his friend Dignum, of the Golden Posts, as a trump and a brick, and the nicest little creature he ever saw, almost.

Mr. Vane Trevor, who had called at Gilroyd that morning, but found all things in confusion and panic, called again in the evening, and had the pleasure of an interview with Winnie Dobbs; but he could not see Miss Darkwell. The young lady had given peremptory directions respecting all visitors, and would not leave Miss Perfect's room.

Doctor Drake was honoured that evening by a call from the proprietor of Revington, and gave him a history of the case; and Trevor accompanied him back again to Gilroyd, where he was about to make his evening visit, and awaited his report in the little gravel court-yard, stealing, now and then, a wastful glance up to the old-fashioned stone-faced windows. But Violet did not appear. It might have been different—I can't say—had she known all that had passed between Miss Perfect and Vane Trevor respecting her. As it was, the young gentleman's long wait was rewarded only by the return of Doctor Drake, and a saunter with him back again to Saxton.

Pretty nearly the same was the routine of several subsequent days. Fruits and vegetables, too, with messages came down from Revington; and in his interviews with old Winnie Dobbs he betrayed a great solicitude that the young lady should not wear herself out with watching and attendance.

On Sunday he was in the church-yard almost as early as the doors opened, and loitered there till the bell ceased ringing; and sat in his pew so as to command an easy view of the church door, and not a late arrival escaped his observation. But Violet Darkwell did not appear; and Vane Trevor walked home with little comfort from the Rev. Dr. Wagget's learned sermon; and made his usual calls at Gilroyd and at Doctor Drake's, and began to think seriously of writing to Violet, and begging an interview, or even penning the promptings of his ardent passion in the most intelligible terms. And I have little doubt that had he had a friend by him, to counsel him ever so little in that direction, he would have done so.

——o——

CHAPTER LV.

SUSPENSE.

One day Trevor actually made up his mind to bring about the crisis; and, pale as a man about to be hanged, and with the phantom of a smile upon his lips, after his accustomed inquiries, he told Mrs. Podgers, the cook, who, in the absence of Winnie Dobbs, officiated as hall-porter, to ask Miss Violet Darkwell if she would be so good as to give him just a moment. And on getting through his message his heart made two or three such odd jumps and rolls, that he was almost relieved when she told him that old Doctor Wagget had come by appointment, and that Miss Violet and Winnie were receiving the sacrament with the mistress, who, thank God, was getting on better every day.

"It's wiser for me to wait," thought Trevor, as he walked away, determined to take a long ride through the Warren, and over Calston Moor, and to tire himself effectually. "They never think what they're doing, girls are so hand-over-head—by Jove, if she had not Miss Perfect to talk to she might refuse me, and be awfully sorry for it in a day or two. I must only have patience, and wait till the old woman is better. I forget how the woman said she is to-day. No matter—old Drake will tell me. It's hanged unlucky, I know. I suppose she eat too much dinner with that great fellow, Maubray; or some nonsense—however, I'll think it over in my ride; or, by Jove, I'll take my gun and have a shot at the rabbits."

Miss Perfect was, indeed, better, and Doctor Drake, though a little reserved, spoke on the whole, cheerily about her. And she saw a good deal of her kind old friend, Parson Wagget; and also, was pronounced well enough to see her lawyer, Mr. Jones, not that Doctor Drake quite approved of business yet, but he thought that so eager a patient as Miss Perfect might suffer more from delay and disappointment. So there were a few quiet interviews on temporal matters.

William was a little disquieted at receiving no letter from Gilroyd for some days after his arrival. But there came at last a short one from Doctor Drake, which mentioned that he had seen the ladies at Gilroyd that morning—both as well as he could desire; and that Miss Perfect had got into a troublesome dispute with some tenants, which might delay her letter a little longer, and then it passed to shooting anecdotes and village news. Such as it was, he welcomed it fondly—enclosing as it did the air of Gilroyd—passing, as it must have done, in its Town-ward flight from Saxton, the tall gait of Gilroyd, penned by the hand which had touched Violet Darkwell's that very day, and conned over by eyes on whose retinas her graceful image lingered still. Even tipsy Dr. Drake's letter was inexpressibly interesting, and kept all the poetry of his soul in play for that entire evening.

Miss Violet consulted with Miss Wagget, and agreed that in a day or two they might write a full account of Miss Perfect's attack and recovery to William, whom it had been judged best, while there was still any anxiety, to spare the suspense of a distant and doubtful illness.

But this is an uncertain world. The message, when it did go, went not by post but by telegraph, and was not of the cheery kind they contemplated.

When William returned to his lodgings that evening, oddly enough projecting a letter to Aunt Dinah, in the vein of the agreeable Baron de Grimm, whose correspondence he had been studying, he found upon his table a telegram, only half an hour arrived.

It was sent "from the Rev. J. Wagget, Saxton Rectory, to M. William Maubray," &c., &c., and said simply—

"Miss Perfect is dangerously ill. Come to Gilroyd immediately."

A few hours later William was speeding northward in the dark, for a long time the only occupant of his carriage, looking out from time to time from the window, and wondering whether train had ever dragged so tediously before—thinking every moment of Gilroyd and dear old Aunt Dinah—reading the telegram over and over, and making for it sometimes a cheery, and sometimes the most portentous interpretation; then leaning back with closed eyes, and picturing a funereal groupe receiving him with tears, on the door-steps at home. Then again looking out on the gliding landscape, and in his dispairing impatience pressing his foot upon the opposite seat as if to impel the lagging train.

When William reached London he found at his old lodgings two letters, one from Doctor Sprague, the other from Miss Perfect, which had been lying there for some days. Having a wait of two hours for his train he was glad to find even this obsolete intelligence. That which, of course, interested him most was written with a very aged tremble in the hand, and was very short, but bore the signature of "poor old auntie." It was as follows—

"My dear Willie,

"I suppose they given you some account

of my indisposition—not much, and need not not you be disquieted. My old head is a little confused, some medicine I dare say, but shall well again in a day or two two. This note is under the rose. The doctor says I must not write, so you need not it. I have eaten a morsel for three days—so the pen a little. Do remember, dear boy, all told you, dear, about the five years. I dreamed much since. If you think of such a thing, I must do it. Willie, sorry I should be you shoul fear or dislike me. I should haunt torment Willie. But you will do right. When you go go to France, I will send £4 to amuse yourself with sights, &c. And Heaven bless and guard my precious Willie by every and influence, says his fond

"poor old AUNTIE.

"Better."

William Maubray's trouble increased on reading this letter. The slips and oddities of style instinctively alarmed him. There was something very bad the matter, he was sure. The letter was eight days old, the telegram scarce four-and-twenty hours. But however ill she might be, it was certain she was living when the message was despatched. So he went on assuring himself, although there lay on his mind a dreadful misgiving that he was summoned not to a sick bed, nor even to a death-bed, but to a funeral.

Early that evening William drove from the station toward Gilroyd. The people at Dolworth had heard nothing of Miss Perfect's illness. How should they living so far away, and hardly ever seeing a Saxton face, and not caring enough about her to be very likely to inquire.

At last, at the sudden turn in the road, as it crosses the brow of Drindle Hill, the pretty little place, the ruddy brick and tall chestnuts, touched with the golden smile of sunset, and throwing long gray shadows over the undulating grass, revealed themselves. The small birds were singing their pleasant vespers, and the crows sailing home to the woods of Wyndleford, mottled the faint green sky, and filled the upper air with their mellowed cawings. The very spirit of peace seemed dreaming there! Pretty Gilroyd!

Now he was looking on the lawn, and could see the hall-door. Were the blinds down? He was gazing at Aunt Dinah's windows, but a cross-shadow prevented his seeing distinctly. There was no one on the steps, no one at the drawing-room window, not a living thing on the lawn. And now that view of Gilroyd was hidden from his eyes, and they were driving round the slope of the pretty road to the old iron gate, where, under the long shadow of the giant ash tree opposite, they pulled up. The driver had already run at the gateway.

Pushing his way through the wicket, William Maubray had reached the porch before any sign of life encountered him. There he was met by honest Tom. He looked awfully dismal and changed, as if he had not eaten, or slept, or spoken for ever so long. Aunt Dinah was dead. Yes, she was dead. And three or four dark shadows, deeper and deeper, seemed to fall on all around him, and William Maubray went into the parlour, and leaning on the chimney-piece, wept bitterly, with his face to the wall.

———o———

CHAPTER LVI.

SOME PARTICULARS.

THE air is forlorn—the house is vocal no more—love is gone.

"When was it, Tom, at what hour?" asked he.

"Late cock-crow, just the gray of the morning. She was always early, poor little thing—somewhere betwixt five and six—it must 'a' bin. Will you please have something a'ter your ride?"

"Nothing, Tom, nothing, thanks, but I'd like very much to see Winnie. Call her, Tom, and I'll wait here—or no—I'll be in the drawing-room, tell her."

And to that room he went, standing for a while at the threshold, and making his desolate survey; and then to the window, and then from place to place.

The small table at which she used to sit in the evenings stood in its old place by the sofa. Her little basket of coloured worsted balls, the unfinished work with the ivory crotchet-needles stuck through it, were there awaiting the return that was not to be. There lay the old piano open. How well he knew that little oval landscape over the notes mellow by time, the lake and ruined tower, and solitary fisherman—poor enough, I dare say, as a work of art; but to William's mind always the sweetest and saddest little painting the world contained. Under that roofless tower that lonely fisherman there had heard all Violet's pretty music, and before it poor Aunt Dinah's grand and plaintive minutes, until, years ago, she had abdicated the music-stool in favour of the lighter finger and the rich young voice.

He remembered dear Aunt Dinah's face as she, sitting by that little table there, would lower her book or letter and listen to the pretty girl's song, sadly, in some untold poetry of memory. Oh, Aunt Dinah!—He did not know till now how much you were to him—how much of Gilroyd itself was in your kindly old face. The walls of Gilroyd speak and smile no more.

He heard old Winnie Dobbs talking to Tom in the passage, and her slow foot approaching. Poor Aunt Dinah's light step and pleasant tones would come no more on stair or lobby.

Such a welcome at Gilroyd, or anywhere, as the old one, for him would be no more—no, nowhere—never.

In came old Winnie. Could old Winnie be quite old Winnie, and Aunt Dinah gone? The yearnings of love were strong within him, and he hugged good old Dobbs on the threshold, and her fat arms were round him, and her fat fingers were grotesquely patting his back, and the sounds of sobbing were heard by the servants in the kitchen through the silent house. At last old Winnie, drying her eyes, related all she had to tell.

"It happened, early this morning, a little before sunrise, she went very quit—like a child. She talked a deal about Master William, when she was well enough, an' more loving-like than ever. She did not wish to live; but she thought she would though—ay, she thought she'd do well, poor thing. Miss Vi was with her all the time—she was breaking her heart like about it; and Miss Wagget came down in the carriage, and took her away wi' her—and better, sure it was. This was no place for her—poor Miss Vi. Doctor Drake was very kind, and sat up all the night wi' her. And sure was Winnie, if doctors could a' saved her she would a' bin on her feet still; but everyone has their time. It's right, of course, to have the doctors in; but, dear me, we all know 'tis no more use than nothink—there's a time you know and all is one, first or last. I have mine, and you yours, and she had hers—the dear mistress; and time and tide waits for no man; and as the tree falleth so it lieth; and man is born unto trouble, as the sparks fly upward—and, indeed, *that's* true, dear knows. Would you like to see her, Master William?"

"Does she look happy—does she look like herself?" inquired William.

"Ah! that she does—asleep like, you'd say. You never saw quieter—just her own face. She is a very pretty corpse—poor little thing, she is."

"Perhaps, by-and-by—*not* yet. I could not now. You'll come with me to her room, perhaps, in a little while, *perhaps*. But oh! Winnie, I don't think I could bear it."

"It is not in her room," said Winnie Dobbs. "She was very particular, you know, poor little thing, and would have her way; and she left a note in the looking-glass drawer for the Rector—Mr. Wagget, you know, that now is; and she made him promise it should be done as ordered, and so he did—only a scrap of a note, no bigger than a playing card; and I don't think you knew, unless she told you, but she had her coffin in the house this seven years—nigh eight a'most—upright in the little press be the left of the bed, in her room—the cupboard-like in the wall. Dearie me! 'twas an odd fancy, poor little thing, and she'd dust it, and take it out, she would, wi' the door locked, her and me, once a month. She had a deal o' them queer fancies, she had; but she was very good, she was—very good to every one, and a great many will miss her."

And old Winnie cried again.

"I knew it must a' happened some time for certain—her or me must go—but who'd a' thought 'twas to be so soon?—who'd a' thought it ever? There's a great plate, silvered over, wi' her name on't, as Doctor Wagget took away to get her years and date put on; 'twill be back again to-morrow—poor thing—and she's not in her room—out in the gardener's house."

This was a disused out-building; for it was many a year since Gilroyd had boasted a gardener among its officers.

"Do you mean to say she has been carried out *there?*" inquired William, in unfeigned astonishment.

"Them was her directions—the little note as I told you—and Doctor Wagget went by her orders strict, as he said he would; and sure 'twas right he should, for she would not be denied."

So this odd conversation proceeded, and, indeed, with this strange direction of poor Aunt Dinah's, whose coffin lay on tressels in the little tiled room in the small two-storied cubical brick domicile, which stood even with the garden wall, old Winnie's revelations ended.

William walked down to Saxton, and had a long talk with Doctor Drake, who was always sober up to nine o'clock, about poor Aunt Dinah's case; and he wrote to Doctor Wagget, not caring to present himself at the Rectory so late, to report his arrival. And in the morning Doctor Wagget came down and saw him at Gilroyd, when a conversation ensued, which I am about to relate.

———o———

CHAPTER LVII.

DOCTOR WAGGETT: FURTHER PARTICULARS.

Doctor Waggett found William in the study at Gilroyd; he met him without the conventional long face, and with a kindly look, and a little sad, and shaking his hand warmly, he said,

"Ah, sir, your good aunt, my old friend, Miss Perfect, we've lost her. My loss is small compared with yours, but I can grieve with you."

The Doctor laid his hat, and gloves, and cane upon the table, and fixing his earnest eyes on William, he went on—

"We had a great deal of conversation in her last illness which will interest you. On religious subjects I found her views—poor lady—all very sound; indeed, if it had not been for that foolish spirit-rapping, which a little led her away—that is, confused her—I don't think there was anything in her opinions to which exception could have been taken. She had the sacrament twice, and I visited and prayed with her constantly, and very devout and earnest she was, and indeed her mind was in a very happy state—very serene and hopeful."

"Thank you, sir, it is a great comfort."

"And about that spiritualism, mind you, I don't say there's *nothing* in it," continued the Rector, "there *may* be a great deal—in fact, a great deal too much—but take it what way we may, to my mind, it is too like what Scripture deals with as witchcraft to be tampered with. If there be no familiar spirit, it's *nothing*, and if there be, *what* is it? I talked very fully with the poor lady the last day but one I saw her on this subject, to which indeed she led me. I hope you don't practise it—no—that's right; nothing would induce *me* to sit at a séance, I should as soon think of praying to the devil. I don't say, of course, that every one who does is as bad as I should be; it depends in some measure on the view you take. The spirit world is veiled from us, no doubt in mercy—in mercy, sir, and we have no right to lift that veil; few do with impunity; but of that another time. She made a will, you know?"

"No, I did not hear."

"Oh, yes; Jones drew it; it's in my custody; it leaves you everything. It is not a very great deal, you know; two annuities die with her; but it's somewhere about four hundred a year, Jones says, and this house. So it makes you quite easy, you see."

To William, who had never paid taxes, and knew nothing of servants' wages, four hundred a year and a house was Alladdin's lamp. The pale image of poor Aunt Dinah came with a plaintive smile, making him this splendid gift, and he burst into years.

"I wish, sir, I had been better to her. She was always so good to me. Oh, sir, I'd give anything, I would, for a few minutes to tell her how much I really loved her; I'm afraid she did not know."

"Pooh! she knew very well. You need not trouble yourself on that point. You were better to her than a son to a mother. You are not to trouble yourself about that little—a—a—difference of opinion about taking orders; for I tell you plainly, she was wrong, and you were right; one of her fancies, poor little thing. But that's not a matter to be trifled with, it's a very awful step; I doubt whether we make quite solemnity enough about it; there are so few things in life irrevocable; but however that may be, you are better as you are, and there's nothing to reproach yourself with on that head. When I said, by-the-bye, that she had left you everything, I ought to have excepted her little jewellery, which she has left to Miss Darkwell, and a few books to me, that mad fellow, Bung, you know, among them, and an old silver salver to Saxton church, which there was a tradition was stolen by a Puritan tenant of Sir—what's-his name—that had the tobacco-box, you know, from some church, she did not know what, in this county, when his troop was quartered at Hentley Towers. And—and she had a fancy it was that spirit, Henbane, you know, that told her to restore it to the church—*any* church—and there are a few trifling legacies, you know, and that's all."

Then their conference diverged into the repulsive details of the undertaker, where we need not follow, and this over, the Rector said:—

"You must come down and see us at the Rectory; Miss Darkwell, you know, is with us at present; something likely to be in that quarter very soon, you are aware," he added, significantly; "very advantageous, everything, but all this, you know, delays it for a time; you'll come over and see us, as often as you like; a very pretty walk across the fields—nothing to a young athlete like you, sir, and we shall always be delighted to see you."

Well, this dreadful week passed over, and another, and William Maubray resigned his appointment at Paris, and resolved on the bar; and with Mr. Sergeant Darkwell's advice, ordered about twenty pounds' worth of law-books, to begin with, and made arrangements to enter his name at Lincoln's Inn, which was the learned Sergeant's, and to follow in the steps of that, the most interesting of all the sages of the law, past or present.

Vane Trevor looked in upon William very often. Gilroyd, William Maubray, even the servants, interested him; for there it was, and thus surrounded, he had seen Miss Violet Darkwell. There, too, he might talk of her; and William, too, with a bitter sort of interest, would listen, an angry contempt of Vane rising at his heart; yet he did not quite hate him, though he would often have been glad to break his head.

Trevor, too, had his grounds for vexation.

"I thought she'd have gone to church last Sunday," he observed to Maubray, and I must allow that he had made the same statement in various forms of language no less than five times in the course of their conversation. "I think she might; don't you? I can't see why she should not; can you? The relationship between her and poor Miss Perfect was a very round-about affair; wasn't it?"

"Yes, so it was; but it isn't that—I told you before it couldn't be that; its just that she was so fond of her; and really, here, I don't see any great temptation to come out; do you?"

"No—perhaps—no, of course, there may not; but I don't see any great temptation to shut one's self up either. I called at the Rectory yesterday, and did not see her. I have not seen her since poor Miss Perfect's death, in fact."

"So did I; I've called very often," answered William; "as often as you, I dare say, and I have not seen her; and that's odder, don't you think? and I gather from it, I suppose, pretty much what you do."

"Very likely; what is it?" said Vane.

"I mean that she doesn't expect much comfort or pleasure from our society."

William had a fierce and ill-natured pleasure in placing his friend Trevor in the same boat with himself, and then scuttling it.

Vane remarked that the rain was awfully tiresome, and then looking from the window, whistled an air from "I Puritani" abstractedly, and he said suddenly—

"There's a lot of affectation, I think, about grief—particularly among women—they like making a fuss about it."

"To be sure they do," replied William

"when any one dies they make such a row—and lock themselves up—and all but take the veil; but, by Jove, they don't waste much compassion on the living. There are you, for instance, talking and thinking all day, and night-mared all night about her, and for anything you know she never troubles her head about you. It's awfully ridiculous, the whole thing."

"I thought you said she was very fond of your poor aunt!" said Vane, a little nettled.

"So I did—so she was—I was speaking of *us*—*you* and *me*—you know. I'm an old friend—the earliest she has almost—and you are a lover—no one's listening—you need not be afraid—and you see how much she distinguishes—by Jove, she likes old Wagget better!" and William laughed with dismal disgust, and proposed a walk—to which Vane, with a rueful impression that he was a particularly disagreeable fellow, acceded.

——o——

CHAPTER LVIII.

REVINGTON FLOWERS.

That very afternoon William did see Violet Darkwell; and he fancied he never saw her look so pretty as in her black silk dress. There was no crying—no scene—she met him gravely and sadly in the old-fashioned drawing-room of the Rectory, and was frankly glad to see him, and her wayward spirit seemed quite laid. His heart smote him for having acquiesced in Trevor's fancy that there could be affectation in her grief.

Good Miss Wagget being in a fuss with the schoolmistress of the Saxton Ragged School (why will benevolent people go on leavening the bread of knowledge which they offer with the bitterness of that insulting epithet?)—counting out copy-books, and primers, and slate-pencils, and rustling to and fro from the press to the hall-table, where they were getting those treasures into order—was little in the way of their conversation, except for an interjectional word now and then, or a smile or a nod, as she bustled in and out of the room, talking still to the matron in the hall.

Violet had a great deal to ask about told Winnie Dobbs, and the servants, and even little Psyche, and the bird, which latter inmate William did not somehow love, and regarded him in the light of an intruder who had established himself under false pretences, and was there with a design.

"I think papa means to take me with him to London," said Violet, in reply to William's question, "Mr. and Mrs. Wagget—they are so kind—I think they would make me stay here a long time, if he would let me; but he says he will have a day in about three weeks; and will run down and see us, and I think he intends taking me away."

"What can the meaning of that be?" thought William. "More likely he comes to see Trevor, and bring matters to a decisive issue of some sort," and his heart sank at the thought; but why should William suffer these foolish agitations—had he not bid her farewell in his silent soul long ago? What of this business of Trevor of Rivington! Was it not the same to him in a day, or three weeks, or a year, since be it must! And thus stoically armed, he looked up and saw Violet Darkwell's large eyes and oval face, and felt the pang again.

"In three weeks? Oh! I'm *sorry* if he's to take you away—but I was thinking of going up to town to see him—about the bar—he has been so kind, and there are two or three things I want advice about; I'm going to the bar, you know."

"Papa seems always doubtful whether it is a good profession," said Miss Violet, wisely, "though he has succeeded very well; but it's sad, don't you think, being so shut away from one's friends as he is?"

"Well, for him I'm sure it is—in his case, I mean. I miss him I know, and so do you, I'm sure. But *my* case would be very different. I've hardly a friend on earth to be cut off from. There's *he*, and Doctor Sprague, and Doctor Wagget here, and there's poor Winnie, and Tom—I can count them up you see, on the fingers of one hand—and I really don't think I've another friend on earth; and some of these I could see still, and none I think would miss me, very much; and the best friends I believe, as Doctor Wagget says, are books, they never die, or what's worse, change; they are always the same, and won't go away, and they speak to you as they used to do, and always show you the same faces as long as you have sight to look at them."

"How sensible and amiable of Doctor Wagget to like his Johnson's Dictionary so much better than his sister," exclaimed Miss Vi, with a momentary flash of her old mood. "There's certainly one thing about books, as you say, they NEVER grow disagreeable; and if there—" she was going to be sarcastic, but she reined in her fancy, and said sadly, instead, "About books I know very little—nothing; and about friends—you and I have lost the best friend we'll ever know."

And as she spoke tears glimmered under her lashes, and she looked out of the window over the wooded slope toward Gilroyd, and after a little pause said in a gentle, cheerful voice, with perhaps a little effort—

"How pretty it all looks to-day, the slanting sun—poor Grannie used to like it so—and it *is* the sweetest light in the world, look!"

And William did look out on the familiar landscape, faintly gilded in that aerial light, and looking still he said—

"You ought to come over some day with Miss Wagget, to see old Winnie."

"I should like very much in a little time, but not now; it would be very sad. I was looking at it from a distance, yesterday, from where you see the ash tree there; you know that view; Gilroyd looks so pretty from it; but I could not go in yet. I feel as if I never could go into the house again."

"And about friends," she resumed, "I sometimes think one has more than one suspects. Of course you like them differently in degree —and differently even in the—the kind of liking, I reckon little Psyche among *my* friends."

"And the bird?" said William.

"Yes, the bullfinch," said Miss Vi, firmly; and at this moment Miss Wagget entered the room with a great bouquet in her hand, and exclaimed—

"Isn't this perfectly beautiful; it's positively *wonderful* for this time of year; look at it, my dear, all from the conservatory. It's a very nice taste. I wonder how he keeps it so beautifully, and very kind, I'm sure, to think of us; these are Revington flowers, Mr. Maubray. It is very kind of Mr. Trevor; you'll arrange them, won't you dear?"

This was addressed to the young lady, and at the same time she held the bouquet toward William, to gaze on, and he stooped over and smelled at the flowers, which were really odourless, in some confusion, and then turned his eyes on Violet, who blushed first a little, and then in a brilliant glow all over her face, and William looked down and smelled at the flowers again, and then he recollected it was time for him to go; so he bid Miss Wagget good-bye, and took his leave of Violet, whose large eyes he thought, looked vexed, and on whose cheeks the fading scarlet still hovered; had he ever beheld her so handsome before, or with a sadder gaze; and he took her hand extended to him rather coldly, he fancied, and with a pale smile left the room, feeling as if he had just heard his sentence read. So he stood on the steps for a moment, bewildered, and answered good Doctor Wagget's cheery salutation and pleasantry that issued from the study window, rather confusedly.

——o——

CHAPTER LIX.

VANE TREVOR SEES MISS VIOLET.

NEXT morning William was surprised by a visit from Vane Trevor.

"Just dropped in to see how you are, old fellow, this morning."

"Very good of you," rejoined William with ironical gravity.

"Well, but *are* you well—is there anything wrong?" inquired Vane, who was struck by his friend's savage and distracted looks.

"Nothing—I'm quite well; what could go wrong with a fellow so magnificently provided for? The Lord of Gilroyd, with such lots of small talk, and fine friends, and lavender gloves, and clothes cut so exquisitely in the fashion," and William laughed rather horribly.

"Well, I admit you might get better traps, and if you like decent clothes, why the devil don't you?"

Trevor could perceive that the whole of William's ironical sally was inspired by envy of him, and was gratified accordingly; and thought within himself, "Your shy, gawky, ill-dressed men always hate a jolly fellow with a good coat to his back just because the women know the difference, and I wonder where poor Maubray has been trying his arts and fascinations, he has been awfully shut up, that's clear," so thought Vane Trevor, as he added aloud—

"If you're going to London, as you say, I'll give you a note with pleasure to my man, if you like the sort of things he makes," said Trevor; "but I give you notice he won't do his best unless you seem to—to take an interest, you know."

"Thanks—no," laughed William, a little fiercely, the tailor might do his office, but I should still want too many essentials. Where would be the good in that sort of thing without the rest, and I never *could* go the whole animal—the whole *brute*, and if I could I *would* not. You may smile—"

"I am *not* smiling."

"But I swear to you I wouldn't."

"Oh, you're very well," said Trevor, encouragingly. "Quiet man. What good could that sort of thing do you at the bar, for instance? And when *you're* Lord Chancellor with your peerage and your fortune up in London, I shall be still plain Trevor of Revington down here, vegetating, by Jove!"

"I'll never be *that*, but I may do *some* good —a little, perhaps. Enough to interest me in life, and that's all I want," said William, who was fiercely resolved on celibacy.

"I am going over to see the people at the Rectory—jolly old fellow old Wagget is; and I thought I'd just look in on you. You're not for a walk, are you?"

"*No*, thanks," said William very shortly, and added, "I'm sorry I can't, but I've letters this morning, and must be ready for the post."

"Well, good-bye then," said Trevor, and shook hands like a man going a long journey; and William glanced in his eyes, and saw what he was about, and thought, "He'll be sure to see her this morning."

So William took leave of him, and stood for a while in a troubled brown study on the steps, with a great weight at his heart, and after a while recollecting himself he said, "Pish! Pshaw!" and lifting his head defiantly, he strode into the parlour, and sat himself down grimly to write, but could not get on; and took a walk instead in the direction of the London railway, with his back to the Rectory and to Revington.

Our friend Vane Trevor had made up his mind to see Miss Darkwell this day, and speak, and in fact arrange everything; and as usual the crisis being upon him, his confidence in himself and his surroundings began to wane, and he experienced the qualms of doubt and the shiver of suspense. So as there was usually between the prison and the gallows-tree a point at which the gentleman on the hurdle drew up and partook of a glass of something comfortable, Mr. Vane Trevor halted on his way at Gilroyd and had his word or two, and shake of the hand with William Maubray, and went on.

On he went looking much as usual, except for a little pallor, but feeling strange sensations at his heart, and now and then rehearsing his speech, and more and more agitated inwardly as he drew near the door of the Rectory.

It was early, but Miss Wagget and Miss Darkwell were at home, and Vane Trevor, wondering whether an opportunity would occur, crossed the hall and was announced.

Miss Darkwell was sitting near a window copying music, and he went over and shook hands and felt very oddly; and after a word or two, she looked down again and resumed her work. Old Miss Wagget led the conversation, and began with a speech on her flowers, and was eloquent in admiration and acknowledgements. Now, poor Miss Perfect had told Miss Wagget the whole story of the Revington courtship, and the Rector's sister had quite taken Aunt Dinah's view of the case, and agreed that it was better the subject should be opened by the suitor himself; and, willing to make the opportunity desired at once, and dreaded, she recollected, on a sudden, that she had a word to say to her brother before he went out, and, with apologies, left the room and shut the door.

Miss Violet raised her eyes and looked after her a little anxiously, as if she would have liked to stop her. I think the young lady guessed pretty well what was in Vane Trevor's mind; but there was no averting the scene now, and she went on writing in a bar of crochets in the treble, but placed the minim wrong in the bass.

There was a silence, during which the little French clock over the chimneypiece ticked very loud, and Miss Wagget's lap-dog yawned and chose a new place on the hearth-rug, and the young lady was looking more closely at her music, and, though with a little blush, very gravely industrious. Trevor looked through the window, and down at the dog, and round the room, and up at the clock, but for the life of him he could not think of anything to say. The silence was growing insupportable, and at last he stood up, smiling the best he could, and drew near the window where Miss Violet was sitting, and tapped his chin with his cane, and said:—

"Music—a ha!—copying music!—I—I—a—I used to copy music pretty well; they said I did it uncommonly well; but I used to make those pops round like the copperplate, you know; *you* make them oval. They have a bookful of my copying at Kincton. They said—Clara did—they could read it just like print—and—and I wish you could give me some employment that way—I really wish you would. I'm afraid you find it awfully slow—don't you?"

"No—thanks; no, indeed—I'm very much obliged though, but I rather *like* it; I don't think it tiresome work at all."

"I—I should so like—and I was so glad to hear from Miss Wagget that you thought the flowers pretty—yesterday, I mean. These are beginning to look a little seedy—aren't they? I'll send over more to-day—I only wish, Miss Darkwell, I knew your pet flowers, that I might send a lot of them—I—I assure you I do."

Miss Darkwell here looked closer at her work, and drew two parallel lines connecting the stems of her semi-quavers very nicely.

CHAPTER LX.

THE MOMENTOUS QUESTION

"I—I REALLY would be so *very* much obliged if you would," resumed Trevor. "Do now, *pray*—tell me *any* one you like particularly!"

"I like all flowers so well," said Miss Violet. compelled to speak, "that I could hardly choose a favourite—at least, without thinking a great deal; and I should feel then as if I had slighted the rest."

"And awfully jealous I'm sure they'd be—*I* should—I know I should, indeed—I should, indeed. If I—if you—if I were a flower—I mean, the—the ugliest flower in the garden, by Jove, and that you preferred—a—a *anything*—I—I think I'd almost wither away—I—I swear to you I do—I'd tear my leaves out—I would, indeed—and—and—I'm in earnest, I assure you—I am indeed, Miss Darkwell—I'm—I'm awfully in love with you—I'm—I'm—I've been waiting this long time to tell you. I wrote to your father for leave to speak to you—and poor Miss Perfect also—I—she was very kind; and I've come to—to say—that—that I hope you can like me enough—that if a life of the greatest devotion to your happiness—and—and the greatest devotion to your happiness,"—he was trying here a bit of the speech he had prepared, but it would not come back, and so he shook himself free of it, and went on: "I'll—I'll try always to make you happy—I will, indeed—and you shall do just as you please—and there's no one—I don't care what her birth or rank, I should be prouder to see in the—the—as—as mistress of Revington than you; and I—I hope—I—I hope very much you can like me enough to give me some encouragement to—to—hope."

And Miss Darkwell answered very low—

"I—I'm so sorry, Mr. Trevor—I'm very sorry; but I couldn't—I can't, indeed, say anything but—but just how sorry I am, and how much obliged for your liking me—and I—it could not be." And Miss Violet Darkwell, with a very beautiful and bright colour, and eyes that looked darker than ever, stood up to go.

"I—pray don't—I—I'm sure you misunderstood me—I think I could—I—do pray—just a minute," said Vane Trevor, awfully confounded.

Miss Darkwell waited where she stood, looking down upon the carpet.

"I—I don't want you to answer me now; I—I'd rather you did'nt. I—I—you'll not answer me for a week. I—I'd rather you thought it over just a little—*pray*."

"It would make no difference, I assure you, Mr. Trevor. It would merely prolong what is very painful to me. It is very kind of you to think so well of me, and I'm very much obliged; but I think I'll go." And she extended her hand to take leave, and was on the point of going.

"But really, Miss Darkwell," said Mr. Trevor, who began to a little feel insulted, and to remember the Trevors, the Vanes, and the historic fame of Revington "I—I don t quite see—I think I—I—I *do* think I have a right to—to some explanation.

"There's nothing to explain; I've said everything," said Miss Vi very quietly.

"That's very easy, of course to say; but I —I don't think it's using a fellow quite"——

"Did I ever lead you to think I thought otherwise?" exclaimed Miss Violet with a grave but fearless glance.

There was a pause. Trevor was angry, and looked it. At last he said—

"I did not say that, but—but I know—I know I'm not a mere nobody here. The Trevors of Revington are pretty well known, and they have always married in—in a certain rank; and I think when I've spoken to you as I have done, I might have expected something more than a simple *no*, and—and I think, if you did not appear to like me—at all events there was nothing to make me think you *didn't*, and that's why I say I think I've a right to ask for an explanation?"

"You can have no right to make me say one word more than I please. I've said all I mean to say—more than I need have said—and I won't say more," said Miss Violet Darkwell, with eyes that glowed indignantly, for there was an implied contrast in the lordly marriages of the Trevors with his own tender of his hand to the young lady which fired her pride.

Before he recovered she had reached the door, and with her fingers upon the handle she paused, and returned just a step or two, and said, extending her hand—

"And I think we might part a little more kindly, for you have no cause to blame me, and when you think a little you'll say so yourself. Good-bye."

Trevor did not well know how he shook hands with her. But she was gone. It was all over.

Grief—rage—dissappointment—something like insult! He could not say that he had been insulted. But Revington was. The Trevors were. What a resource in such states of mind—denied to us men—are tears. Good furious weeping—the thunder and the rain—and then the air refreshed and the sky serene.

Mr. Vane Trevor felt as if he had been drinking too much brandy and water, and had been beaten heavily about the head; he was confounded and heated, and half blind. He walked very fast, and did not think where he was going until he stopped close to the gate of Gilroyd.

He went in, and rang the bell at the hall-door, which stood open. William came into the hall.

"Come in, Trevor," said he. He had taken his walk of a couple of miles, and was more serene.

"No. Come out and have a walk with me, will you?" answered Vane.

"Where?" asked William.

"Any where. Wherever you like—here among the trees."

"I don't care if I do," said William, who saw that in Trevor's countenance which excited his curiosity; and out he came with his wide-awake on, and Trevor walked beside him, looking very luridly on the ground, and marching very fast. William walked beside him, quietly waiting till the oracle should speak.

At last, wheeling round by the trunk of a huge old chestnut, he came suddenly to a full stop, and confronted his companion.

"Well, that's off my mind; all over; the best thing I dare say could happen me, and I think she's a bit of a—a—I think she has a temper of her own. I didn't like any more shilly-shally, you know, in that undecided way, and I thought I might as well tell you that it's all off, and that I'm very well pleased it is. She's very pretty, and all that; but, hang it, there are other things, and it never would have done. I have not much of a temper of own, I believe." (Trevor was really a good-humoured fellow, but chose to charge himself with this little failing for the occasion), "and I could not get on with that kind of thing. It wouldn't have done—it *couldn't*—I thought I'd just come down and tell you; and I think I'll run up to town; they want me to go to Kincton, but it's too slow; and—and Revington's such a wilderness. I wish some one would take it. I don't want to marry for ever so long. I don't know what put it in my head."

Mr. Vane Trevor resumed his walk at a slower pace, and he whistled a low and contemplative air, looking down on the grass with his hands in his pocket, and then he said again—

"I thought I'd just come down and tell you; and you're not to mention it, you know—not to that fellow Drake, or any one, mind—not that I much care, but it would not do to be talked about, and you won't I know, thanks, and the Waggets are honourable people, *they* won't talk either I suppose; and—and I *depend* on you; and—and you know you and I are friends all the same."

"Certainly no *worse*," said William, very truly, shaking his hand cordially.

"And I'll be off to-day. I'll go to the opera, or something to-night. I've been too long shut up; a fellow grows rusty, you know, in this tiresome corner. I wish some fool of a fellow would take a lease of it. Good-bye, old fellow; you must come up to town and see me when I'm settled, mind."

And so they parted.

—o—

CHAPTER LXI.

A DOUBT TROUBLES MAUBRAY.

I COME now to some incidents, the relation of which partakes, I can't deny, of the marvellous. I can, however, vouch for the literal truth of the narrative; so can William Maubray; so can my excellent friend Doctor Wagget; so also can my friend Doctor Drake, a shrewd and sceptical physician, all thoroughly cognizant of the facts. If therefore, anything related in the course of the next two or three chapters should appear to you wholly incredible, I beg that you will not ascribe the prodigious character of the narrative to any moral laxities on the part of the writer.

I believe William Maubray liked Vane Trevor very honestly, and that he was as capable of friendship as any man I have ever met with; but this I will aver, that he had not been so cheerful since poor Aunt Dinah's death as for the remainder of the day on which he had heard the authentic report of his friend's overthrow.

Down to the town of Saxton that evening, walked William, for in his comfortable moods he required human society, as he yearned for sympathy in his affections. He visited his hospital friend Doctor Drake, now in his pardonable elation on the occasion of his friend's downfall, as he had done when writhing under the thunderbolts of poor Aunt Dinah.

In this case, however, he could not disclose what lay nearest to his heart. It would not have done to commit poor Trevor's little secret to Doctor Drake, nor yet to tell him how wildly in love *he* was, and how the events of this day had lighted up his hopes. In fact, Doctor Drake had long ceased to be the sort of doctor whom a gay fellow suffering from one of Cupid's bow-shot wounds would have cared to consult, and William visited him on this occasion simply because he was elated, excited, and could not do without company of some sort.

At about half past nine o'clock Doctor Drake was called away to visit Mr. Thomas, the draper.

"Gouty pain in the duodenum—*there's* a man, now, wansh—a—kill himself. He *is* killing himself. Advice! You might as well advise that ub—bottle. You might, a bilious fellow—lithic acid—gouty—'sgouty a fellow, by Jove, sir, as you'd like to see, and all I can do he wone 'rink his—his little—whatever it is, anyway but hot—hot, sir, and with *sugar*—sugar, and you know that's *poison*, simple p—poison. You see *me*, any li'l' thing I take—sometimes a liddle she'y, sometimes a li'l' ole Tom, or branle; I take it *cole*, with*out*—*quite* innocent—rather *use*fle—shlight impulse—all the organs—*never* affec' the *head*—never touch the *liver*—that's the way, sir; that's how you come to live *long*—lots o' waw'r, cole waw'r, and just sprinkle over, that's your sort, sir, stick a' that, sir; cole, cole *waw'r—lots* o' waw'r, sir; never make too stiff, you know, an' you may go on all *nigh'*—don' go, you know, I mayn be half 'n hour, all *nigh*, sir, an' no harm done—*no* harm, sir, rather *use*fle."

By this time the Doctor had got himself into his surtout, and selecting Mr. Thomas's gouty cordials, ether and both bottles from his drawer, he set forth on his sanitary expedition, and the symposium ended.

So William walked musingly homeward. What a tender melancholy over everything! What a heavenly night! What a good, honest, clever fellow Doctor Drake was! By Jove, he had forgotten to ask for Miss Drake, who was no doubt in the drawing-room—a jolly old creature was Miss Drake! Should he go back and drink some of her tea? He halted and turned, not right about, but right face, and hesitated in the moonlight. No, it was too late—he forgot how late it was. But he'd go down specially to drink tea with Miss Drake another evening. And so he resumed that delicious walk homewards.

There was no use in denying it any longer to himself—none—he knew it—he felt it—he *was* in love with Violet Darkwell—awfully in love! And as every lover is an egotist, and is diposed on the whole to think pretty well of himself. The hypothesis did cross his fancy frequently, that the downfall of his friend Trevor was somehow connected with the fortunes of William Maubray. Was there—might there not be—did he not remember signs and tokens, such as none but lover's eyes can read or see, that seemed to indicate a—a preference; might there not be a pre-occupation?

What a charm in the enigmatic conditions of a lover's happiness! How beautiful the castles in the air in which his habitation is! How she stands at the open portal, or leans from the casement, in beautiful shadow, or golden light divine! How he reads his fate in air-drawn characters, in faintest signs, remembered looks, light words, a tone! How latent meanings hover in all she says, or sings, or looks, or does; and how imagination is enthralled by the mystery, and he never tires of exploring, and guessing, and wondering, and sighing. Those deep reserves and natural wiles of girls are given to interest us others, with those sweet doubts and trembling hopes that constitute the suspense and excitement of romance.

William Maubray sat himself down in a delightful melancholy, in his great chair by the drawing-room fire, and ordered tea, and told old Winnie that she must come and have a cup, and keep him company; and so she did very gladly, and William made her talk a great deal about poor Aunt Dinah, and this retrospect went on with a stream of marginal anecdote about Miss Violet, to every syllable of which, though maundered over in honest Winnie's harum-scarum prose, he listened breathlessly, as to the far-off music of angels. And when all was told out, led her back artfully, and heard the story bit by bit again, and listened to her topsy-turvey praises of Violet in a delightful dream, and would have kept her up all night narrating, but honest Homer nodded at last, and William was fain to let the muse take flight to her crib.

Then, leaning back in his chair, he mused alone, revolving sweet and bitter fancies, thinking how well Sergeant Darkwell thought of him, how near Violet still was, what easy access to the Rectory, how sure he was of the old people's good word, how miserable he should be, what a failure his life without her. How she had refused Vane Trevor—refused Revington. Was that a mere motiveless freak? Was there no special augury to *his* favour discernable in it? He had the Bar before him now—could not Sergeant Darkwell bring him forward, put him in the way of business? He was not afraid of work—he liked it. Anything—everything, for sake of her. Besides, he was no longer penniless. He could make a settlement now. Thanks to poor dear Aunt Dinah, Gilroyd was his. Aunt Dinah!

And here the thought of her odd threatenings and prohibition crossed his brain. Five years! Nonsense! Madness! *That* would never do. Five years before so young a man, looks like fifty. In a lover's chronicle it is an age. Quite impracticable. He would lay the case before Sergeant Darkwell and Doctor Wagget. He well knew how *they*, conscientious, good, clear-headed men would treat it. But, alas! it troubled him—it vexed him. The menace was in his ear—a shadow stood by him. There were memoranda in his desk, and poor Aunt Dinah's last letter. He would read them over. He had fancied, very likely, that she meant more, and more *seriously*, than a re-perusal would support. So eagerly he opened his desk, and got out those momentous papers.

———o———

CHAPTER LXII.

THE FURNITURE BEGINS TO TALK.

He read Aunt Dinah's letters over again, and marked the passage with his pencil, and read again.

"Do you remember, dear boy, all told you, dear, about the five years. I dreamed much since. If you think of such a thing I must do it."

This last sentence he underlined, "*If you think of such a thing, I must do it.* Sorry I shoul" (she meant *should*) "fear or dislike me. I should haunt, torment Willie. But you will do right." *Do right.* She meant wait for five years, of course. My poor darling aunt! I wish you had never seen one of those odious books of American bosh—Elihu Bung! I wish Elihu Bung was sunk in a barrel at the bottom of the sea.

Then William looked to his diary, for about that period of his life he kept one for two years and seven months, and he read these entries:

"—— Dear Aunt Dinah pressed me very much to give her a distinct promise not to marry for five years—marry indeed! I, poor, penniless William Maubray! I shall never marry—yet I can't make this vow—and she threatened me, saying, 'If I'm dead there's nothing that spirit can do, if you so much as harbour the thought, be I good, or evil, or mocking, I'll not do to prevent it. I'll trouble you, I'll torment you, I'll pick her eyes out, but I won't suffer you to ruin yourself.' And she said very often that she expected to be a *mocking* spirit; and said again, 'Mind I told you, though I be dead, you shan't escape me.' 'That night I had an odious night-mare. An apparition like my aunt came to my bedside, and caught my arm with its hand, and said, quite distinctly, "Oh! my God! William, I am dead; don't let me go." I fancied I saw the impression of fingers on my arm; and I think I never was so horrified in my life. And afterwards in her own bedroom, my aunt having heard my dream, returned to the subject of her warning, and said, "If I die before the time, "I'll watch you as an old gray cat watches a mouse, if you so much as think of it. I'll plague you; I'll save you in spite of yourself, and mortal was never haunted and tormented as you shall be, till you give it up."' And saying this she laughed."

"The whole of this new fancy turns out to be one of the Henbane delusions. How I wish all those cursed books of spiritualism were with Don Quixote's library!"

William had now the facts pretty well before him. He had, moreover, a very distinct remembrance of that which no other person had imagined or seen—the face of the apparition of Aunt Dinah, and the dark and pallid stare she had actually turned upon him, as he recounted the particulars of his vision. It had grown very late, and he was quite alone, communing in these odd notes, and with these strange remembrances with the dead. Perhaps all the strong tea he had drunk with old Winnie that night helped to make him nervous. One of his candles had burnt out by this time, and as he raised his eyes from these curious records, the room looked dark and indistinct, and the slim, black cabinet that stood against the wall at the further end of the room startled him, it looked so like a big, muffled man.

I dare say he began to wish that he had postponed his scrutiny of his papers until the morning. At all events he began to experience those sensations, which in morbid moods of this kind, dispose us to change of scene. What was it that made that confounded cabinet, and its shadow, again look so queer, as he raised his eyes and the candle; just like a great fellow in a loose coat extending his arm to strike?

That was the cabinet which once, in a confidential mood, poor Aunt Dinah had described as the spiritual tympanum on which above all other sympathetic pieces of furniture in the house she placed her trust. Such a spirit-gauge was in no other room of Gilroyd. It thrummed so oracularly; it cracked with such a significant emphasis.

"Oh! I see; nothing but the shadow, as I move the candle. Yes, only that and nothing more. I wish it was out of that, it *is* such an ugly black beast of a box."

Now William put poor Aunt Dinah's letter carefully back in its place, as also his diary, and locked his desk; and just then the cabinet uttered one of those cracks which poor Aunt Dinah so much respected. In the supernatural silence it actually made him bounce. It was the first time in his life he had ever fancied such things could have a meaning.

"The fire's gone out; the room is cooling, and the wood of that ridiculous cabinet is contracting. What can it do but crack? I think I'm growing as mad as—he was on the point of saying as poor Aunt Dinah, but something restrained him, and he respectfully substituted as a March hare."

Here the cabinet uttered a fainter crack, which seemed to say, "I hear you;" and William paused, expecting almost to see something sitting on the top of it, or emerging through its doors, and he exclaimed, "such disgusting nonsense!" and he looked round the room, and over his shoulder, as he placed his keys in his pocket. His strong tea, and his solitude, and the channel into which he had turned his thoughts; the utter silence, the recent death, and the lateness of the hour, made the disgusted philosopher rise to take the candle which had not a great deal of life left in it, and shutting the door on the cabinet, whose loquacity he detested, he got to his bedroom in a suspicious and vigilant state; and he was glad when he got into his room. William locked his door on the inside. He lighted his candles, poked his fire, violently wrested his thoughts from uncomfortable themes; sat himself down by the fire and thought of Violet Darkwell. "Oh that I dare think it was for my sake she refused Vane Trevor!" and so on, building many airy castles, and declaiming eloquently over his work. The old wardrobe in the room made two or three warning starts and cracks, but its ejaculations were disrespectfully received.

"Fire away old fool, much I mind *you!* A gentlemanlike cabinet may be permitted, but a vulgar cupboard, impudence."

So William got to his bed, and fell asleep; in no mood I think to submit to a five years' wait, if a chance of acceptance opened; and in the morning he was astonished.

Again, my reader's incredulity compels me to aver in the most solemn manner that the particulars I now relate of William Maubray's history are strictly true. He is living to depose to all. My excellent friend Doctor Drake can certify to others, and as I said, the Rector of the parish, to some of the oddest. Upon this evidence, not doubting, I found my narrative.

—o—

CHAPTER LXIII.

WILLIAM MAUBRAY IS TORMENTED.

On the little table at his bedside, where his candle stood, to his surprise, on awaking, he saw one of the boots which he had put off in the passage on the previous night. There it was, no possible mistake about it; and what was more it was placed like one of his ornamental bronze weights; one of those indeed was fashioned like a buskin upon some papers.

What were these papers? With growing amazement he saw that they were precisely those which he had been reading the night before, and had carefully locked up in his desk—poor Aunt Dinah's warning letter—and his own notes of her threatening words!

It was little past seven now; he had left his shutters open as usual. Had he really locked his door? No doubt upon that point. The key was inside, and the door locked. The keys of his desk, what of them? There they were, precisely where he had left them, on the chimney-piece. This certainly was *very* odd. Who was there in the house to play him such a trick? No one could have opened his door; his key stuck in the lock on the inside; and how else could any one have entered? Who was there to conceive such a plot? and by what ingenuity could any merry devil play it off? And who could know what was passing in his mind? Here was a symbol such as he could not fail to interpret. The heel of his boot on the warnings and entreaties of his poor dead aunt! could anything be more expressive?

William began to feel very oddly. He got on his clothes quickly, and went down to the drawing-room. His desk was just as he had placed it; he unlocked it; his papers were not disturbed; nothing apparently had been moved but the letter and his diary.

William sat down utterly puzzled, and looked at the black japanned cabinet, with its straggling bass-reliefs of gold Chinamen, pagodas, and dragons glimmering in the cold morning light, with more real suspicion than he had ever eyed it before.

Old Winnie thought that day that Mr. William was unusually "dull." The fact is, that he was beginning to acquire, not a hatred, but a fear of Gilroyd, and to revolve in his mind thoughts of selling the old house and place, or letting it, and getting out of reach of its ambiguous influences. He was constantly thinking over these things, puzzling his brain over an inscrutable problem, still brooding over the strange words of Aunt Dinah, "A mocking spirit; I'll trouble; I'll torment you. You shan't escape me. Though I be dead, I'll watch you as an old grey cat watches a mouse. If you so much as think of it, I'll plague you!" and so forth

William walked over to the Rectory. He asked first for Miss Wagget—she was out; then for the Rector—so was he.

"Are you *quite* sure the ladies are out—*both?*" he inquired, lingering.

"Yes, sir. Miss Darkwell drove down with the mistress to the church, about the new cushions, I think."

"Oh! then I'll call another time;" and William's countenance brightened as he looked down on the pretty spire, and away he went on the wings of hope.

The church door was open, and sexton and clerk were there, and William, looking round the empty pews and up to the galleries, inquired for Miss Wagget. He was not lucky. The sexton mistook the inquiry for Mr. Wagget, and directed William to the vestry-room, at whose door he knocked with a beating heart, and entering, found the Rector examining the register for the year '48.

"Ha!—found me out? Tracked to my lair," said he, saluting William with a wave of his hand, and a kindly smiling. "Not a word, though, till this is done—just a minute or two. Sit down.

"I'll wait in the church, sir," said William, and slipped out to renew his search. But his news was disappointing. The ladies had driven away, neither clerk nor sexton could tell whither, except that it was through High Street; and William mounted the elevated ground about the yew tree, and gazed along the High Street, but all in vain, and along the upward road to Treworth, but equally without result: and the voice of the Rector, who thought he was admiring the landscape, recalled him.

Mr. Wagget was not only an honourable and a religious man—he was kindly and gay; he enjoyed everything—his trees and his flowers, his dinner, his friends, even his business, but, above all things, his books; and herein was a powerful sympathy with the younger student, who was won besides to confidence by the general spirits of the good man.

The loneliness of Gilroyd, too—insupportable, had it not been for the vicinity of Violet—made his company very welcome. So, falling into discourse, it naturally befel that William came to talk of that which lay nearest his heart at that moment—his unaccountable adventure of the night before.

Very curious, and, as it seems to me, quite inexplicable," said Doctor Wagget, very much interested. "The best authenticated thing I've heard—*much* the best—of the kind. You must tell it all over again. It's the best and most satisfactory case I know."

Thus oddly encouraged, William again recounted his strange story, and unfolded something of the horror with which his doubts were fraught.

"You *said* nothing?" asked the parson.

"Nothing."

"Ha! It *is* the very *best* case I ever heard or read. Every one knows, in fact, there *have* been such things. *I* believe in apparitions. I don't put them in my sermons, though, because so many people *don't*, and it weakens one's influence to run unnecessarily into disputed subjects, and it's time enough to talk of such things when people are visited, as you have been. You must not be frightened, though; you've no need. If these things *be*, they form part of the great scheme of nature, and any evil that may befal you in consequence is as much a subject for legitimate prayer as sickness or any other affliction; indeed, more obviously so, because we are furnished with no other imaginable means than prayer alone, and a life conformable to God's will, to resist them. Poor little thing! She talked very flightily. I had a great deal of conversation, and latterly she listened, and I had hoped with some effect. Especially I urged her to clear her mind of all idea of spiritual action, except such as is presented for our comfort and warning in the Holy Scriptures. But here, you *see*, she, poor little thing, is restless, and you troubled. It's the oddest case I ever heard of."

"Pray don't mention what I've told you, sir, to any one."

"Certainly not, for the world—not a human being, not even my sister. By-the-bye, couldn't you come over and dine with us, and sleep; you must sleep to-night by way of experiment."

So William promised, well pleased, and went; but, alas! this was a day of disappointments. Violet had gone again to make a short stay at the Mainwarings.

"What can the Mainwarings want of her? She's always going there; what *is* there about them so charming?" demanded William of himself; and an outline of the military son of the family, Captain Mainwaring, possibly on leave and at home, disturbed him.

Now, to the further wonderment and even delight of Doctor Wagget, a very curious result followed from the "experiment" of William's one night's sojourn at the Rectory. At his host's request, he had locked his bed-room door, just as he had done at Gilroyd, and in the morning he found his stick, which he had left in the *hall*, tied fast in the loops in which in the daytime the curtains were gathered. There it hung across the bed over his head, an image, as it seemed to him, of suspended castigation.

The Doctor was early at William's door, and found his guest's toilet half completed. In real panic, Maubray pointed out the evidence of this last freak.

"What an absurd ghost!" thought Mr. Wagget, in a pleasing terror, as he examined and pondered over the arrangement.

"It only shows that change of place won't

do," said the Rector. "Consider this, however," he resumed, after an interval consumed in search of consolation, "these manifestations, and very characteristic they are, if we assume they come from my poor friend, are made in furtherance of what she conceives your interests, in the spirit of that love which she manifested for you all your life, and you may be well assured they will never be pushed to such a point as to hurt you.

William got on the bed, and untied his stick, which on his way home he broke to pieces, as a thing bewitched, in a nervous paroxysm, and flung into the little brook that runs by Revington.

At breakfast, Miss Wagget asked of her brother,

"Did you hear the noise at the hat-stand in the hall last night? Your hat was knocked down and rolled all across the hall." (The parson and William glanced at one another here.) "It was certainly that horrid grey cat that comes in at the lobby window."

At mention of the grey cat the remembrance of poor Aunt Dinah's smile struck William.

"By Jove! my stick was at the hat-stand," exclaimed he.

"Your stick? but this was a hat," replied Miss Wagget, who did not see why he should be so floored by the recollection of his stick.

"Ha! your stick? so it was—was it," exclaimed Doctor Wagget, with a sudden awe, equally puzzling.

And staring at her brother, and then again at William, Miss Wagget suffered the water from the tea-urn to overflow her cup and her saucer in succession.

—o—

CHAPTER LXIV.

AN AMBUSCADE.

Gilroyd was awfully slow, and even the town of Saxton dull. Cricket was quite over. There was no football there. William Maubray used to play at the ancient game of quoits with Arthur Jones, Esq., the Saxton attorney, who was a little huffy when he lost, and very positive on points of play; but on the whole a good fellow. Sometimes in the smoking-room, under the reading-room, he and Doctor Drake played clattering games of backgammon, with sixpenny stakes, and called their throws loudly, and crowed ungenerously when they won. But these gaieties and dissipations failed to restore William altogether to his pristine serenity. Although he had been now for four nights quite unmolested, he could not trust Gilroyd. It was a haunted house, and he the sport of a spirit. The place was bewitched, but so, unhappily, was the man. His visit to the Rectory proved that change of place could not deliver him. He was watched and made to feel that his liberty was gone.

Violet Darkwell was not to return to the Rectory for a week or more, and William called on Doctor Wagget, looking ill, and unquestionably in miserable spirits. To the Rector he had confessed something vaugely of his being in love, and cherishing hopes contrary to the terms which poor Aunt Dinah had sought to impose upon him.

A few nights later, emboldened by his long respite, he had written some stanzas, addressed to the young lady's *carte de visite*, expressive of his hopes, and in the morning he had found his desk in his bed-room, though he had left it in the drawing-room, and his bed-room door was as usual locked. His desk was not open, nor was there any sign of the papers having been disturbed, but the verses he had that night written had been taken out and torn into small pieces, which were strewn on top of the desk.

Since then he had not had a single quiet night, and the last night was the oddest, and in this respect the most unpleasant, that they had set the servants talking.

"Tom, he's a very steady old fellow, you know," related William, "waked me up last night at about two o'clock. I called through the door not knowing but that it might be something."

"I *know*," said the Rector, with a mysterious nod.

"Yes, sir; and he told me he had been awake and heard a loud knocking in the drawing-room, like the hammering of a nail, as indeed it proved to be; and he ran up to the drawing-room, and saw nothing unusual there, and then to the lobby, and there he saw a tall figure in a white dress run up the stairs, with a tread that sounded like bare feet, and as it reached the top it threw a hammer backward which hopped down the steps to his feet. It was the kitchen hammer, unhung from the nail there which we found had been pulled out of the wall. Without waiting to get my clothes on, down I went with him, but our search showed nothing but one very curious discovery."

"Ha? Go on, sir."

"I must tell you, sir, there was a print, a German coloured thing. I had forgotten it—it was in my poor Aunt's portfolio in a drawer there, of a great tabby cat pretending to doze, and in reality slily watching a mouse that half emerges from its hole, approaching a bit of biscuit, and this we found nailed to the middle of the door."

"The inside?"

"Yes."

"You did not *see* anything of the apparition yourself?" asked Doctor Wagget.

"No, I was asleep. I've seen nothing whatever but such things as I've described; and the fact is I'm worried to death, and I don't in the least know what to do."

"I tell you what," said the clergyman, after a pause. "I'll go down and spend the night at Gilroyd, if you allow me, and we'll get Doctor Drake to come also, if you approve, and we'll watch, sir, we—we'll spy it out—

we'll get at the heart of the mystery. Drake's afraid of nothing, no more am I—and—and what do you say, may we go?"

So the bargain was concluded, and at nine o'clock that evening the Parson and Doctor Drake in friendly chat together walked up to the door of Gilroyd, and were welcomed by William, who led these learned witch-finders into his study, which commanded easy access to both drawing-room and parlour, and to the back and the great staircase.

The study looked bright and pleasant—a cheery fire flashed on the silver tea-pot and cream-ewer, and old China tea things, and glimmered warmly over the faded gilded backs of the books. This and the candles lighted up the room so brightly that it needed an effort—notwithstanding the dark wainscot—to admit a thought of a ghost.

I don't know whether the parson had really any faith in ghosts or not. He thought he had, and cultivated in private a taste for that curious luxury, though he was reserved on the subject among his parishioners. I don't think, however, if his nerves had been as much engaged as they might, he could have turned over the old tomes of the late Dean of Crutched Friars with so much interest as he did, or commented so energetically upon the authors and editions.

Doctor Drake was utterly sceptical, and being "threatened with one of his ugly colds," preferred brandy and water to tea—a little stimulus seasonably applied, often routing the enemy before he had time to make an impression. So, very snugly they sat round their table. The conversation was chiefly between the Rector and the Doctor, William being plainly out of spirits and a good deal in the clouds. The churchman sipped his tea, and the physician his strong drink, and there was adjusted a plan for the operations of the night.

"Now, Mr. Maubray, you must do as we order, when we bid you, you go to bed—do you see—everything must proceed precisely as usual, and Doctor Drake and I will sit up and watch here—you go, at your accustomed hour and lock your door—mind, as usual—and we'll be on the alert, and ready to—to——"

"To arrest the Cabinet—egad!—and garrotte the Clock, if either so much as cracks while we are on duty," interposed Doctor Drake, poking William's flagging spirits with a joke, in vain.

"I dare say," was William's parting observation; "just because you are both here there will be nothing whatever to-night—I'm quite certain; but I'm awfully obliged to you all the same.

He was quite wrong, however, as all who please may learn from the sequel.

——o——

CHAPTER LXV

PURSUIT.

William Maubray, in obedience to orders went to his bed, having locked his chamber door. He grew tired of listening for sound or signal from the picket in the parlour, as he lay in his bed reading, his eyes failed him. He had walked fifteen miles that day, and in spite of his determination to remain awake, perhaps partly in consequence of it he fell into a profound slumber, from which he was awakened in a way that surprised him.

The sages in the study had drawn their arm-chairs about the fire. The servants had gone to bed—all was quiet, and it was now past one o'clock. The conversation was hardly so vigorous as at first—there were long pauses, during which the interlocutors yawned furtively into their hands, and I am sorry to add, that while Mr. Wagget was, at the Physician's request, expounding to him the precise point on which two early heresies differed, Doctor Drake actually sank into a deep slumber, and snored so loud as to interrupt the speaker, who smiled shrugged, shook his head, and, being a charitable man, made excuses for his drowsiness, and almost immediately fell fast asleep himself.

The clergyman was awakened by some noise. He must have been asleep a long time, for the fire had subsided, and he felt cold, and was so stiff from long sitting in the same posture that he could hardly get up—one of the candles had burned out in the socket, and the other was very low.

On turning in the direction of the noise, the clergyman saw a gaunt figure in white gliding from the room. On seeing this form I am bound to confess the clergyman was so transported with horror, that he seized the sleeping doctor by the head, and shook it violently.

Up started the doctor, and also saw in the shadow the spectre which had paused in the hall, looking awfully tall.

The doctor's hand was on the candlestick, and uttering a prayer, he flung it, in a paroxysm of horror; but it was a wild shot, and hit the sofa near the study door, and rebounded under the table. The study was now dark, but not so the hall. One tall window admitted a wide sheet of moonlight. The clatter of the doctor's projectile seemed to affect the apparition, for it suddenly began to run round and round the hall, in wide circles, regularly crossing the broad strip of moonlight and displaying its white draperies every time for half a second; the philosophers in the study could not tell whether each new revolution might not bring it into the room, to deal with them in some unknown way. One word they did not utter, but groped and pulled one another, fiercely, and groaned, and panted, and snorted, like two men wrestling, and I am afraid that each would have liked to get his friend between himself and the object, which, after whirling some half dozen times round the hall, passed off as it seemed in the direction of the kitchen or the back-stair.

The gentlemen in the study, still holding one another, though with a relaxed grasp, were now leaning with their backs to the chimney-piece.

"Ha, ha, ha, ha!" panted Doctor Drake nervously, and the Rector sighed two or three times in great exhaustion. The physician was first to speak.

"Well! Hey! Where's your scepticism now?" said he.

"My friend—my good friend," replied the parson, "don't be alarmed. Where's your faith?"

"Was there a noise?" whispered the doctor; and they both listened.

"No," said the parson. "Pray shut the door. We must not be so—so unmann'd, and we'll light the candle if you can find it."

"Come along then," said the physician, who preferred the cleric's company just then.

"To the door," said the clergyman, gently pushing him before him.

When the candle was found and relighted, the gentlemen were much more cheerful. They looked about them. They stole into the hall and listened. They looked like Christian and Hopeful making their escaoe from Doubting Castle.

They hastened toward the back stair and the kitchen, and were satisfied without exploring. Then side by side they mounted the great stair, and reached William's door. They had to knock loudly before he awaked.

"Hollo!—I say!" shouted William from his bed.

"Let us in; Doctor Drake and I; we've a word to say," said the clergyman mildly.

"*Will* you open the door, sir?" wildly shouted Doctor Drake, who hated the whole affair.

And they heard the pound of William's feet on the floor as he got out of bed, and in another moment the key turned, and William, candle in hand, stood at the open door.

"Well, any news—anything?" asked William.

"Get some clothes on and come down with us. *Yes.* We have seen something odd," said the clergyman.

"Could it have been Rebecca?" inquired William.

"Hoo! no, sir—two feet taller," said the Rector.

"*Four* feet taller," said Doctor Drake.

"Did you see its face?" asked William, using, awfully, the neuter gender.

"No," said the Parson.

"But I did," said Drake—"as long as my arm."

The learned gentlemen stood very close together on the lobby, and looked over their shoulders.

"Come into my room, sir—won't you? You may as well" (the "sir" applying to both gentlemen), said William, doing the honours in his night-shirt.

"I don't see any great good," observed Doctor Drake, turning the key again in the door, as he followed the clergyman in, "we can do by going down again. If there was a chance of *finding* anything, but whatever it is, its gone by this time, and going down would be a mere flourish, don't you think?"

"I wish we had the bottle of Old Tom that's in the locker," said William, who, behind the curtain, was making an imperfect toilet; "but I suppose it's too far," and they all looked a little uneasy.

"No, no," said the clergyman morally, "we've had enough—quite enough."

"Unless we all went down *together* for it," said Doctor Drake

"No, no, *pray* no more to-night, said the Rector, peremptorily.

"I've pipes and a lot of latchia here," said William, emerging in trowsers and dressing-gown. "I've been trying it for the last ten days. Suppose we smoke a little."

"Very good idea," said the Rector, who had no objection to an occasional pipe under the rose.

So they poked up the fire, and laid a block of coal on, and found that it was half-past four o'clock, and they chatted thoughtfully, but no more upon the subject of the apparition; and when daylight appeared they made a hasty toilet, had an early breakfast in the parlour; and the good Doctor Wagget, with his eyes very red, and looking as rakish as so respectable a clergyman could, appointed William an hour to meet him at the Rectory that day, and the party broke up.

CHAPTER LXVI.

THE GHOST REAPPEARS.

So soon as he was alone, the real horror of his situation overpowered William Maubray.

"They won't say so, but the Rector and Doctor Drake, from totally different points—with minds constituted as dissimilarly as minds can be—have both come to the conclusions that these persecutions are supernatural. No jury on their oaths, having all the facts before them, could find otherwise. I see and know that they are unaccountable, except in this way; and go where I will, I am dogged by the same cruel influence. Five years' bondage! Where shall I be at the end of that time? What will have become of Violet Darkwell? I must abandon all my hopes—honestly abandon them—it is the price I must pay for the removal of this curse, which otherwise will extend itself, if there be meaning in the threat, to the unconscious object of my hopes."

So raved William, "pacing up and walking down" in his despair.

That night he had his old night-mare again, and was visited by what poor Miss Perfect used to call "the spirit key." In a horror he awaked, and found his wrist grasped by a cold hand precisely as before. This time the grip was maintained for a longer time than usual, and William traced the hand to its real owner of flesh and blood. Thus was there a gleam of light; but it served him no further.

In the evening, still agitated by his discovery, he visited Dr. Drake, who listened first with surprise, and then with downcast thoughtful look, and a grim smile.

"I'll think it over," said he. "I must be off now," and he poked his finger toward the window, through which were visible his cob and gig; "they don't leave me much time; but I'll manage to be with you by nine this evening, and—and—I don't care if we try that old Tom," and the Doctor winked comfortably at William. "We'll be more to ourselves, you know; our Rector's all for tea. Good-by, and I'll turn it over carefully in my mind. I have an idea, but—but I'll consider it—and—nine o'clock to-night, mind."

Thus said the Doctor as he climbed into his gig, and nodding over his shoulder to William Maubray, away he drove.

Like a restless soul as he was, William toiled hither and thither through the little town of Saxton with his hands in his pockets, and his looks on the pavement, more like an unfortunate gentleman taking his walk in a prison yard, than the proprietor of Gilroyd pacing the High Street of Saxton, where he ranked second only to Trevor, Prince of Revington.

Repose is pleasant, but that of Saxton is sometimes too much for the most contemplative man who is even half awake. There are in the town eleven shops, small and great, and you may often look down the length of the High Street, for ten minutes at a time, and see nothing in motion but the motes in the sunshine.

William walked back to Gilroyd, and paid himself as it were a visit there, and was vexed to find he had missed the Rector, who had called only half an hour before. The loss of this little diversion was serious. The day dragged heavily. Reader, if you repine at the supposed shortness of the allotted measure of your days, reside at Saxton for a year or two, and your discontent will be healed.

Even Doctor Drake was half an hour late for his appointment, and William was very glad to see that pillar of Saxton society at last.

When they had made themselves comfortable by the fire, and the physician had adjusted his grog, and William had got his cup of tea by him, after a little silence the doctor began to ask him all sorts of questions about his health and sensations.

"I don't think," said William, except perhaps, my spirits a little, and my appetite, perhaps, this thing has affected my health at all."

"No matter, answer my questions," said the Doctor, who after a while fell into a mysterious silence, and seemed amused, and after a little time further, he expressed a great wish to remain and watch as on the former occasion.

"But," said William, very glad of the offer, "the Rector is not coming, and you would wish some one with you."

"No—no one—I don't mind," said the Doctor, smiling with half-closed eyes into his tumbler. "Or, *yes*, we'll have your man up when you go to bed; that will do."

"I missed Dr. Wagget to-day; he called here," said William.

"Not after nightfall, though," said the physician, with a screw of his lips and eye-brows. "I saw him early to-day; he's awfully frightened, and spoke like a sermon about it."

William looked sorely disquieted at this confirmation of his estimate of Dr. Wagget's opinion of the case. He and Drake exchanged a solemn glance, and the Doctor lowering his eyes sipped some grog, and bursting into a mysterious fit of laughter which rather frightened William, who helplessly stood at the tea-table, and gazed on the spectacle, Everything began to puzzle him now; the Doctor was like an awful grotesque in a dream. How could a good-natured and shrewd man laugh thus, amid suffering and horrors such as he had witnessed?

"I beg your pardon, but I could not help laughing when I thought of the Rector's long face to-day, and his long words, by Jove," and in a minute or two more, the Doctor exploded suddenly again, with the old apology on recovering his gravity, and William's bewilderment increased.

The Doctor insisted on William's adhering strictly to his tea and his hours, precisely as if he were alone.

And Tom came in, and the Doctor, who was in no wise ceremonious, made him sit down by the fire, and furnished him with a glass of the grog he so recommended.

He then delivered to Tom a brief popular lecture on the subject he desired him to comprehend, and, having thus charged him, silence reigned; and then the Doctor, after an interval, smoked half a dozen pipes, and by the time the last was out it was past three o'clock.

The Doctor had left the study door open. The moon was shining through the great hall window.

"Put off your shoes, make no noise, and follow me close, with the candle, wherever I go. Don't *stir* till I do," whispered the Doctor, repeating the directions he had already given—"Hish!"

The Doctor had seen a tall, white figure in the hall—in the shade beyond the window.

"Hish!" said the Doctor again, seizing Tom by the arm, and pointing, with a mysterious nod or two, towards the figure.

"Lawk!—Oh! oh!—*Law* bless us!" murmured the man; and the Doctor, with another "Hish," pushed him gently backward a little.

———o———

CHAPTER LXVII.

THE PHANTOM IS TRACKED.

As the Doctor made this motion, the figure in white crossed the hall swiftly, and stood at the study door. It·looked potentiously tall, and was covered with a white drapery, a corner of which hung over its face. It entered the room, unlocked William Maubray's desk, from which it took some papers: then locked the desk, carrying away which, it left the room.

"Follow, with the light," whispered the Doctor, himself pursuing on tiptoe.

Barefoot, the figure walked towards the kitchen, then turning to the left, it mounted the back stair; the Doctor following pretty closely, and Tom with his candle in the rear.

On a peg in the gallery opposite to the door of William Maubray's bed-room, hung an old dressing-gown of his, into the pocket of which the apparition slipped the papers it had taken from his desk. Then it opened William's door, as easily as if he had not locked it upon the inside. The Doctor and Tom followed, and saw the figure approach the bed and place the desk very neatly under the bolster, then return to the door, and shut and lock it on the inside. Then the figure marched in a stately way to the far side of the bed, drew both curtains, and stood at the bedside, like a ghost, for about a minute; after which it walked in the same stately way to the door, unlocked it, and walked forth again upon the gallery; the Doctor still following, and Tom behind, bearing the light. Down the stairs it glided, and halted on the lobby, where it seemed to look from the window fixedly.

"Come along," said the Doctor to Tom; and down the stairs he went, followed by the torch-bearer, and, on reaching the lobby, he clapped the apparition on the back, and shook it lustily by the arm.

With the sort of gasp and sob which accompany sudden immersion in cold water, William Maubray, for the ghost was he, awakened, dropped the coverlet which formed his drapery, on the floor, and stood the picture of bewilderment and horror, in his night-shirt, staring at his friends and repeating—"Lord have mercy on us!"

"It's only Tom and I. Shake yourself up a bit, man. Doctor Drake—here we are—all old friends."

And the Doctor spoke very cheerily, and all sorts of encouraging speeches; but it was long before William got out of his horror, and even then he seemed for a good while on the point of fainting.

"I'll never be myself again," groaned William, in his night-shirt, seating himself, half dead, upon the lobby table.

Tom stood by, holding the candle aloft, and staring in his face and praying in short sentences, with awful unction; while the Doctor kept all the time laughing and patting William on the shoulder and repeating, "Nonsense!—nonsense!—nonsense!"

When William had got again into his room, and had some clothes on, he broke again into talk:

"Somnambulism!—walk in my sleep. I could not have believed it possible. I—I never perceived the slightest tendency—I—the only thing was that catching my own wrist in my sleep and thinking it was another person who held me; but—but actually walking in my sleep, isn't it frightful?"

"I don't think you'll ever do it again—ha, ha, ha!" said the Doctor.

"And why not?" asked William.

"The fright of being wakened as you were, cures it. That's the reason I shook you out of your doldrum," chuckled the Doctor.

"I'm frightened — frightened out of my wits."

"Glad of it," said the Doctor. "Be the less likely to do it again."

"Do you think I—I'm really cured?" asked William.

"Yes, I do; but you must change your habits a bit. You've let yourself get into a dyspeptic, nervous, state, and keep working your brain over things too much. You'll be quite well in a week or two; and I really do think you're cured of this trick. They seldom do it again—hardly ever—after the shock of being wakened. I've met half a dozen cases—always cured."

The Doctor stayed with him the greater part of that night, which they spent so cheerfully that Drake's articulation became indistinct, though his learning and philosophy, as usual, shone resplendent.

It was not till he was alone, and the bright morning sun shone round him, that William Maubray quite apprehended the relief his spirits had experienced. For several days he had lived in an odious dream. It was now all cleared up, and his awful suspicions gone.

As he turned from the parlour window to the breakfast table, the old Bible lying on the little book-shelf caught his eye. He took it down, and laid it beside him on the table. Poor Aunt Dinah had kept it by her during her illness, preferring it to any other.

"I'll read a chapter every day—by Jove, I will," resolved William, in the grateful sense of his deliverance. "It's only decent—it's only the old custom. It may make me good some day, and hit or miss, it never did any man harm."

So he turned over the leaves, and lighted on an open sheet of note paper. It was written over in poor Miss Perfect's hand, with a perceptible tremble; and he read the following lines, bearing date only two days before her death:—

"DEAR WILLIE,

"To-day I am not quite so, but trust to be better; and wish you to know, that having convers much with Doctor, my friend, the Rector, I make for future the Bible my only guide, and you are not to mind what I said about waiting five — only do all things — things—with prayer, and marry whenever you see goo seeking first God's blessing by pra——.

"So, lest anything should happen, to remove from your mind all anxiet, writes

"Your poor old fond

"Auntie."

Thus ended the note, which William, with a strange mixture of feelings, kissed again and again, with a heart at once saddened and immensely relieved.

—o—

CHAPTER LXVIII.

SOME SMALL EVENTS AND PLANS.

William Maubray heard from Trevor, who affected boisterous spirits and the intensest enjoyment of his town life, though there was not a great deal doing just then to amuse anybody. He had been thinking of running over to Paris to the Sourburys, who had asked him to join their party, but thought he must go first to Kincton for a week or two, as the ladies insisted on a sort of promise he had made, and would not let him off. He hinted, moreover, that there was a perfectly charming Lady Louisa Sourbury, of whom he spoke in a rapture; and possibly all this, and a great deal more in the same vein, was intended to reach the ear of Miss Violet Darkwell, who was to learn that "there are maidens in Scotland more lovely by far, who would gladly," &c., &c., and also, that young Lochinvar was treading his measures and drinking his cups of wine with remarkable hilarity, notwithstanding the little scene which had taken place.

But Vane Trevor was not a topic which William would have cared to introduce, and it was in relation to quite other subjects that he was always thinking of Violet Darkwell.

"So," said the old Rector, walking into the hall at Gilroyd, shaking his head, and smiling as he spoke, "We've found you out—the merry devil of Edmonton—hey? I don't know when I was so puzzled. It was really—a-ha!—a most perplexing problem—and—and Doctor Drake has been our Matthew Hopkins, our witch-finder, and a capital one he has proved. I dare say, between ourselves," continued the Rector, in a low tone, like a man making a concession, "that several cases of apparently well authenticated apparitions are explicable—eh?—upon that supposition;" and, indeed, good Doctor Wagget devoted time and research to this inquiry, and has written already to two publishers on the suject of his volume, called "The Debatable Land;" and when, last summer, I passed a week at the Rectory, my admirable friend read to me his introduction, in which he says, "If apparitions *be* permitted, they are no more supernatural than water-spouts and other phenomena of rare occurrence, but, *ipso facto, natural.* In any case a Christian man, in presence of a disembodied spirit should be no more disquieted than in that of an embodied one, *i.e.*, a human being under its mortal conditions."

And the only subject on which I ever heard of his showing any real impatience is that of his night-watch in the study at Gilroyd, as slily described by Dr. Drake, who does not deny that he was himself confoundedly frightened by William Maubray's first appearance, and insinuates a good deal about the Rector, which the Rector, with a dignified emphasis, declares to be "unmeaning travesty."

In the meantime, Mr. Sergeant Darkwell made a flying visit to the Rectory, and Maubray had a long walk and a talk with him. I do not think that a certain shyness, very hard to get over where ages differ so considerably, permitted the young man to say that which most pressed for utterance; but he certainly did talk very fully about the "bar," and its chances, and William quite made up his mind to make his bow before the world in the picturesque long robe and whalebone wig, which every one of taste admires.

But the Sergeant, who remained in that part of the world but for a day, when he donned his coif, and spread his sable wings for flight towards the great forensic rookery, whither instinct and necessity called him, carried away his beautiful daughter with him, and the sun of Saxton, Gilroyd, and all the world around was darkened.

In a matter like love, affording so illimitable a supply of that beautiful vaporous material of which the finest castles in the air are built, and upon which every match-maker—and what person worthy to live is *not* a match-maker?—speculates in a spirit of the most agreeable suspense and the most harmless gambling, it would be hard if the architects of such chateaux, and the "backers" of such and such events, were never in their incessant labours to light up a prophetic combination. Miss Wagget was a free mason of the order of the "Castle in the Air." Her magical trowel was always glittering in the sun, and her busy square never done adjusting this or that block of sunset cloud. She had, some little time since, laid the foundations in the firmament of such a structure for the use and occupation of William Maubray and Violet Darkwell; and she was now running it up at a rate which might have made sober architects stare. The structure was even solidifying, according to the nebulous theory of astronomers.

And this good lady used, in her charity, to read for William in his almost daily visits to the rectory, all such passages in Violet's letters as she fancied would specially interest him.

Her love for the old scenes spoke very clearly in all these letters. But—and young ladies can perhaps say whether this was a good sign or a bad one—she never once mentioned William Maubray; no, no more than if such a person did not exist, although certainly she asked vaguely after the neighbours, and I venture to think that in her replies, Miss Wagget selected those whom she thought most likely to interest her correspondent.

All this time good Miss Wagget wrote constantly to remind the barrister in London of his promise to allow Violet to return to the Rectory for another little visit. It was so long delayed that William grew not only melancholy, but anxious. What might not be going on in London? Were there no richer fellows than he, none more—more—what should he say?—more that style of man who is acceptable in feminine eyes? Was not Violet peerless, go where she might? Could such a treasure remain long unsought? and if sought, alas! who could foresee the event? And here he was alone, at Gilroyd, well knowing that distance, silence, absence, are sure at last to kill the most vigorous passion; and how could a mere fancy, of the filmiest texture—such as his best hopes could only claim, by way of interest in her heart or in her head—survive these agencies of decay and death?

"Next week I think I shall run up to town. I must arrange about attending an equity draughtsman's. I'm determined, sir, to learn my business thoroughly," said William.

"Right, sir! I applaud you," replied the Rector, to whom this was addressed. "I see you mean work, and are resolved to master your craft. It's a noble profession. I had an uncle at it who, everybody said, whould have done wonders, but he died of small-pox in the Temple, before he had held a brief, I believe, though he had been some years called; but it would have come. *Macte virtute.* I may live to see you charge a jury, sir."

——o——

CHAPTER LXIX

WILLIAM MAUBRAY IN LONDON.

VIOLET DARKWELL's stay in London lengthened. Saxton was growing intolerable. William began to despond. He ran up to town, and stayed there for a few weeks. He eat his dinner in Lincoln's Inn Hall for two terms, and dined every Sunday, and twice beside, at the 'Darkwells.' The Sergeant was so busy that, on these occasions, he appeared like a guest—an unexpected presence, and wes still evidently haunted by briefs—fatigued and thoughtful; but very kind to William. In their short after-dinner sittings I do not think that William ever opened the subject that was nearest his heart. He had, I think, and with a great deal better reason than poor Vane Trevor of Revington, whose pale phantom sometimes flitted warningly before his imagination — horrible qualms about his money qualification.

After one of these Sunday dinners William and Sergeant Darkwell *tête-à-tête*, the barrister, in his quiet cheery way, had been counselling the student on some points, and relating bar stories, always pleasant to hear when told by bright and accurate men like him; and said he, as they rose, "and the first term you make a hundred pounds I give you leave to marry."

William looked hard at his host. But his countenance was thoughtful, he had wandered away already to some other matter. In fact he looked quite innocent, and I believe he was, of thought of Violet.

"I give you leave to marry." Of course it was quite out of the question that he could have meant what the young man fancied he might mean. Still he thought he might lay down this general rule, and leave it to him to make the particular inference.

"I see," said William, in conference with himself, as he trudged home that night, dejectedly. "He wishes me to understand that I shan't have his consent till then. A hundred pounds in a term! *He* had been seven years called before he made that? Could William hope to succeed so well? Not quite, he rather thought." And then grasping his stick hard he swore it was like Jacob's service for Rachel—a seven years' business; and all for a Rachel, who had no thought of waiting.

On all these occasions he saw Violet. But was there not a change, a sense of distance, and above all, was there not that awful old "she-cousin" (to borrow Sam Papy's convenient phrase), of Sergeant Darkwell, silent, vigilant, in stiff silk, whose thin face smiled not, and whose cold gray eyes followed him steadily everywhere and who exercised an authority over Violet more than aunt-like?"

William called again and again, but never saw pretty Violet without this prudent and dreadful old lady. *Her* indeed he twice saw alone. In a *tête-à-tête* she was not more agreeable. She listened to what few things, with a piteous ransacking of his invention and his memory he could bring up, and looked upon him with a silent suspicion and secret aversion under which his spirit gradually despaired and died within him. Glimpses of Violet, under the condition of this presence, were tantalizing, even agonizing sometimes. The liberty of speech so dear to Englishmen was denied him, life was gliding away in this speechless dream, the spell of that lean and silent old lady was upon him. How he yearned for the easy country life with its kindly chaperons and endless opportunities. Love, as we all know, is a madness, and it is the property of madmen to imagine conspiracies, and William began to think that there was an understanding between Sergeant Darkwell and the "she-cousin," and that she was there to prevent his ever having an opportunity of saying one confidential word in Violet's ear. It seemed to him, moreover, that this was unspeakably worse, that Violet was quite happy in this state of things. He began to suspect that he had been a fool, that his egotism had made him, in a measure, mad, and that it was time for him to awake and look the sad truth in the face.

William left London. He wavered in his allegiance to the Bar. He doubted his fitness for it. Had he not money enough for all his wants? Why should he live a town life, and grieve his soul over contingent remainders, and follow after leading cases in objectless pursuit, and lose himself in Bacon's interminable Abridgment, all for nothing ?

He returned to keep his next term, and suffer a like penance. It seemed to him there was a kind of coldness and reserve in Violet that was hardly tangible, and yet it was half breaking his heart. She was further away than ever, and he could not win her back. He sate there under the eye of silent Miss Janet Smedley—the inexorable she-cousin. There was no whispering in her presence. She was so silent you might hear a pin drop. Not a syllable escaped her observant ear. There was no speaking in her presence, and that presence never failed—though Violet's sometimes did. The situation was insupportable. Away went William again—and this time he made a portion of that charming tour of Brown, Jones, and Robinson, which for any comfort it gave his spirit, he might as well or better have made within the covers of Mr. Doyle's famous quarto.

Back to England with the home sickness of love came William. He had still a week before his term commenced.

"I can't stand it any longer," said he, as he paced the platform of the "Railway" by which he had taken not an "up" but a "down" ticket. "I know I'm right. I must go down and see Miss Wagget. I'd rather talk to her than to the Doctor. I know very well she sees how it is, and she'll tell me what she thinks, and if she advises, I'll speak to the Sergeant when I go to town, and so I shall soon know one way or other," and he sighed profoundly, and with a yearning look town-wards he took his place, and flew away toward Gilroyd.

——o——

CHAPTER LXX.

VIOLET DARKWELL TELLS MISS WAGGET THAT QUEEN ANNE IS DEAD.

THE sun was near the western horizon, and sky and clouds were already flooded with the sunset glow, as William Maubray drove up to the high and formal piers of Gilroyd, with their tall urns at top—decorations which belong to old-world fancy—a little formal, like the stately dress of by-gone beauties and beaux, but with a sentiment and a prettiness of their own. Sad looked to him the smile of the old building and lordly trees in the fading sunlight; the windows sparkled redly in it, the ivy rustled in the light air, and the sparrows twittered and fluttered up and down among its glittering leaves—the time, the sights, and sounds recalling many an arrival at the same pleasant hour, and many a welcome look and tone—gone now—faint and far away in memory, and ever to grow more and more distant.

The hall door was open—in went William without a summons—and in the hall he heard voices issuing from the drawing-room. Old Miss Wagget's kindly and cheering tones were distinctly audible, and Winnie Dobbs was making answer as he entered. From the two old women, as he stepped in, there was a simultaneous ejaculation; and Winnie's two hands were lifted in amaze, and she beamed on him with a ruddy smile of welcome, crying aloud, "Well, law! 'Tis him, sure enough!" and "There you are; what a charming surprise!" exclaimed Miss Wagget, trotting up to him with her hands extended, and shaking both his with a jolly little laugh.

"We walked over to pay our respects to good Winnie Dobbs here, little expecting to meet the lord of the Castle. Ha, ha, ha! why we thought you were at Hamburg, and lo and behold! Here we have you! And I ventured to bring a friend, will you allow me to introduce?"

But Violet Darkwell—for she was the friend—not waiting for Miss Wagget's mock ceremony, came a step or two to meet him, and again, in Gilroyd, he held that prettiest of slender hands in his.

"Oh! pretty Vi, who could forget you? How I wish you liked me ever so little! Oh! that you were the mistress of Gilroyd!" These were his thoughts as with a smile and a quiet word or two of greeting he took her hand.

"Did you come through London?" asked Miss Wagget.

"No; direct here," he answered.

"Surprised to find us, I dare say?" and she glanced at Violet. "Our friend here—like a good little creature, as she is—came down to keep me company for a week, and as much longer as I can make her stay, while my brother is at Westthorpe, and you must come over with us to tea."

William acquiesced.

"And, Winnie Dobbs, you must tell me all you know of that Tummins family at the mill—are they really deserving people?—there was a rumour, you know—young people, do you go out and take a ramble in the lawn, and I'll join you. Winnie and I must talk for a minute or two."

So Violet and William did go out, and stood for a minute in the old familiar porch.

"How pretty it looks—always in the setting sun—it's the light that suits Gilroyd. There's something a little melancholy in this place, though cheery along with it—I don't know how," said William.

"So do I—I always thought that—like those minutes I used to play, that dear old grannie liked so well—something brilliant and old fashioned, and plaintive," replied the sweet voice of Violet Darkwell.

"Come out into the sunlight," said William. "Oh! how pretty! isn't it? isn't it?"

Violet looked round with a sad smile that was beautiful on her girlish face.

"And the chestnut trees—I wonder how old they are," said William. "I must see you once more, Violet, among the chestnut trees;" and he led her towards them, she going willingly, with a little laugh that sounded low and sadly.

Among their stems, he stopped before that of a solitary beech tree.

"Do you remember that tree?" said William, speaking very low.

"I do indeed," said Violet with the faintest little laugh in the world.

"It's more than three years ago—it's four years ago—since I carved them." He was pointing to two lines of letters, already beginning to spread and close in as such memorials on the living bark will do—but still legible enough. They were—

Vi Darkwell,
William Maubray.

"These are going," he said with a sigh, "like the old inscriptions in Saxton churchyard; I believe it is impossible to make any lasting memorial; even memory fails as we grow old; God only remembers always; and this little carving here seems to me like an epitaph, times are so changed, and we—Vi Darkwell—William Maubray"—(he read slowly). "Little Vi is gone—dead and buried—and William Maubray—he did not know a great many things that he has found out since. He is dead and gone too, and I am here. He did not know himself; he thought the old things were to go on always; he did not know, Vi, how much he loved you—how desperately he loved you. *You* don't know it—you *can't* know it—or how much rather I'd die than lose you."

She was looking down, tne point of her little foot was smoothing this way and that the moss on the old roots that over-laced the ground.

"If I thought you could like me! Oh! Violet, can you—ever so little?" He took her hand in both his, and his handsome young face was as that of a man in some dreadful hour pleading for his life. There were the glow of hope, the rapture of entreaty, the lines of agony

"I like you, William. I do like you," she said, so low that no other ears but his, I think, could have heard it, and the little wood anemonies nodded their pretty heads, and the groups of wood-sorrel round trembled, it seemed with joy; and William said in a wild whisper—

"My darling—oh! Vi—my darling. My only love—dearer, and dearer, every year. Oh! darling, my love is everlasting!" and he kissed her hand again and again, and he kissed her lips, and the leaves and flowers were hushed, nature was listening, pleased, and, I think, the angels looking down smiled on those fair young mortals, and those blessed moments that come with the glory of paradise, and being gone, are remembered for ever.

"Why, young people, what has become of you?" cried the well known voice of Miss Wagget. Ho! here you are. I guessed I should find you among the trees, grand old timber Mr. Maubray." The guilty pair approached Miss Wagget side by side, looking as unconcerned as they could, and she talked on. "I sometimes think, Mr. Maubray, that Gilroyd must be a much older place than most people fancy. That house, now, what style is it in? My brother says there were such houses built in Charles the Second's time, but the timber you know is—particularly the oaks down there—the trees *are* enormously old, and there are traces of a moat. I don't understand these things, but my brother says, at the side of the house toward the road," and so on kind Miss Wagget laboured, little assisted by William, upon topics about which none of them were thinking.

That evening Miss Wagget was seized with a sort of musical frenzy, and sat down and played through ever so many old books of such pieces as were current in her youth, and very odd and quaint they sound now—more changed the fashion of our music even than of our language.

I'm afraid that the young people were not so attentive as they might, and William whispered incessantly, sitting beside Violet on the sofa.

It was rather late when that little musical party broke up.

To Gilroyd, William walked in a dream, in the air, all the world at his feet, a demigod. And that night when Vi, throwing her arms about Miss Wagget's neck, confided in her ear the momentous secret, the old lady exclaimed gaily—

"Thank you for nothing! a pinch for stale news! Why I knew it the moment I saw your faces under the trees there, and I'm very happy. Im delighted. I've been planning it, and hoping for it this ever so long—and poor fellow! He *was* so miserable."

——o——

CHAPTER LXXI.

THE CHIMES OF SAXTON.

Next morning Miss Wagget was busy, in a great fuss, writing the news to her brother and the Sergeant, and for the benefit of the latter she drew such a picture of William Maubray's virtues and perfections in general as must have made that sagacious man long to possess such a son-in-law. The good lady enclosed a dutiful little note to him from Violet, and wound up with an eloquent lecture, in which she demonstrated that if the Sergeant were to oppose this palpable adjustment of Providence, he should be found to fight against heaven, the consequences of which enterprise she left him to conjecture.

William also spent the entire forenoon over a letter to the same supreme authority; and the letters despatched. there intervened a few days of suspense and wonderful happiness, notwithstanding.

William was waiting in the little post-office

of Saxton when the answering letters came. Mrs. Beggs having sorted the contents of the mail with an anxious eye, delivered his letters and at his desire, those for the rectory, to William. There was a letter from the Sergeant for him. There was no mistaking the tall and peculiar hand. There were two others addressed severally to the ladies at the rectory. William did not care to read his in Mrs. Begg's little parlour, so he took his leave cheerfully, even gaily, with an awful load at his heart.

In his pocket lay his fate sealed. Hardly a soul was stirring in the drowsy little street. Here and there a listless pair of eyes peeped through the miniature panes of a shop window.

He could not read the letter where any eye could see him. He hurried round the corner of Garden Row, got on the road leading to Gilroyd, crossed the style that places you upon the path to the rectory, and in the pretty field, with only half a dozen quiet cows for witnesses, opened and read his London letter.

It told him how well Mr. Sergeant Darkwell liked him, that he believed wedded happiness depended a great deal more on affection, honour, and kindness, than upon wealth. It said that he had aptitudes for the bar, and would, no doubt, do very well with exertion. It then mentioned what the Sergeant could do for his daughter, which William thought quite splendid, and was more, Miss Wagget afterwards said, than she had reckoned upon.

For some years at least they were to live with the Sergeant, "putting by your income, my dears, and funding at least five or six hundred a year," interposed Miss Wagget, who was in a wonderful fuss. "You'll be rich before you know where you are—you will, indeed! He's an admirable man—your father's an *admirable* man, my dear! I don't know such a man, except my brother, who's a man by himself, you know. But next after him, your papa, my dear, is the very best man I ever heard of. And you'll be married here, at Saxton—you shall, indeed. You must remain with us, and be married from this, and I wonder my brother stays so long away, he'll be as glad as I. The Sergeant shall come down to us for the wedding, and give you away at Saxton, and there's that beautiful spot, Wyndel Abbey, so romantic and charming, the very place for a honey-moon, and only fifteen miles away."

And so, on and on, ran good Miss Wagget, arranging everything for the young people, and as it were, counting the turnpikes, and packing the trunks for the happy excursionists, and making them comfortable in the pretty little inn at Wyndel Abbey, where she had once spent a week.

Well would it be for castle-builders in general if their dreams proved all as true as those of fanciful and kindly Miss Wagget did, on this occasion.

It was agreed it was to be a very quiet wedding. At secluded Saxton, indeed it would not have been easy to make it anything else. Sergeant Darkwell of course gave pretty Violet away.

Honest Dr. Drake was there, in an unprofessional blue coat and buff waistcoat, and with a bouquet in his button-hole, in which not a single camomile flower figured. Miss Drake, too, in a lavender silk; and wishing the gay couple every good from her heart, notwithstanding her surprise that Sergeant Darkwell should have permitted his *child* to marry at so early an age as eighteen—*nineteen?* Well, one year here or there doesn't signify a great deal, she fancied. Good old Winnie Dobbs, too, in a purple silk and new bonnet, which must have been quite in the fashion, for all Saxton admired it honestly. A little way from the communion rails, behind the gentlefolks, she stood or kneeled, edified, only half credulous, smiling sometimes, and crying a great deal—thinking, I am sure, of kind old Aunt Dinah, who was not to see that hour. Winnie, I mention parenthetically, is still housekeeper at Gilroyd, and very happy, with nothing but a little rheumatism to trouble her.

Here every year William and Violet pass some time, and the happiest month of all the twelve, though the estates and title have come to him, and he is Sir William and she Lady Maubray. But the change has not spoiled either. The honest affections and friendly nature delight in the old scenes and associates; and in summer sunsets, under the ancient chestnuts, they ramble sometimes, her hand locked in his; and often, I daresay, he runs over those delightful remembrances, still low—still in a lover's tone, she looking down on the grass and wild flowers, as she walks beside him and listens as she might to a sweet air, always welcome, the more welcome that she knows it so well; and they read the inscription on the beech tree, time has not effaced it yet, they read it smiling, in their happy dream, with that something of regret that belongs to the past, and all the tenderness that tones the uncertain mortal future.

Sometimes William says a word of Trevor, and she laughs, perhaps a little flattered at the remembrance of a conquest. Vane Trevor is very well, not married yet, they say, grown a little stout, not often at Revington. He does not put himself much in the way of Sir William, but is very friendly when they correspond on Saxton matters, Workhouse, and others. He has not renewed his attentions at Kincton. Clara has grown "awfully old," he has been heard to remark. She has latterly declined gaieties, has got to the very topmost platform of high-churchism, from which a mere step-ladder may carry her still higher. Dean Sancroft, who fought the Rev. John Blastus in the great controversy, you must remember, on credence tables, candles, and super-altars, is not unfrequently an inmate of Kincton, and people begin to canvass probabilities.

But whither have I drifted? Let us come back to quiet old Saxton Church, and the marriage service. The Miss Mainwarings and a pretty Miss Darkwell a cousin of the bride's, attended as bridesmaids. And with Sergeant Darkwell had arrived the "silent woman." She could not help her taciturnity any more than her steady gray eyes, which used to terrify William so, while he haunted the drawing-room in town, she attended, in very handsome and appropriate costume, and made Vi a very pretty present of old-fashioned jewellery, and was seen to dry her gray eyes during the beautiful "solemnization of matrimony," as good Doctor Wagget, in the old church, under the oak-roof which had looked down for so many centuries on so many young kneeling couples, in the soft glow of the old stained windows whose saints looked smiling on with arms crossed over their breasts; read the irrevocable words aloud, and the village congregation reverently listening, heard how these two young mortals, like the rest, had "given and pledged their troth, either to other, and declared the same by giving and receiving of a ring, and by joining of hands," and how the good Rector pronounced that "they be man and wife together," in the name of the glorious Trinity.

As we walk to the village church, through the church-yard, among the gray, discoloured headstones that seem to troop slowly by us as we pass, the lesson of change and mortality is hardly told so sublimely as in the simple order of our services. The pages that follow the "Communion" open on the view like the stations in a pilgrimage. The "Baptism of Infants"—"A Catechism"—"The Order of Confirmation"—"The Solemnization of Matrimony"—"The Visitation of the Sick"—"The Burial of the Dead." So, the spiritual events of life are noted and provided for, and the journey marked from the first question—"Hath this child been already baptized or no?" down to the summing up of life's story—"Man that is born of a woman, hath but a short time to live, and is full of misery. He cometh up and is cut down as a flower, he fleeth as it were a shadow, and never continueth in one stay."

And so Doctor Wagget after the blessing invoked, and his beautiful office ended, smiling bids William "Kiss your wife," and there is a fluttering of gay ribbons, and many smiling faces, and a murmuring of pleased voices, and greetings and good wishes, as they go to the vestry-room to sign Dr. Wagget's ancient ledger of all such doings.

And now while the sun is shining and the bells of Saxton trembling in the air, I end my story

THE END.

www.ingramcontent.com/pod-product-compliance
Lightning Source LLC
LaVergne TN
LVHW050539100826
845148LV00002B/622

* 9 7 8 1 4 2 5 5 7 6 1 8 9 *